# BILLIE'S BLUES

# BILLIE'S BLUES

*Billie Holiday's Story*
*1933-1959*

## JOHN CHILTON

Foreword by Buck Clayton

**SD** STEIN AND DAY/*Publishers*/New York

To Max and Betty Jones, fans and friends of Billie Holiday

First published in the United States of America, 1975
Copyright © 1975 by John Chilton
All rights reserved
Printed in the United States of America
Stein and Day/ *Publishers*/Scarborough House,
Briarcliff Manor, N.Y. 10510

*Library of Congress Cataloging in Publication Data*

Chilton, John, 1931 or 2-
    Billie's blues.

    Includes bibliographies, discographies, and
index.
    1.   Holiday, Billie, 1915-1959.   I.   Title.
ML420.H58C5        784'.092'4   [B]        75-8837
ISBN 0-8128-1821-0

## Grateful acknowledgements to:

Robin Aitken
Steve Allen
Walter C. Allen
Ernie Anderson
Jack Armitage
Jeff Atterton
Harry Avery
Eddie Baker
Clyde Bernhardt
Johnny Best
Per Borthen
Michael Brooks
Floyd Brady
Beryl Bryden
Milt Buckner
Paul and Kay Burgess
Billy Butterfield
Niger Carr
Adolphus 'Doc' Cheatham
Wilbur 'Buck' Clayton
Bill Coleman
Ian Crosbie
Stanley Dance
Jean Delaney
Bertrand Demeusy
Roy Eldridge
Leonard Feather
Gerry Finningley
Gilbert Gaster
Bob Haggart
Corky Hale
John Hammond

Dr Herbert Henderson
Daphne Hellman
John Hine
Norman Jenkinson
Cynthia Jones
Jonah Jones
Max and Betty Jones
Barney Josephson
Harold Kay
John Kendall
Irene Kitchings
Brian Knight
Norman Lees
Albert McCarthy
Jimmy McPartland
Marian McPartland
David Marks
Babe Matthews
Joyce Melina
Johnny Mercer
Louis Metcalf
Jack Millar
Alun Morgan
Benny Morton
Tommy Moulds
Paul Nossiter
Frank Owens
Margaret Paterson
Brian Peerless
Bernie Privin
Rudy Powell
Frank Rosolino

Annie Ross
Jimmie Rowles
Charles Saunders
R. 'Skip' Schrammel
Tony Scott
Jimmy Sherman
Hal Singer
Johnny Simmen
Roland Smith
Joe Springer
Richard Sudhalter
Jack Surridge
Peter Tanner
Charlie Teagarden
Joe Thomas
Françoise Trainaud
Bobby Tucker
U.S. Department of Justice
U.S. General Services
 Administration
Mal Waldron
George Wein
Fred Welstead
Dave Wilborn
Johnny Williams
Ean Woods
Roy Woomer
Michael Wyler
James 'Trummy' Young
Dorothy Zaidins
Earle Warren Zaidins
Fred Zentner

The proprietors of:

*Melody Maker, Jazz Journal, Down Beat, Metronome, Jazz Record, Ebony, Jazz, Coda*

*Photographs*

p. 30 – Brian Knight: p. 106 – Max Jones: p. 111 Bill Mark: p. 147 – Frank Kurchirchuk: p. 153 – Beryl Bryden: p. 155 – Max Jones: p. 166 – Flair Photography: p. 173 – Jean-Pierre Leloir: p. 175 – Tony Scott: p. 184 – Buck Hoeffler

Because originals of many of the photographs are no longer in existence, several of the illustrations in this book are of poor quality. Despite the lack of sharpness they are included in order that the illustrations should cover as wide a part of Billie's life and career as possible.

# FOREWORD

## by  Buck  Clayton

When I first met Billie Holiday she lit up,
but I must say that it was her face that lit up. John Hammond
first introduced me to Billie, at the first recording date of my
life, and I was surprised to see that she was such a young,
healthy, robust and pleasant girl, the kind that I grew up with
when I was a boy in Kansas.

That first recording date was in January 1937, and I was
so surprised when I walked into the studio and saw for the
first time Benny Goodman. Previously, I had only heard
Benny, and his great band of the 1930s, on records and radio.
I knew Teddy Wilson would be on the date as he made
practically all of Billie's first records. Freddie Greene I didn't
know at all. He was just a New York guy sitting on a tall
stool holding his guitar. Little did I know that he was one of
the world's greatest guitarists.

Billie was running over a song at the piano with Teddy
Wilson. After getting an introduction together we proceeded
to start what was my first recording (I had not yet recorded
with Count Basie). Billie sang just beautifully on this date and
after several coffee breaks and a few visits to the nearest bar I

1

began to get a little closer to Billie and found her to be a very warm person.

Before coming to New York, when I was in Los Angeles, I heard Billie's first recordings. After meeting her and getting to know her I liked her singing even more than I had in California. I'll never forget the mornings I would awake to 'If You Were Mine' in my hotel-room on Central Avenue in Los Angeles. I'd never heard Roy Eldridge and Benny Morton in person, and to hear them together with Billie was a perfect combination.

After making several more recording dates with Billie we began to be great friends, and she would take me to all of the 'joints' in Harlem; well-known to Billie, but unknown to me. At the time of my first meeting with Billie she also met up with Lester Young − and there was one of the greatest companionships that I've ever seen, and that is all it was, and ever would be. They were so close that many believed them to be in love, but that never was the case. If you've ever seen two guys become great pals, then you can see the companionship of Billie and Lester. I know this, because I was one of the 'Unholy Three', as we used to call ourselves when we were together in some pad in Harlem. Lester had his girl friends, and Billie had her boy friends and there was never any confusion. However, I do believe that if they had to, they would have given up all the girl friends and all the boy friends, and still they would have remained no more than great friends. Billie admired Lester's playing, and he obviously admired her singing and they complimented each other. 'Lady Day' and 'Pres' made one of the greatest combinations together that I've seen in my life, but were never in any way more than just great buddies.

I think that during those days I may have been in Billie's company a bit more than Lester was, even though we were all together quite often. Sometimes, Billie and I would cover as many as ten or twelve Harlem pads in a matter of a few hours, because she didn't like to stay in one place too long. She was always anticipating going to the next one. Pads with soft lights, pot, incense and good jazz records − mostly by

Louis Armstrong, Duke Ellington and Billie Holiday. Billie knew every corner of Harlem, and I got the best introduction to Harlem that anyone could possibly get. It seems that everyone in Harlem knew Billie personally, and there were always little stories that would circulate through Harlem about some episode that involved Billie, but Billie never gave a damn what people might say and she retained that attitude all through her life. Some of the tales were probably true, some of them false, Billie became one of the most talked-of personalities of Harlem. Good or bad.

Later, when she joined Count Basie's band it was one of the joys of our lives. To have the great Billie Holiday singing with our band was something we never thought possible – a pleasure we never thought we would have. It was through John Hammond, and her acquaintanceship with me and Lester, that Billie joined Basie. I think she was as happy to join as we were to have her. She asked me to make a big band arrangement, as she had no music for a band the size of Basie's, and the first one she wanted was 'I Can't Get Started With You'. She made her debut in Pennsylvania, and I was pretty proud, the arrangement was good and she sounded marvellous. During her stay with Basie, I must say that like the rest of us, she lived in a bus on 'one nighters'. She would, like all of us, shoot craps, sing and drink to get over the rigours of the one-nighters.

Many mornings about five o'clock, when everyone else was asleep on the bus, Billie and I would talk of the highlights of our lives. I'd tell her of some of my experiences in Shanghai, which especially interested her. Later on, whilst visiting her home, I noticed in her room a picture that was painted for her by an artist friend, of the head of a Chinaman lying in a Shanghai street – after a battle with the Japanese. It seemed pretty gruesome to me, but it was a favourite with Billie. She would tell me all of her experiences, and believe me there were many.

During Billie's whole time with Count Basie she only became involved with one musician, and that was Freddie Greene. Many think it impossible that this was all that

3

happened with Billie but it's true. Freddie was the only one, and sometimes they would fight all over the bus – but only as people fight when they care for each other. Freddie was always an admirable guy, and the only one that Billie admired.

Billie remained with Count Basie for some time and then, for a reason that I never knew, she left the band. I suppose it was the politics that occurred in big bands during those days, but I never knew for sure. A few months later she was singing with Artie Shaw's Band.

I saw and worked with Billie periodically after that. During the 1940s she worked and lived in California quite a bit. One afternoon, while I was with the 'Jazz At The Philharmonic' group, under Norman Granz, I was among several musicians who were having a jam-session at Billy Berg's Club in Hollywood when Billie showed up. She didn't sing that Sunday afternoon, but she told me that the night before she had been introduced to heroin by an artist who lived in Hollywood. She went on to tell me how good it was, and that it wasn't as harmful as people had led her to believe. 'Come on Bucket,' she said, 'it will make you feel like you've never felt before.' I listened to her, but then I told her 'No, Lady, that's not for me.'

After that, she became more deeply involved with narcotics, and it began to take its toll. Gradually she became very thin, gone was the plump girlish Billie that I first met. She always had trouble with narcotic agents, and she was an easy mark for the many unscrupulous men in her life. She was preyed on by so many hangers-on, who were out for either a fix or some money, and being always big-hearted and sympathetic she was taken advantage of numerous times.

During the latter part of the 1950s we played the Art Ford Jazz Show, a television show out of Newark, New Jersey, and I noticed that Billie was more and more in a bad way. She was very thin, her skin was sallow, and her voice cracked – which was something I never thought I'd hear. Shortly afterwards, she entered hospital for the last time. Even though Billie is gone now, every time I play or hear a Billie

4

Holiday record it brings back many memories of the wonderful, kind, tough, and sympathetic person that I was very proud, or rather, that I am very proud to have known.

I am very pleased that John Chilton has asked me to write the introduction to his book, and I sincerely give it all of my very best wishes.

*Buck   Clayton.*

# PROLOGUE

'This month, there has been a real find in the person of a singer called Billie Halliday ... though only eighteen, she weighs over 200 pounds, is incredibly beautiful, and sings as well as anybody I ever heard.' Thus, John Hammond, then twenty-two, gave Billie Holiday the first critique of her career.

The report was published in the April 1933 issue of the British publication, the *Melody Maker*. Hammond, who provided the New York news column for the magazine at that time, had already gained a reputation for spotting outstanding jazz talent. His visit to hear Billie became an important part of her career; before the year had ended he had arranged for her to make her first recordings. The published details of Hammond's discovery are also important for a researcher, since they represent the first immovable landmark in the quest for factual detail on Billie's early career.

Few hard-and-fast facts are available on Billie's vocal work in the years before 1933. In her fascinating autobiography *Lady Sings The Blues** (written in collab-

*Published by Barrie & Rockliffe

oration with William Dufty). Billie chose to cite Jerry Preston's club as the place where she made her debut as a paid singer. However, some musicians can remember hearing Billie sing professionally long before then.

Tenor saxophonist Kenneth Hollon (who later recorded with Billie) took her to some of her first club dates, during 1930 or 1931. The venue was the Gray Dawn, a cabaret club on Jamaica Avenue and South Street in Queens, New York. Billie sang there with Hat Hunter's Band. Hollon recalled: 'At that time the audience used to throw money on the floor – Billie made her first dollar in New York that night.'

Billie was then living with her mother at 7 Glenada Place in Brooklyn. The two of them had made their own separate ways to New York from their home city of Baltimore, where Billie said she was born on 17 April 1915. Her original name was Eleanora (during the late 1920s, she took the first name of her then-favourite film star Miss Billie Dove); her parents were two black youngsters, Sadie Fagan and Clarence Holiday. They were teenagers when their daughter was born, and, according to Billie, still teenagers three years later when they married.

Unfortunately, it is impossible to ascertain if these statements are facts. Neither birth certificates nor wedding certificates are available from Maryland's Division of Vital Records. Sight of these documents is reserved only for close relatives, and as Billie's close relatives died before her, the documents – if they exist – could well remain unseen by researchers until legislation is altered. The stone that marks Billie's mother's grave in St Raymond's Cemetery, New York, indicates that Sadie was born in 1896 and died in 1945. If this was the case, it would mean that Sadie was eighteen or nineteen before she had Billie, assuming that Billie's correct birth-date was 1915.

Billie's childhood was apparently packed with traumatic incidents, so it is small wonder that she found great difficulty in giving exact recollections. She could be positive that she had heard Louis Armstrong's recording of 'West End Blues' (made in 1928) before she left Baltimore in the year that

7

Lindbergh first flew the Atlantic (1927); she was certain that her father left home to join McKinney's Cotton Pickers in the early 1920s, yet none of the survivors of that band can remember Clarence working with them, and they point out that it was not until 1926 that the band became known as McKinney's Cotton Pickers. No useful purpose is served in dissecting Billie's story and pointing out other anomalies. Rather than present the reader with a chronicle of riddles I have chosen to cover the great singer's career from the time she began recording (1933) until the time of her death (1959).

# PART ONE

# CHAPTER ONE

Monette's Supper Club on 133rd Street in Harlem, where John Hammond first heard Billie, was similar to hundreds of other little night-spots that flourished in New York during the Prohibition era.

The name 'Monette's' was a temporary one. Some New York club owners had devised a system for side-stepping certain police restrictions; if the law moved in and closed a club, it was possible to begin operating immediately at the same address by re-naming the place — the new 'reserve' name having been previously registered by one of the staff. Legend has it that many clubs changed their names more often than they did their table-cloths.

Most of the business at Monette's was done after midnight, a six a.m. closing wasn't unusual and a nine a.m. finish wouldn't have made history, but in those times it was possible to shop for anything in Harlem from hams to hardware until past two a.m. The clientele at Monette's consisted mostly of black people, though there were a few white regulars who also used the club. John Hammond, then writing a regular music column, was invited to the club by Monette herself — Monette Moore the vocalist.

Monette and Billie Holiday were both accompanied by Dot Hill on piano. Dot (wife of guitarist Howard Hill) was the club's resident piano player, she backed everyone who sang there. During these early years, Billie wasn't earning anything like enough money to retain her own accompanist; in 1933, pianists were at a premium in New York – a good soloist could earn as much as 300 dollars a week (about ten times the national average wage). Bobby Henderson, who later worked with Billie at Pod's and Jerry's (a club at 168 W. 133rd Street) said that he never earned less than eighty-five dollars a night during this era. Not that the club's owners were excessively generous: the pianist's salary was only fourteen dollars a week – the rest came in tips.

The formal name of 'Pod's and Jerry's' was 'The Patagonia', but the regular clientele knew the club by the nicknames of the two owners, Charles 'Pods' Hollingsworth and Jeremiah 'Jerry' Preston; after the repeal of Prohibition in 1933 the club was re-named 'The Log Cabin'. In a letter to Swiss jazz-writer Johnny Simmen, Bobby Henderson recalled his days at the club, and outlined the technique taught him by a predecessor, fellow-pianist Willie 'The Lion' Smith. To ensure that all tips reached the kitty, 'The Lion' placed a mirror over the piano so that he could clearly see a vocalist going from table to table collecting money. 'As the big shots put their dollars, and even silver on the table, the girls would pull up their dresses and take the money off between their legs. At that time, this was an established part of any female entertainer's act in Harlem.'

The wily 'Lion' could spot any attempt by the girls to hide the money, 'in their handkerchiefs, in their bosoms, or you know where...' Later, 'The Lion' would insist that the gratuities be recovered from their various hiding places and placed in the 'entertainers' fund'. After the money had been counted it was divided evenly between the pianist and the singers (sometimes numbering four or five) who worked at the club.

Billie always disliked the method of collection, and at Pod's and Jerry's her disdain was obvious enough for the other girls to sarcastically name her 'Lady'; to make matters worse, 'Lady' also disagreed with the system of kitty sharing. Singer Mae Barnes, who worked at the club with Billie clearly remembered the other girls' chagrin that Billie chose to share her tips only with the pianist, deliberately excluding the rest of the entertainers.

But, Billie, then eighteen years old, had a special reason for wanting to share only with Bobby Henderson: they were deeply involved in a love affair. In her autobiography, Billie refers to him anonymously: 'It was the first time I was ever wooed, courted, chased after. He made me feel like a woman. He was patient, and loving; he knew what I was scared about and he knew how to smooth my fears away.' Henderson, who died in 1969, never understood why Billie chose not to use his name; their love affair was no secret, and when it ended, the *New York Age* of 1 December 1934 told its readers: 'Bobbie Henderson, pianist, no longer engaged to Billie Halliday'.

Billie's name would not have meant much to that paper's average reader. True, she had made a record, but in spite of John Hammond's high hopes the sales had been negligible and the resultant publicity almost nil. On the recordings, made in late 1933, Billie sang with Benny Goodman's specially assembled nine-piece studio-band. Goodman, who had often heard Billie sing in the clubs, became a close personal friend of hers, but for some of the band the recording marked their first meeting with Billie. Trumpeter Charlie Teagarden recalls that at the time he had never heard of Billie, he was told 'that she was a youngster who had been discovered in Harlem'.

Billie recalled her debut session in a 1956 'Voice of America' radio interview with Willis Conover. She spoke of being nervous as she entered the recording studio: 'I got there and I was afraid to sing in the mike ... I was scared to death of it. Buck (Washington) played the piano on that date. Can you imagine all those studio men and Buck, he can't read a note.'

Buck, Billie, and trumpeter Shirley Clay were the only Negro participants in the session, the rest of the band were

13

white. Buck used this uneven factor as a lever to make Billie sing out, she remembered his words 'You're not going to let *these* people think you're a square are you? Come on, sing it!' Billie sang it, and although she had only one chorus and an eight-bar reprise to work on, she gave a competent performance.

Billie gave her latter-day opinion of the record to Conover, 'Well, I get a big bang out of "Your Mother's Son-in-Law". It sounds like I'm doing comedy. My voice sounded so high and funny.'

Billie got thirty-five dollars for making the record; she casually mentioned the session to her friends, but didn't regard it as being anything particularly important. She chose not to include either of the songs, '... Son-in-Law', or 'Riffin' The Scotch' in her club repertoire.

Perhaps the clearest picture of Billie's style of working in the early 1930s comes from British musician—writer Spike Hughes, who like John Hammond heard Billie sing at Monette's. In his book *Second Movement,* Hughes gives his impressions of Billie; 'She was tall, self-assured girl with rich golden-brown skin, exquisitely shown off by the pale blue of her full-skirted and low-cut evening frock, her black, swept-up hair and a pair of long, sparkling paste earrings. Billie was not the sort you could fail to notice in a crowd at any time; in the cramped low-ceilinged quarters of a Harlem speak-easy she not only registered, but, like a gypsy fiddler in a Budapest cafe, she came over to your table and sang to you personally. I found her quite irresistible.'

Billie was perceptive in her assessment of the situation regarding her record debut, the results of the session made no difference whatsoever to her life-style. She carried on doing club-dates as usual, and continued to share a small apartment with her mother.

Billie's mother and father, Sadie and Clarence, were divorced during Billie's childhood, Clarence, best known for his work as a guitarist with Fletcher Henderson's Orchestra, married again soon after moving from Baltimore to New York in the mid-1920s. Sadie also re-married; her second husband, Philip Gough, was a Baltimore dock-worker. However, Gough died soon after the marriage and Sadie stayed a widow for the rest of her life. She remained popular with a wide range of men, but chose never to get heavily involved again.

Sadie, who had had very little formal education, had worked since childhood at various domestic jobs. During the 1920s, when Sadie left Baltimore to work for higher wages in Philadelphia and New York, she left Billie in the care of her relative Cousin Ida. Billie's maternal grandparents also shared the house, as did Billie's great-grandmother, who according to Billie had begun life as a slave; Billie's half-Irish grandfather, Charles Fagan, had been born as a result of a liaison between the plantation owner and the slave.

But many of Billie's recollections about the early period of her childhood were very hazy, and such details of her family tree that she pieced together were assembled from scraps of gossip that she had gleaned from her mother. Sadie moved back to Baltimore and bought a house on Pennsylvania Avenue, but the home was only temporary, she soon returned to New York, and in the spring of 1927 sent for Billie to join her there.

Although Sadie was shorter, plumper and a shade darker than Billie, she could easily pass as an elder sister. For a time, the two girls worked together at Jerry Preston's Club, where Sadie had a job in the kitchen; at the Log Cabin they would often pull a 'sister routine' on strangers, much to Sadie's delight.

Billie left Preston's club to begin a residency at Frank Bastone's Alhambra Grill at 2120 7th Avenue, but she was soon on the move again, this time to the nearby Hot-Cha Bar and Grill on the corner of 134th Street and 7th Avenue. It was whilst working there that Billie got the chance to make her debut at Harlem's famous Apollo Theater, and at the time, the booking meant much more to her than the recording debut.

The Apollo is situated halfway between 7th and 8th Avenues on the north side of 125th Street, New York; its large two-balconied structure holds close to two thousand people. For over thirty years it has been regarded as an important testing ground for talent, and its predominantly black audience is acknowledged as superb judges of entertainment. Some white bands and singers have appeared at the theatre, but the majority of those who have played there are black. The Apollo's Amateur Nights could be a harrowing experience for an indifferent or immature performer, but the audience's intuitive appreciation for real talent discerned super-stars in embryo more accurately than any other crowd in the world. Sarah Vaughan, Billy Eckstine, La Vern Baker, the Isley Brothers and dozens more all appeared on Amateur Nights and their initial successes proved a springboard for their careers.

Billie's big chance came when Ralph Cooper, then working as a master of ceremonies at the Apollo, called into the Hot-Cha Club and heard Billie sing (accompanied by pianist Don Frye). Cooper, who later became a nationally famous disc-jockey, had led his own band (the Kongo Knights) during the early 1930s. He had a discerning ear for talent and immediately realised that Billie was a unique vocalist. He advised Frank Schiffman, the Apollo's owner, to book Billie, describing her style in vague, but enthusiastic, terms: 'You never heard singing so slow, so lazy, with such a drawl ... it ain't the blues – I don't know what it is, but you got to hear her.' Schiffman was convinced and booked Billie for the week of 19 April 1935. In a 1952 *Down Beat* interview, Ralph Cooper described how he equipped Billie for the debut by buying her an evening gown and slippers; he also rehearsed the Apollo House Band for the numbers that Billie had written arrangements for, 'Them There Eyes' and 'If The Moon Turns Green'.

In spite of being almost paralysed by stage-fright, Billie had an amazingly successful debut. Comedian-singer Alamo 'Pigmeat' Markham, a regular favourite at the Apollo, gave Billie a well-timed push from the wings just as she appeared to have decided that she didn't want to begin her stage career. Once in the spotlight she quickly settled down. The public

16

loved what they heard – in Billie's own words, 'The house broke up'. She sang 'The Man I Love' as an impromptu encore, then beaming and bowing she left the stage, the sounds of the enthusiastic audience still reaching her ears. The Apollo's owner, Frank Schiffman, gave Billie's confidence a huge boost by promising a return booking. He kept his word. Billie returned to the theatre for the week of 2 August 1935, only this time she changed her billing: instead of Halliday she called herself Holiday.

# CHAPTER TWO

Billie felt that the Apollo booking was a god-send, she said that she couldn't believe her luck. In fact, it would have only been a matter of time before a talent-scout from the theatre world spotted her. The sight of this tall, buxom, beautiful girl with the exquisite colouring was enough to make any neck swivel. On looks alone, Billie was potential 'star' material, but her voice was her greatest asset, for she sang in a style that was new to the world.

The timbre of her voice was completely individual, and her incredible sense of rhythm and intuitive knowledge of harmony enabled her to phrase songs in a unique way. She could reshape the bleakest melody into something that offered a vast range of emotions to her listeners; her artistry and timing gave her the ability to make poetry out of the most banal lyrics. No one appreciated Billie's talents more than musicians, and many jazzmen (black and white) began to pay regular visits to the clubs where Billie sang.

Trumpeter Bill Coleman heard Billie for the first time at the Hot-Cha Club. He recalls: 'I was not an authority on singing, but when Billie started to sing I could tell instantly that she sounded different from any female singer that I had

19

heard before. I didn't know who she was, but Don Frye (who I had worked with in Cecil Scott's Band) was playing piano for her, and he told me that she was Clarence Holiday's daughter.' Drummer Cozy Cole, who played on many of Billie's records, first heard her at the same club, and he still remembers the initial impact that her voice made: 'Then and there, I was certain that she would make it, and make it big.'

One person who made a special point of hearing Billie in the clubs during these early years was Mildred Bailey, a woman whose entire adult life was beset by weight problems. Mildred, part-Cherokee, was one of the few singers of the 1930s who managed to achieve widespread success, without amputating the jazz content of their work. She was for many years married to vibes-player Red Norvo. During the early 1930s the couple's passion for jazz led them to hear any newcomer to the New York Jazz Scene, whether the venue was uptown or downtown. Years later, Red Norvo recalled that Mildred assessed Billie's potential within seconds of first hearing her. The brevity of her comment, 'That girl's got it', seems to reveal that Mildred was quick to realise that she had a top-class rival. This initial jealousy became a malignancy with Mildred; she chose an oblique way of showing her spite. After hearing that Billie's mother was looking for work she offered Sadie a job as cook and maid at her Forest Hills apartment. Soon afterwards, Mildred began telling anyone who would listen that she had hired a woman who was the laziest maid and the worst cook in the world combined – inevitably, the name of Sadie's daughter was mentioned in the tirade. A friend gave Billie warning signs, without revealing the exact nature of Mildred's vindictiveness; simultaneously, Sadie left the job. Thereafter, Billie kept a very wary eye on Mildred. The two singers never achieved any degree of friendship, but Red Norvo retained a life-long admiration for Billie's singing; during the 1940s and 1950s his groups accompanied her on many occasions. Looking back, in 1968, he said, 'Billie said that she always felt happy working with me, and at one time especially asked that I form up the band for her Californian dates.'

The Cecil Scott mentioned by Bill Coleman was a regular at the Hot-Cha, he was then playing tenor-saxophone in Vernon Andrade's Band at the nearby Renaissance Casino. Billie got to know several of Cecil's thirteen children, and for a while, one of his daughters was a friend and confidante, but Billie's closest friend in the 1930s was Irene Wilson, then married to pianist Teddy Wilson. Irene was also a pianist; as Irene Eadie she had led her own band in Chicago during the late 1920s, she quit professional playing when she married, and from then on devoted her time to composing. She and Teddy were later divorced; Irene has since remarried. She remembers meeting Billie for the first time at the Hot-Cha Club, 'I had been asked by Teddy Wilson, then my husband, to contact Billie for a recording session. It culminated in her cutting her first recording with Teddy, the "Miss Brown to You" session.' The two girls became great friends, and later Billie recorded three of Irene's compositions.

Back in 1935, a month before Billie made her Apollo debut, she made a brief appearance in a film called *Rhapsody in Black*, a short movie filmed on the East Coast. Duke Ellington's Orchestra were the main musical stars, and the Three Rhythm Kings and Florence Edmondson were also featured. Billie had a small acting role playing 'his other woman' as a preliminary to singing a twelve-bar blues chorus on Duke Ellington's 'Saddest Tale'. Billie had appeared in one earlier film, as an extra in a Paul Robeson film, and she had also done some radio 'bit parts' in *Love Story*, a 'soap opera' series produced by composer Shelton Brooks. The appearance in *Rhapsody in Black*, brief though it was, greatly pleased Billie as she had always been a movie fan, and the glamour of a film star's life seemed to her, at that time, to be the perfect existence.

Glamour itself had a fascination for Billie; she loved to be in style both in dress and in jargon. She had a natural dignity, and during the last of her teen years she augmented this with a panache which, while not being overbearing, certainly meant that people noticed her when she entered a club or bar. Despite her weight (she was around the 200-210 pound mark during the mid-1930s) she moved well, and on first sight appeared brimful of confidence whereas in fact she was unsure of herself, and remained so for all of her life, as people discovered when they got to know her. Max Kaminsky, a life-long friend of Billie's, first met her in 1935. In his book, *My Life in Jazz,* he describes her, 'A large, fleshy, but beautifully boned woman, with a satin-smooth beige skin. She had a shyness so vast that she spoke in practically a whisper. An uncompromising, devastatingly honest kind of girl, and always, in the deepest sense, a Lady.'

Billie's schedule was hardly one that a vocal-coach would ever recommend to a pupil. If there was a lively scene in the offing – home or away – she would quite happily miss a night's sleep. She drank steadily – rather than excessively – but she supplemented her fifty cigarettes a day with a regular intake of marihuana: a habit she picked up before her fifteenth birthday. However, at twenty-one, she was always in control of the situation, and several musicians who knew her at that time have stressed that there was no question of Billie being addicted to anything in the 1930s – except good living. One who saw her often at the Hot-Cha said, 'I never saw her drunk nor high at that time.'

Billie had a succession of casual men-friends in the mid-1930s. Someone who knew her at this time described her sexual activities: 'healthy ... plus,' the man said, 'she had a craving for experiences, an appetite for sensations, she loved to hear about weird scenes, and it was no surprise to me that she eventually tried the dike scene [lesbianism] just for kicks I guess.' Sadie's reaction to her daughter's behaviour was usually taciturn. One of Billie's lovers who spent the night at her apartment was alarmed when Billie's mother entered the room early next morning, but he soon relaxed when he saw that she was carrying two cups of coffee. However, Sadie could turn very salty if she thought that anyone was trying to harm Billie. One of Billie's affairs was with Ben Webster, a famous tenor-saxophone player noted for his robust attitude towards love and life. Billie gained a blackened eye and a bruised jaw after an outing with this musician, and although

22

she herself had no objections at all, her mother noticed the marks and was very angry. On the next occasion that Ben dated Billie he chose not to enter the apartment but announced his arrival by tooting his car-horn. Sadie quietly followed her daughter down the stairs and as the man opened the car-door to let Billie enter, she rushed forward and struck him several times with an umbrella, telling him he'd get worse if ever he hurt her daughter again. Years later Ben said 'Naturally I could see that Billie's ma was real mad, but what made it worse was that Billie was just busting with laughter at the sight of me being whupped, that made me mad, but we all ended up friends.'

Despite the revelry, Billie was singing superbly; just before she played her return dates at the Apollo she began making the series of recordings that laid the foundation of her reputation. In July 1935, she made four titles with Teddy Wilson and his Orchestra, a seven-piece pick-up band (assembled in the studio for one date only). This septet was very different in style from the Benny Goodman group which had backed Billie twenty-one months before. Goodman did play on Teddy Wilson's July 1935 date, but only as a sideman – the rest of the band were black.

John Hammond was again the organiser of the session; this time he opted for a more informal 'jam-session' style backing, and his strategy paid rich dividends. It was the type of accompaniment that Billie might have got at a Harlem party, or at her club when top-class visiting musicians sat in. To avoid problems he had most of the band rehearsing on the day before the recording. He wanted the session – the first under Teddy Wilson's new contract – to go off as smoothly as possible; he recalled that 'the recording moguls were sitting around, anxious and sceptical'.

In order to get the musicians as relaxed as possible Hammond avoided a morning session and arranged that the recording had a late afternoon start. Soon after the date he told *Melody Maker* readers: 'The recording was set to start at 5.30 sharp. Two men had not shown up at that time. At 5.35 the phone rang and Benny Goodman was on the wire busily explaining that he would not be able to come, despite earlier promises. Just at that moment I put on a greater burst of temperament than the New York Telephone Company has ever before had to suffer. Result: in ten minutes Benny was sitting and playing in the studio better than ever.' Goodman on clarinet joined Teddy Wilson on piano, Roy Eldridge on trumpet, Ben Webster on tenor sex, John Trueheart on guitar, John Kirby on bass and Cozy Cole on drums.

Billie's relaxation in this exalted company is apparent. She sounds completely at ease on the slow wistful 'I Wished on the Moon', and on 'What a Little Moonlight Can Do', the second title recorded that day, she seems out to prove that her talents weren't restricted to slow torch-songs; her great sense of rhythm and versatility are highlighted as she swings her way through an amazingly fast version of the song.

Billie recorded another session with Teddy Wilson before the end of July 1935. Wilson re-thought his policy for the follow-up date and wrote out arrangements for the accompanying band. The effect of using written parts meant that the backings sounded less exciting, as Wilson later admitted: 'On the second Brunswick session, when we made "Too Hot for Words", etc., you'll notice that I added a man to get a trumpet-and-three-reeds line-up, so that I could write fuller arrangements for the date. The results were actually far less interesting, in my opinion.'

Fortunately, Wilson decided to revert to the more informal style of backing that the band had used on the first session, a format that ideally suited Billie. The method precluded long rehearsals for the entire band; Billie and Teddy Wilson sometimes got together before a session for vocal and piano run-throughs if Billie needed to familiarise herself with new songs.

Usually publishers' song-pluggers sent copies of the sheet music to Teddy and to Billie; before the session, they and the recording manager (usually Harry Gray) selected four or five numbers from a mound of song copies. When the musicians got to the studio, song introductions were worked out, and endings organised; the leader (in this case Wilson) designated

24

who was to take solos. Occasionally a riff was sketched out, but generally no written music was used; the musicians memorised their parts in what they called 'a head arrangement'.

As neither Billie nor Teddy were yet classed as stars, they usually had to make their selections from a batch of tunes that well-known artists had declined to record. Teddy Wilson explained the procedure in an interview with Don DeMichael: 'In those days the publishers made the hits. They had what they called number one, number two and number three plugs – the songs they were pushing. We never got into the plug tunes. We had our choice of the rest. That's why many of those songs we recorded you never heard anybody singing besides Billie.'

Trombonist Benny Morton, who began recording with Billie in August 1935, emphasised that Billie often had to work wonders with very trite material. In 1973 he said 'I have seen Billie turn the melody line around completely simply because a lot of those tunes sang as written were pretty dull. She definitely knew how she wanted to sing any song that she sang, she had an excellent ear and her diction was very good. She had something that you can't teach; this was a very beautiful woman – skin as smooth as could be, and it looked the colour of a peach. She and Teddy Wilson worked very well together, Teddy had the taste whereby he didn't overplay on any of the numbers, he always gave the right fill-ins.

'On the recording sessions Billie did a lot of composers favours. I remember one particular experience. We had gone through a couple of numbers that were accepted, when in walked a man who had composed one of these tunes. He heard the playback of his composition then said, "That's a nice job, but it isn't my tune." Billie said "That's the way I've done it. If you don't like it we'll just cancel it, we have several tunes here we could do instead." The man said "Oh, no, oh, no." I can't remember what the tune was, but it turned out to be one of Billie's hit songs.'

Billie liked all of the Irene Wilson compositions that she recorded: 'I'm Pulling Through', 'Ghost of Yesterday' and

25

'Some Other Spring'; she often said that the last named was her favourite tune. The composer tells how Billie first heard 'Some Other Spring'. 'This song was introduced to Billie at a dinner at the home of Helen Oakley, who is now Mrs Stanley Dance. Present were Carmen McRae, Billie and myself. The song was sung by Carmen, and played by me. Since Billie knew the inspiration for this song, and the facts surrounding it, she asked permission to record it. It became her favorite song, and one that she mentioned wherever she went – she saw fit to use it as the title of the opening chapter in her book.' Thirty years later, in 1968, Carmen McRae gave her early impressions of Billie, 'In her visualisation of song, and in her aura she was, to me, then a young hopeful, a combination of idol, alter ego, and mentor.'

Teddy Wilson recalled that he (as leader) got seventy-five dollars a session, this was for four titles recorded – usually a three-hour task. Billie averaged fifty dollars; the sidemen got a basic rate of twenty dollars – in accordance with scales laid down by the American Federation of Musicians.

Wilson gave the background: 'The sessions were highly co-operative affairs between John Hammond and me, we'd choose the personnel. It would depend on who was in town. If Basie was in we'd get Lester, Buck Clayton, Jo Jones and so on. If Duke Ellington was here we'd get Johnny Hodges and Cootie Williams. We'd get the best men we could find. There was always a nice attitude in the studio. Billie was wonderful to work with. We always tried to pass out solos so everybody would get sixteen or eight bars. The early sessions were held during the day at the Brunswick Studio on Broadway, between 57th and 58th.'

In 1973, John Hammond recalled the record company's attitude toward these early sessions: 'In the mid-30s Billie was so uncommercial that if I had tried to make a business arrangement with the American Record Company they would have laughed me out of the studios. They figured they were really indulging me by recording Billie and Teddy Wilson. I believe that on the first sides Billie made with Teddy she received twenty-five dollars a side, which was later increased to fifty dollars. Since we almost always did four tunes per session, it meant that she rarely got less than a hundred dollars.'

John Hammond estimates that the average sale per release was around the 3,000 mark, ludicrously low by today's figures, but in those times above the break-even figure. Hammond points out that the record company were quick to see how economical these informal jam-session-styled dates were: only small bands were employed, no arrangers needed to be paid, the ratio of rejects and wasted masters was very low. By 1935, the juke boxes were beginning to be regular features of many small bars all over the United States, and if a tune caught the public's attention via this medium, sales figures were sure to improve. Billie's 'I Cried For You' got a lot of plays on the jukes and consequently sold an impressive 15,000 copies.

In general, the Wilson–Holiday recordings were favourably reviewed, particularly in Britain. Billie was flattered to receive fan letters from Europe long before she ever got any from people in her own country. When her first American fan-letter did arrive, it was an extremely unusual one, sent by a long-term prisoner who enclosed an elaborate picture-frame made from 5,000 matchsticks. The model was granted a place of honour in Billie's apartment.

Before 1937, no music magazine had published an interview with Billie, and her British devotees were hazy as to who she actually was. Initially (in 1933) she was described to the *Melody Maker* readers as Clarence Holiday's step-daughter – jazz fans knew of Clarence because of his work with Fletcher Henderson. Later on (in 1935) she was called Clarence's niece.

Apparently, Clarence would not have minded if Billie had been described as his sister. His colleagues remember him as an easy-going companion, something of a lady's man who gained his nick-name 'Lib-Lab' for an inclination to do more than his share of talking if any girls were around. When Fletcher Henderson's Band played on their home-pitch at the Roseland Ballroom in New York, a continually changing

27

entourage of ladies waited on Clarence's exits. To his consternation, Billie occasionally turned up at the ballroom, usually to discuss her mother's failing finances. Rex Stewart remembered Lib-Lab's look of alarm as he spotted his daughter in the ballroom foyer. At first, colleagues thought that the consternation was a dutiful concern to protect his daughter from the wiles of randy musicians. Later, they realised that his annoyance emanated from a concern that his particular sweetheart of the hour might be less enthusiastic if she knew that her sugar-daddy was the real-life father of someone. in her own age group. Nevertheless, Clarence usually gave Billie a hand-out to tide his ex-wife over. Billie herself never asked for anything from her father, she never wanted to be accused of trading on his name, and accordingly she originally billed herself 'Hallidav'.

When Clarence left Fletcher Henderson to rejoin Billy Fowler's Band, his drinking buddy in Fowler's band was trombonist-vocalist Clyde Bernhardt. Clyde remembers: 'Clarence and myself would put our money together and buy a bottle of "Canadian Club" whiskey, or pints of "Golden Wedding" — in those [Prohibition] days the musicians and entertainers could always get the best, because we played for the people who had power and influence. Clarence was a nice fellow to know, a very regular likeable fellow, and he was friendly to all the people that he met. He wasn't like his daughter Billie, who was very moody at times. Billie was starting to sing professional jobs in those days. She had some very hard knocks, and lots of disappointments in those days, because she was young and green. The agents and bandleaders didn't understand or dig her style when she first started to sing in public. I always did like her singing, because she was different from anybody that I had ever heard in those days.'

John Hammond vividly recalled Clarence's reaction when he first congratulated him on his daughter's vocal skills. ' "I heard your daughter Billie last night. She's the greatest thing I ever heard." He frowned at me, so I waited until intermission. Then he told me, "John, for God's sake don't talk about Billie in front of the guys. They'll think I'm old." '

By 1935, Clarence was openly acknowledging the compliments that many musicians were making about his daughter's singing, the proud parent was gradually emerging. In 1932, Clarence had told Clyde Bernhardt that he didn't think that Billie would ever get any place as a singer because, in his opinion, 'she didn't have the kind of smooth voice that the public would take to'. Clarence knew that Billie was buying every Louis Armstrong record she could lay hands on, and he told Bernhardt that 'he didn't think that a girl singer should copy Louis Armstrong because there were already too many musicians copying Louis.' But Billie chose to disregard Clarence's advice on music, and on her style of living. Bernhardt remembers Billie's father saying that she was 'very hot-headed at times, and that she would fight him if he made her mad'. Clarence said philosophically that he guessed Billie 'loved him and her mother, but she wouldn't let them tell her what to do in her private life'. Clarence's disapproval of Billie's singing style gradually disappeared. In 1935, Bernhardt told him that he had heard Billie at the Hot-Cha Club and said how much he liked her singing. Clarence admitted that there had been 'a big improvement' and added 'if she keeps on trying she will get some place in the future'.

Just before Billie returned to the Apollo, Clarence made a special point of visiting her at the Hot-Cha to wish her luck; being a seasoned professional he was more impressed by a re-booking than a try-out. Billie was delighted and it seems that this overt sign of her father's approval was the factor that caused her to finally take his surname for her professional billing.

However, there was one area of Billie's professional activities that irked Clarence, and that was her recording sessions. His close friend, drummer Kaiser Marshall, told writer Johnny Simmen that 'Clarence was very salty because his successful daughter, who now had a regular recording contract, hired every guitar player in town bar himself for her dates.'

29

Later, when Billie began to attract more attention, Clarence took pride in telling people that his daughter was 'the Billie Holiday', but he and Billie never enjoyed a feeling of great family closeness, and subsequently Billie regretted that she hadn't made more of an effort to really get to know her father before his early death in 1937. Years later, she would talk eagerly to almost anyone who had known, or worked with, her father. Trombonist Floyd 'Stumpy' Brady, who played in Billie's 1945 big band, had also worked with her father in Don Redman's Band. He remembers Billie's set procedure in broaching the subject of her father. She'd down a few brandies then call him over saying, 'Come on, Stumpy, tell me about Lib-Lab.' She positively swelled with pride as Stumpy went through the ritual of saying, 'He was the tops, a great musician, and having you around is the living proof of his greatness.' Billie would always say aloud to the company: 'Hear that, that's my daddy he's talking about.'

However, Billie never ever discussed her father with someone who knew him well, trombonist Benny Morton.

Benny, who began recording with Billie in October 1935, has grateful reasons for remembering Clarence Holiday. Back in 1924, Clarence recommended Benny for a vacancy in Billy Fowler's Band — the change of job had meant a 100% increase in Benny's salary. Later, Benny and Clarence also worked together in Fletcher Henderson's Band and in Don Redman's Orchestra. It was whilst Clarence was with Don Redman that Benny first met Billie; by way of introduction Clarence simply said, 'Meet my daughter,' and that was the only occasion that Benny ever saw the two together. He says, 'She and I never talked about Clarence at all, even when we worked together in Basie's Band. I think she inherited some of her talent from Clarence, he played guitar and banjo well, and also sang, not that he taught her, they never lived together. Of course, he didn't sing in the style that she sang in, he was what you might call a shouter.'

The lack of close rapport between father and daughter meant that Billie lost out on a valuable source of advice on how she might handle her business affairs, particularly in such vital areas as the selection of suitable keys for her vocals. In later years, Billie spoke of her early musical inexperience, and how it led to a quick rejection from the big Harlem carbaret club Small's Paradise, where she had applied for the job of singing with Charlie Johnson's Band. 'At Ed Small's ... I went there, I was about thirteen, and I'll never forget it. Myra Johnson got me the audition. I was all ready to sing, and this cat asked me, "What key you singing in?" I said, "I don't know man, you just play." They shot me out of there so fast, it wasn't even funny.'

However, Clarence offered Billie good advice when he told her that the success of her Apollo dates would mean that she could work at many other theatres in and around New York. But Billie decided against seeking more theatre work, possibly influenced by the memory of a troubled date at a theatre in Philadelphia. Agent Irving Mills was prepared to give Billie a try-out with one of his black touring orchestras, the Mills Blue Rhythm Band. He sent her off to do a week with the band in Philadelphia. Among the numbers that she chose to sing was the 1932 hit, 'Underneath the Harlem Moon', a song that Ethel Waters, a featured artiste on the same bill, had also chosen. Stage protocol defined that Billie should give way to Miss Waters; the theatre owner's wife was detailed to point this out to Billie. Billie rarely brushed aside any professional guidance proffered by men, but throughout her life she regarded female comment as dispensable when complimentary and totally superfluous when destructive. Still in her teens at the time of this show-down, she made no effort to disguise her annoyance at the woman's suggestion. One word led to another, and after the owner's wife had told Billie that she couldn't stand her singing, Billie let out a series of linked oaths that greatly impressed the eavesdropping musicians. The engagement ended there and then, but its memory induced Billie to shun theatre work for some while afterwards.

She chose to accept a booking at a newish club in New York called the Famous Door, a basement venue that had opened in February of 1935. The syndicate that owned the club was comprised almost entirely of musicians, among them, Lennie Hayton, Gordon Jenkins, Manny Klein, Jimmy Dorsey and Glenn Miller.

A small band led by trumpeter Louis Prima had a highly successful inaugural season, then fellow white New Orleanian trombonist George Brunies took a band into the club in September 1935. It was during this run that Billie Holiday, (with Teddy Wilson at the piano) was persuaded that the club would make a marvellous showcase for her, enabling her to sing regularly to booking-agents, recording-managers and musicians. However, Billie's style of singing didn't capture the undivided attention of the clientele, many of whom felt that their entertainment should be raucous and obvious rather than subtle and artistic. Billie appeared ill at ease during her sets, and her uneasiness was increased by the fact that during her breaks she was not allowed to sit with any of the club's customers.

Arnold Shaw, in his excellent survey of the night life of New York's 52nd Street, *The Street That Never Slept*,

32

comments on this surprising aspect of the policy of the musicans who ran the club; he points out that Billie 'was not permitted to mingle, occupy a table, or even sit at the bar. Between frustrating sets, she had to endure the aggravation of sitting upstairs in the foyer just outside the club's toilets.'

The booking was a disaster for a sensitive artist like Billie, who at this stage of her career wilted visibly in front of a disinterested crowd. On 12 September 1935, four days after her opening, Billie was 'let go' by the club's management committee, and thus ended Billie's initiation in singing for a white audience and working for a white management.

During the summer of 1935, Joseph G. Glaser a white thirty-seven-year-old Chicago club-owner and band-booker began to devote more of his time to personal presentation of musicians. For some time previous he had been working in collaboration with a powerful booking agency owned by Tommy Rockwell and Francis 'Cork' O'Keefe. In 1935, Glaser decided to augment his agency activities by signing musicians and singers to an exclusive contract of personal management. He began building his empire of talent by signing Louis Armstrong, who had worked for Glaser years before at the Sunset Cafe in Chicago. During the mid-1930s, Glaser began offering engagements to Billie, and some while later, she too signed an exclusive contract with him.

It has been suggested that Billie might have fared better if she had worked only for black managements and agencies, but it is a sombre fact that during the 1930s, no black agents or managers were operating on a national basis. Some Territory bands and local singers had black managers, and dealt successfully with local black agents, but as soon as the bands moved into New York, Chicago, Detroit, and other major cities they found that white agents and managements had a strangle-hold on most of the entertainment outlets.

Glaser soon provided Billie with an open sesame into a Broadway revue at Connie's Inn. Connie's (named after proprietor Connie Immerman) was famous for its floor shows during the 1920s and 1930s. During the 1930s, the night club moved from Harlem, and the 1936 productions took place at

33

48th Street, between Broadway and 7th Avenue. There Billie joined a cast that included Louis Armstrong, Luis Russell's Orchestra, and Kahloah, 'the amazing dancer'.

The show proved successful and Billie's feature number, 'You Let Me Down' (which she had recorded the previous December) was one of the hits of the production. However, soon after the show's opening Billie suffered ptomaine poisoning and had to leave the cast temporarily. Her replacement was none other than the great Bessie Smith. Billie stressed throughout her life that the two musical forces that shaped her early style were Louis Armstrong and Bessie Smith – by coincidence her booking at Connie's intertwined with her two idols.

Unfortunately, we shall never know what Bessie thought of Billie's singing; she was noted for her lack of interest in the work of other artistes. However, some eighteen months before the Connie's show she had called in to the Hot-Cha Club whilst Billie was singing there. The younger woman was thrilled that 'The Empress of the Blues' had visited the club, but Bessie gave no overt sign that she was impressed, or seeking friendship, and it is uncertain whether Bessie ever bothered to listen to Billie again.

Louis Armstrong, however, always made a point of listening to newcomers on the same bill as himself. He had met Billie before the Connie's booking when two years earlier she had presented herself fan-like at his dressing room at the Lafayette Theater. Louis admired Billie's singing, but he was usually guarded in any public appraisal or criticism of her – mainly because they shared the same management. Knowing of the see-saw relationship that existed between Billie and Joe Glaser, he wisely didn't go out of his way to take sides.

Bessie Smith's contract with Connie's Inn was only for the duration of Billie's absence. Billie soon recovered from ptomaine poisoning, but she delayed her return to the show in order to undertake various auditions and engagements fixed by her management. She auditioned for the representative of a London-based agency with a view to fulfilling dates in

Europe. The regular publicity that she got in the British music magazines, and the healthy Trans-Atlantic sales of her recordings made a tour of Europe a viable proposition. To tie in with this possibility, the *Melody Maker* of 4 April 1936 published its first picture of Billie – answering a telephone, her eyebrows heavily pencilled. The pencilled brows were to appear in several subsequent photographs, they weren't part of a planned image. Billie explained years later, 'My eyebrows were all off 'cause I tried to shape 'em and took half of one off by mistake' (*Down Beat,* 4 June 1947).

Although Billie was fit and well again, Joe Glaser couldn't decide whether she should return to Connie's Inn. He would have preferred that she began working on the lucrative theatre circuits, however he told her outright that he couldn't consider recommending her for that sort of work until she lost weight. Billie, who was at this time an enormous eater, reluctantly, but successfully, began to diet. Glaser's family owned the site of the Grand Terrace Revue Ballroom in Chicago and he thought that it would be good experience for Billie to work with Fletcher Henderson's Band there for the season commencing in March 1936. But Ed Fox, who rented the ballroom from Glaser, couldn't find a spot for Billie in that production. Instead Billie went out of New York for a few theatre dates with the up-and-coming Jimmie Lunceford Band.

Billie's absence from New York, albeit temporary, made it impossible for her to take part in the Teddy Wilson session scheduled for 17 March 1936. Billie's place was taken by Ella Fitzgerald, then a 17-year-old singer with drummer Chick Webb's Orchestra. The records sold about as well as Billie's but in Britain there was a sense of disappointment; Ella was described as a 'charming warbler' but there was muted consternation that this release meant that the Teddy Wilson–Billie Holiday partnership had ended, particularly as the *Melody Maker* story of 1 August 1936 (from Leonard Feather in New York) made no mention of Teddy Wilson. 'Billie Holiday had her first solo recording at Brunswick last week. With Joe Bushkin on piano, Dick McDonough, guitar,

Cozy Cole, drums, Arthur 'Pete' Peterson, bass, Art Shaw, clarinet, and Bunny Berigan, trumpet, she was due to wax four commercial tunes: 'Did I Remember', 'No Regrets', 'Summertime' and another, but when a little trouble cropped up over the fourth side, Bernie Hanighen, that most remarkable and swing-minded supervisor, suggested making a blues. So the blues it was.'

The blues was 'Billie's Blues', a number that Billie was to regularly feature in many of her later programmes. The session passed off smoothly, and left a lasting impression on clarinetist Artie Shaw. Some months later, in an exclusive interview with the *Melody Maker* he said 'Of my own records, one of my favourites is "Billie's Blues" which I made with Billie Holiday, that was a swell session.' Years later, in his book *The Trouble with Cinderella* Shaw summarised his early impressions of Billie: she was 'already beginning to develop that distinctive style of hers which has been copied and imitated by so many singers of popular music that the average listener of to-day cannot realise how original she actually is'.

At the time of recording 'Billie's Blues' Shaw was impressed enough to suggest that Billie join the band he was organising, but Billie, who had heard Benny Goodman talk vaguely in the same way three years earlier, shrugged the suggestion off. She couldn't see a white bandleader and a black vocalist overcoming the Jim Crow restrictions that many ballroom owners and club operators firmly believed in.

It was not that Billie was unduly cynical, but recent events had made her more and more realistic. In June 1936, Joe Glaser again asked Ed Fox if he would feature Billie at the Grand Terrace, Chicago (for seventy-five dollars a week). This time, Fox reluctantly agreed. The engagement was to be one of the shortest of Billie's career. She left New York full of enthusiasm, knowing that she was to be accompanied by Fletcher Henderson's Orchestra, which contained several old friends.

The optimism quickly faded. After one performance, Fox made it clear that he thought Billie's style of singing was entirely unsuitable for one of his shows. Each night, he began shouting at her as soon as she had finished her set. Billie, mindful of previous rows with owners, kept calm for longer than usual. However, when she was called into Fox's office for a show-down the battle was two-sided. Twenty years later Billie recalled the viciousness of the row. She recounted: 'Jesus Christ, they ran me out of Chicago. Ed Fox, who owned the god-damn Grand Terrace said "What the hell, my Grand Terrace. Why the fuck should I pay you 250 (sic) dollars a week to stink my god-damn show up? Everybody says you sing too slow. Get out." ' Fox, who had seen his fair share of violence in Prohibition Chicago, felt that he had met his match when Billie began hurling the office furniture at him. He fired her then and there, no salary, no recompense.

Several of Fletcher Henderson's Band felt that their leader should have helped Billie, either by getting her re-instated, or by obtaining travelling expenses for her. However, Henderson deliberately avoided getting involved. Babe Matthews, then working with Nat Cole's Band at the Panama Cafe, was asked to take Billie's place immediately.

Someone once said that Billie in a full rage was 'as wild as a tigress', but usually her anger passed quickly; soon after the Chicago debacle she was full of despondency. Back in New York she got no sympathy from Joe Glaser. Billie recalled Glaser saying 'You've gotta speed up the tempo, you gotta sing hot stuff.' Billie remembered saying to Glaser, 'I want to sing like I want to sing ... that's my way of doing it.' Later, when the conversation became more heated, Billie ended the meeting by saying 'Look, you son-of-a-bitch, you sing it. I'm going to sing my way. You sing your way.' The outlook soon looked less bleak when Billie heard that the sales of her own recordings were gradually increasing.

Although Billie was now classified as a name recording artist she continued to record with Teddy Wilson's Orchestra; Wilson's records were issued on the seventy-five cent per record Brunswick label, whilst Billie's discs were issued by Vocalion at thirty-five cents each. As neither Wilson nor Billie were on artists' royalties at the time, the label-name and disc-price were only prestige pointers. Billie felt well satisfied that she was having recordings issued under her own name, the label credits were making a difference to her status, if not to her bank balance.

A session fee of seventy-five dollars wasn't enough to retire on, so Billie continued working – mainly in night-clubs. By 1936, most club-owners in uptown New York knew of Billie, and even if they weren't all fighting to book her, at least she could work almost as regularly as she chose.

The recordings and a spate of well-paid bookings convinced Billie that life was improving, and she suggested to her mother that they should move to a new apartment. Sadie needed little persuasion – for a long time she had been planning her own catering venture and after a search she found the perfect set-up, an apartment over a small vacant restaurant.

Sadie got great pleasure from cooking, and her speciality was soul food; opinions differs as to Sadie's prowess in the culinary arts, but whatever kitchen secrets that she had she shared with her daughter, whose cooking won nothing but praise. Billie was delighted to help her mother set-up the barbecued spare-rib snack bar, though she herself took no active part in the venture.

The restaurant wasn't run on any highly organised business system – often the food was given away to anyone who looked needy, and the hours were very variable. Sadie was a devout Catholic, but some of the goings-on in the upstairs part of the restaurant would certainly have surprised the local priest. Someone who knew the set-up said, 'It wasn't exactly a good-time flat, it was just that so many different people used to drop in there, you never knew quite what was happening, it was sort of a mixed resting place for homeless hustlers, chicks or guys who were genuinely down on their luck, or just plain pimps.' Billie's good natured mother never checked credentials, and Billie, who loved the prevailing party atmosphere had no objections. Later, when Billie became more famous, she often invited white people from the jazz world to visit the restaurant. Invariably these visitors were so over-fed downstairs they could scarcely stagger up the stairs to the inevitable party.

Billie broke new territory on 2 September 1936 when she opened at the Onyx Club on West 52nd Street. There she shared billing with violinist Stuff Smith's sextet (which included trumpeter Jonah Jones). Billie's booking scheduled as 'an indefinite engagement' lasted less than a month. Stuff's extrovert performances and Billie's poised restraint were an effective contrast for the audience, but friction soon developed backstage. The sextet received top billing, and although they and Billie appeared separately, Stuff became hyper-sensitive about audience reaction and hinted to Billie that she was 'milking' the applause. Later, he complained to the club's owner that Billie was on stage for too long, and asked that she be forbidden to do encores. After one columnist praised Billie more than the sextet, Stuff demanded that she be dismissed. The club's owner, Joe Helbock, who had been doing sensational business with Stuff Smith's group for most of the year, reluctantly told Billie that her engagement had to end.

One of the musicians who witnessed the contretemps said, 'It was a clash of personalities. If Stuff had liked Billie he wouldn't have let the applause thing get at him. He was a great guy in many respects, but this time he was as stubborn as a mule.' Joe Helbock had no hard feelings towards Billie and re-booked her at the Onyx in December 1936, to sing with the Spirits of Rhythm who were playing the club whilst Stuff Smith and his sextet were away on tour.

This re-booking was a compensation to Billie who was deeply hurt by the dismissal. She suffered from self-doubt all her life; even in later years when critics gave her every accolade she still needed reassurance; as a twenty-one-year-old she must have felt agonies in surveying the year that had just passed. In twelve months she had encountered two humiliating sackings through the indifference of white managements; the third dismissal was due to one of her own race's jealousy, and this was almost more than she could bear. Nevertheless, her dry, laconic approach to the song 'That's Life I Guess', recorded not long after the Onyx debacle, showed she was able to triumph over disappointments that might well have obliterated a lesser artist.

After finishing her return booking at the Onyx, Billie went to work in a basement night club called the Uptown House (on 7th Avenue and 134th Street); there she sang with a quartet that included pianist Vivian Smith (who later married clarinetist Jimmy Hamilton).

Billie's stay at the Uptown House lasted for three months. The residency could have gone on for much longer. Billie enjoyed singing at the club, even though regularity wasn't then the key word for owner Clark Monroe's system of payment. However, during the twelve weeks that she worked there several things happened that were to shape the rest of her life.

# CHAPTER THREE

In December 1936, Count Basie's Band
made its first appearance in New York. At John Hammond's
instigation the band had made its way to New York from its
home territory of Kansas City. Within its ranks was one of
the most remarkably gifted jazzmen who ever lived, the
tenor-saxophone player Lester Young. Lester, who had been
born in Woodville, Mississippi, in 1909, was the son of a
carnival musician. He spent most of his early life travelling
and playing in his father's band, then worked with various
bands: Art Bronson's Bostonians, the Original Blue Devils,
King Oliver's Band, Bennie Moten's Orchestra and others,
before settling down with Basie's Band. Like Billie, he had
suffered his share of disappointments, notably on his previous
visit to New York (in 1934) when his stay with Fletcher
Henderson's Band had been made untenable by fellow
musicians who had remorselessly criticised the sound and the
style of his playing.

Instead of demoralising Lester, this experience
strengthened his resolve to be individual. He had the
reputation of being uncomfortably shy, and it was said that
he appeared more retiring than ever when white reporters

attempted to interview him – even though he was once married to a white woman. His long-time colleague drummer Jo Jones once said that Lester knew only how to talk through his horn. However he did occasionally give interviews; in 1946, he told the black writer Alan Morrison, 'Originality should be the highest goal ... without it, art or anything else stagnates, and eventually degenerates.' Although Billie Holiday would have found it difficult to frame such sentiments, they were the creed of her artistry. It was inevitable that these two kindred souls should feel sympathy for each other.

They first met at a January 1937 recording session, and their mutuality was instantaneous. At that session Billie recorded one of her greatest performances, 'I Must Have That Man'; Lester's obliggato and solo are so close to Billie's mood that one could imagine that the two had worked closely together for years – in fact they had only been introduced a few hours before.

John Hammond was again in charge of the session; he recalled 'Billie Holiday, who met Lester first at one of her Brunswick sessions under Teddy Wilson's name. Their styles fitted, as did their tastes in smoking – the session was nearly cancelled when one of the top American Record Company officials walked in and sniffed the air suspiciously.' (*Jazz,* summer 1959, p. 183).

Billie's and Lester's empathy went a great deal deeper than their mutual liking of marijuana. Amazingly, although their friendship was a very close one, it was purely platonic. Buck Clayton, who knew Billie and Lester very well, has said 'They were the greatest and closest of buddies, but that was all.' Another colleague from Count Basie's Band, Benny Morton, also knew the couple well and he gave a similar summary of the relationship: 'They had something going musically, as well as their friendship, and I'm talking about clean friendship.' After Lester encountered a rat in his shirt-drawer he moved out of his hotel and went to live with Billie and her mother.

Lester's droll style of conversation went with his

predilection for bestowing nicknames on his friends. **Billie** was already known as Lady, but Lester felt that Holiday **was** too long a surname – so Lady Day was born. Lady Day returned the compliment: Lester was to her ears the leading tenor-sax player in the land, thus he was 'The President', informally shortened to 'Pres'. Lester also felt that the mother of a 'Lady' had to be a Duchess, so Sadie too got a new name. These sobriquets, casually endowed, were to stay with all three people for the rest of their lives.

Billie continued her stint at the Uptown House, and whilst working there (on 1 March 1937), she received a dramatic long-distance telephone call from Dallas, Texas. The caller asked if he was speaking to Eleanora Billie Holiday, daughter of Clarence Holiday; when Billie said yes she was told that her father had just died. Fortunately, the club's owner, Clark Monroe, was near the telephone and he culled the details of where the body was located and the cause of death.

During World War I Clarence, as Private 4105715, had served in France with the U.S. Army; he suffered gas poisoning during the fighting and this permanently damaged his lungs. He needed careful nursing during any illness. Whilst touring Texas with Don Redman's Band, Clarence contracted a heavy chest cold. Knowing the segregation problems that he was likely to encounter in that part of the world he delayed seeking medical attention until the band reached Dallas. By then, pneumonia had set in; Clarence died not long after being admitted to a hospital for army veterans.

In spite of the fact that Clarence had re-married in the mid-1920s, both Billie and her mother were full of recriminations when they learnt of his death. Billie, because she felt that she had not spent sufficient time with her father; Sadie, because she now blamed herself for the break-up of the marriage. The funeral was bizarre: Clarence's wife Elizabeth was joined by an unofficial wife who had had two children by Clarence. Former wife Sadie (Billie's mother) got lost en route to the funeral and anger augmented her sorrow when she finally met up with Billie long after the interment had taken place.

That night at the Uptown House, several of Clarence's ex-colleagues dropped in to give Billie and her mother their condolences. Clark Monroe looked after all the funeral arrangements, assisted by his younger brother Jimmy. Billie's friendship with Jimmy Monroe blossomed later when she returned to play casual dates at the club. There was no time for romantic developments in March 1937, for within a week of her father's death, Billie left the Uptown House.

In the March 1937 issue of *Down Beat*, John Hammond again stressed his admiration for Billie's musical talents, describing her as being 'great as ever at the Uptown House'. Hammond, well aware of the teething problems that Count Basie's Band was having during its early days in New York, suggested to Basie, and his agent Willard Alexander, that Lady Day would add both to the band's visual appeal and to its musical versatility. It was agreed that Billie be offered the job at seventy dollars a week, a raise of thirty-five dollars a week on her Uptown House salary.

During the early months of 1937, Billie had got to know several members of the Basie Band at the after-hours jam-sessions that Lester Young had taken her to. The appeal of going on the road with a bunch of young men who were lively company and great jazz musicians was all the incentive that Billie needed. Although the sum total of Billie's touring experience had been a few dates in Canada, accompanied by Louis Metcalf's Band, she readily agreed to the offer of joining Basie and packed her bags there and then.

In the 1930s, musicians usually regarded girl-singers as a necessary evil – an unmusical adornment designed to catch the male customers' eyes, without, if possible, offending their ears. Not so with Billie – all of the Basie Band found her singing inspirational, and although her particular clique consisted of Lester Young, Freddie Greene, Walter Page, and Buck Clayton, she was a popular travelling companion with all of the band, and her laughter on the Blue Goose coach journeys was always a welcome sound. Earle Warren, lead alto-saxophonist with the band, praised Lady's social qualities: 'Billie, like Lester, was always jovial and entertaining, very seldom moody and obstinate.' In an interview with Valerie Wilmer, trumpeter Harry Edison duplicated the same sentiments. 'It would be most beautiful the whole trip, because everybody loved Billie Holiday and everybody loved Pres.'

Part of Basie's schedule of one-night stands involved playing college-dates and amusement-park dance halls. For these bookings, the Basie Band always tried to rent a whole house of self-contained apartments, so that the musicians could economise by cooking their own meals. Earle Warren elaborated, 'We used to set up cooking quarters, and have our meals collectively. Billie was always helpful, she was a great cook.'

However, on one of the band's rare excusions into the South, they found that one particular town had neither apartments nor hotel rooms for them. The call of 'Every Tub' (every man for himself) went out. Billie and bassist Walter Page found that a local clergyman took in lodgers, and they decided to stay with the reverend. In order to enjoy a respite from the restrained atmosphere of the priest's home, Billie and Walter Page took a stroll through the town. Both of the strollers knew that one member of Basie's Band could easily pass for white, but nevertheless they were still absolutely astonished to see this man emerge from an exclusively white-only restaurant with a well-fed look on his face. They hurried up to him to share the joke and he brushed past them, giving out a 'who are these people?' stare. Billie let him go a dozen paces up the street, then she bawled out: 'Life's okay for you, Peola.' A cutting reference to a character attempting to pass for white in a then-current film.

Trombonist Benny Morton well remembers the tours with Basie, 'If the guys played cards, Billie could play cards with them, if they shot craps, she could shoot crap. A lot of men don't like to play with women, because they feel they usually take away their luck, but with Billie it was okay. Mind you, she used to win all the money.

'She liked the boys who liked the things that she liked. I don't drink, smoke or gamble, but we got on fine. These people made their own fun because they needed it, a lot of the time these people were hurting inwardly, because the world was cruel to them.

'Then, Billie laughed her life away, but I believe that this girl cried a whole lot too. You never got an idea that she wasn't enjoying life, but to me this was a cover-up. The laughter, this was a top, this also goes for Lester, He was one of the nicest men I've ever known, so very kind, but I think he felt that the world had short-changed him; he contributed such a lot to Basie's Band.'

In March 1937, one of the jazz world's most distinguished writers, Stanley Dance, was making his first visit to the U.S.A. Stanley, who has lived in the U.S. for many years, has vivid memories of hearing Billie's debut with Count Basie (13 March 1937): 'I heard Billie Holiday for the first time in person at the Uptown House in Harlem, where she was singing with a small band. Artie Shaw took me up there in his car, he sat in and jammed with the band. About a week later, Billie opened with Count Basie in Scranton, about 140 miles from New York. John Hammond and I drove up that evening and it was the first time I heard Basie. Well, I guess it was no night for judging Billie anyway, when she was new and settling in, but it was the impact of the band, its rhythm section and soloists, Basie himself, Lester, Herschel Evans, Buck Clayton and Jimmy Rushing, that meant most to me. The floor was jammed with dancers, the balcony packed, and the whole atmosphere tremendously exciting. As at the Renaissance, something came off the floor from the dancers, but something extra came out of the balcony, something you didn't get at the Savoy, or the Ritz in Bridgeport. They were sitting up there, but really participating.

'The following week, the band and Billie were at the Apollo Theater, New York, where I still remember the band breaking it up with "Honeysuckle Rose". Before I left for home, I heard her again at one of the Hickory House jam-sessions with Joe Marsala's Band.'

Billie's visit to the Hickory House left a lasting impression on Art Shapiro, the bassist with Joe Marsala's Band. In the mid-1950s, Shapiro and pianist Jimmie Rowles did a recording session with Billie (eventually issued in 1973 by Paramount Records); the tapes were left running in between numbers and some fascinating conversations emerge, one of them relating to Billie's visit to the Hickory House. Art Shapiro asks, 'Do you remember coming to the Hickory House? I remember you came down in a little gingham dress, and you sang, sat in with us ... Joe Marsala's Band. First time I laid eyes on you ... about 1937 or 1938.' 'That's right, Joe Marsala, my baby. They had them good steaks, he bought me a steak that night, I was still out of work, and didn't have no loot. I told him, I said "Man, I just got a subway fare to get Uptown and I'm hungry." He said, "Don't worry about that, I'll sign for you." He got me a steak and I got loaded.'

Shapiro then says, 'You were just a baby then yourself, a natural,' and Billie replies 'That's right, I was about eighteen or nineteen,' exercising a lady's prerogative to be cool about her age; the reference to being out of work was possibly a slip of the memory.

A contemporary newspaper review gives a glowing report of Billie's first date at the Apollo with Basie's Band, 'The sensation of the show is statuesque and effervescent Billie Holiday, and braving controversy we dare to place her in superior position to Ella Fitzgerald. When the rhythm-wise redhead swings "I Cried For You" and sings of her "Last Affair", the Apollo, the audience and the fixtures truly belong to her. But it was not until she came across with the beautiful "One Never Knows, Does One?" does she rate tops. There is more force, personality and sparkle in the Holiday voice than we ever noticed in La Fitzgerald's, and that's going some, for Fitzgerald can sing for us anytime of day.' (*Hist. N.Y. Jazz Scene,* pp. 287-8).

News of Billie's success with Basie spread quickly throughout the New York jazz scene, and when she appeared with the band at the Savoy on Sunday 11 April, the packed house included Louis Armstrong, Ella Fitzgerald, Benny Goodman, John Hammond, Lionel Hampton, Allen Reuss,

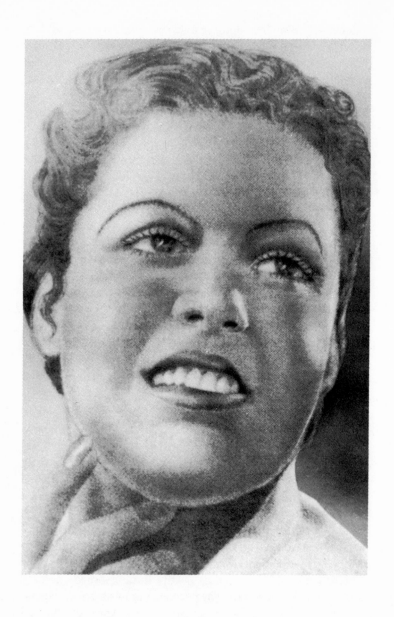

Dave Tough and Chick Webb.

Billie's natural musicianship enabled her to make the transition from small-band to big-band work with complete ease. Count Basie said, 'She fitted in so easily, it was like having another soloist. All she needed was the routine, then she could come in with her eyes closed – no cues or signals.' The success of this musical partnership is apparent on a recording taken from a Savoy Ballroom broadcast originally transmitted in June 1937. Unfortunately, due to contractual reasons there are no studio recordings of Billie with Basie's Band.

Musically, Billie's stay with Basie's Band was almost perfect, but in other ways things became less happy for Billie. Trouble began when Basie's agent wanted her to change her repertoire. Count Basie and John Hammond didn't disagree with this idea in toto; they suggested a compromise whereby Billie sang more blues, which they felt showed the band off at its best. But Billie indicated that she felt best in singing material that she had chosen herself, and also pointed out that in Jimmy Rushing the band already had one of the greatest of all blues singers. There were also rumours that her friendships with various band members were causing jealousy to intrude into the band's work on stage. Billie denied this emphatically. She was on good terms with all of the band, but her only intimate friendship was with guitarist Freddie Greene. One of the Basie Band said long afterwards, 'Hell, Lady was an angel compared to what lots of girl-singers have been, she once made a comment that she was scared of what she might catch from the band on account of the girls we went with, but we were no worse than any other touring band, except back in those early days we weren't getting much money, so there weren't many wine-and-dine romances with girls we met on tour'.

Money was short, the average wage for a Basie sideman on tour was sixty dollars a week – gross; hotel and eating expenses had to come out of that total. Billie had to pay for her own gowns and even the cleaning bill for them made a big hole in the seventy-odd dollars a week that she was getting.

49

But sax-player Earle Warren points out that nobody in the band was starving; by judicious scouting they could economise on rooming expenses. The money that was saved was often used for gambling, and the usual routine on tour was to play card-games and craps in the aisle of the band-coach.

Jimmy Rushing, the band's male vocalist (nicknamed 'Mister Five by Five' because of his enormous girth and lack of height) rarely participated in the gambling games; he neither gave money nor sympathy when the losers came to him for comfort. He also kept well out of the squabbles between Billie and the Basie Band's management. Jimmy had the greatest admiration for Billie's vocal talents, but nevertheless, he did find that her general attitude was, at times, less than what he considered 'professional', in that he always equated professionalism with consistency, and Billie's finest vocal qualities weren't perpetually on display when the band toured. She was really a city-flower, and when the novelty of touring with Basie had worn off, she became progressively disenchanted with life on the road. Dissension between her and the band's management became more regular. Things came to a head early in 1938, and Billie was asked to leave. Lady's stay with the band had lasted less than a year, but to her it seemed much longer; she said 'for almost two years I didn't see anything but the inside of a Blue Goose bus.'

For some years afterwards, Lady Day viewed the whole Basie Band interlude with bad feelings; her relationship with John Hammond was never the same again. Billie's fans were mystified by the dismissal, the *Melody Maker* of 5 March 1938 said 'Billie Holiday has been fired from the Basie Band for reasons not directly connected with music.' Months later, in the August 1938 *Down Beat,* Billie told Ted Locke 'I'm just a poor girl who lost her job.' She blamed John Hammond for her sacking. However, a month later, Basie's manager, Willard Alexander (an executive of the Music Corporation of America) gave some very frank comments to *Down Beat*: 'It was John Hammond who got Billie the job with Count Basie, and he was responsible for Basie keeping her. In fact, if it hadn't been for John Hammond, Billie would have been through six months sooner.' Taking full responsibility for the sacking, Alexander went on, 'The reason for her dismissal was strictly one of deportment, which was unsatisfactory, and a distinctly wrong attitude towards her work. Billie sang fine when she felt like it. We just couldn't count on her for consistent performance.'

Count Basie always retained a high opinion of Billie's singing (or William as he usually called her). In 1938, shortly after he signed Helen Humes as her replacement, he prophetically summarised Lady Day's whole career when he told the *Melody Maker* 'Billie is a marvellous artist who remains unappreciated by the world at large.'

Billie may have been disenchanted with life as a travelling band's vocalist, but she wasn't completely disillusioned. Less than a month after the Basie rumpus she left New York to join the big band led by white clarinetist Artie Shaw, the man who had offered her a job eighteen months before.

Contrary to most sources, Billie was not the first black girl-singer to work with a white band. Over ten years before, Ivie Anderson had guested briefly with Anson Weeks' Orchestra at a Californian hotel and, with far more publicity, tubby June Richmond had worked regularly with Jimmy Dorsey's Band months before Billie joined Shaw in the spring of 1938. However, all of June Richmond's work with Jimmy Dorsey took place in the North, usually in-and-around New York. Despite being liberally-minded, Dorsey was disinclined to take Miss Richmond on a tour of the Southern States.

Throughout the 1940s and the 1950s more and more white bandleaders had to face the dilemma of whether or not to ask their black star-performers to tour the South. There was always the possibility that a Negro might be insulted by someone in the audience, with the result that the band's white sidemen might join in, en masse, on behalf of their affronted colleague. Worse still, were the miserable occasions when some of the band refused to stand-up for the black minority in an up-tight situation, thus antagonising the black musicians *and* the white liberals in the band. Either way, resultant tensions were not conducive to good performances, by anyone concerned.

Artie Shaw would have willingly met both situations head-on. Having suffered a deal of anti-Jewish antagonism, he held outspoken views on racial persecution. He could also count on 100% support from his musicians, they were overjoyed by the news that Billie was to join the band. Billie's first job with Shaw was at the Roseland State Ballroom in Boston, Massachusetts. At that time, Shaw was doing a lot of work in the Boston area, the home territory of the Schribman Brothers who ran an entertainment booking agency that virtually controlled all the band work throughout New England. The Schribmans who guaranteed Shaw's payroll were less delighted by Shaw's signing; they envisaged difficulties in trying to talk reluctant ballroom and club owners into booking a white band with a black singer. The Schribmans were business men and not crusaders, and they wanted no part of the pioneering, but Shaw's initial

*Singing with Artie Shaw's band – Atlantic City – Summer 1938*

enthusiasm persuaded them to keep quiet, albeit temporarily.

However, pressures began to build up soon after Billie's debut. The Boston ballroom crowds took to Billie instantly, but at some of the venues outside the city the enthusiasm was less obvious, and much of this indifference had nothing to do with racial prejudice; it was simply that Billie's style was too uncommercial for the casual listener to enjoy. The average ballroom manager's tactic was to instantly relay any of his customers' complaints back to the band's management – in order to forestall or avoid any price increase that the manager might be planning to suggest concerning the return booking. This situation didn't apply only to Artie Shaw, it was, and is, part of show-business strategy. However, Shaw became weary with continually being informed of every trifling comment that had been made about Billie's performance or her appearance.

Shaw wavered on the wisdom of keeping Billie, and trumpeter John Best, who rejoined Shaw in April 1938, recalls that 'Shaw informed the band that he could no longer keep Billie in the band unless we could help out with her salary. From that point on, for some time, we contributed ten dollars each a week towards her salary We were making about ten dollars a night at that time.'

Two months after Billie had joined Shaw, the *Metronome* issue of June 1938 printed a story headliner 'Holiday remains with Artie Shaw'. During the 1930s, the magazine often described Negro performers in quaint old terms. Billie was no exception: 'Despite wild stories that Artie Shaw has been forced to release Billie Holiday, the dusky songstress is still with the band, and will remain with it indefinitely.' The story went on to say that Shaw had temporarily recalled singer Anita Bradley for the express purpose of singing pop-ballads, allowing Billie more opportunity 'to warble the special material for which she is famous'.

In the *Down Beat* issue of the same month John Munro reviewed Billie's work with Shaw's band: 'Her lilting vocals jibe beautifully with the Shaw style; and her stuff is going big with the customers. Most of all the personality and musicianship of this real jazz gal have won and unified the whole band, and these days more than one solo is being played straight at Billie.'

The relationship between Shaw and Lady Day was for a time more close and complex than the usual bandleader–vocalist situation. One black musician who knew Billie said, 'I'm sure that Lady and Artie were real close for a while, and some even thought that Billie was serious; however, Artie hadn't gotten into his marrying ways, and he was always blowing hot and cold about everything. I think that Billie got hurt, but when she was young she had such a way of laughing things off, you could never be sure.'

Often, she travelled to gigs in Shaw's car, which she candidly admitted was 'no damn good for lovers'; because of band economy the car usually had at least three other passengers for journeys to one-night stands. Billie recalled, with great humour, one such ride. 'One afternoon we were driving along in Artie's car to a one-night-stand. We passed an old man on the road who had a beard. I asked Artie if he had ever worn a beard and that I'd bet he sure would look funny if he wore one. Chuck Peterson, George Auld, Les Jenkins and a couple of other boys in the band were all in the car. So we were all surprised when Artie said "I used to wear one all the time – when I was at my own farm a few years ago." So I asked Artie if he looked not bad with a beard – and I was joking, you know, to make conversation on a long drive. "Indeed I did look fine with a beard," Artie said. "I looked exactly like Jesus Christ when he lived." You should have heard the boys and me roar at that. We got a bang out of it. Artie looked mad, because he had been serious. So I said "We'll just call you Jesus Christ, King of the Clarinet, and his Band".'

All of the Artie Shaw sidemen loved Billie's sense of humour, which despite trying circumstances usually managed to make itself evident. On one occasion, in Parkersburg, West Virginia, it did fail her. The band had embarked on a tour of the South, and despite warnings and head-shakings by advisers, Shaw asked Billie to travel with the band on the trip.

Some months after the tour, Billie told the black newspaper the *New York Amsterdam News,* that there were no racial incidents at all on the tour. However, trumpeter John Best can vividly remember a particular scene in Parkersburg. On this tour, Billie usually rode in Best's car, together with Lester Burness and Zutty Singleton (a famous black drummer who Shaw had temporarily hired to 'coach' the band). When the car reached Parkersburg, Zutty asked to be let out at a black hotel and suggested to Billie that she get out there too, as they were 'down South' and couldn't stay at the 'white only' hotel down town. However, Billie was determined to find this out for herself. She found out – the hard way – and was told that there were no rooms available. John Best recalls 'I had to take her back to the place where Zutty had checked in, and in the meantime he had the only room with a private bath.' For a few minutes it seemed as though Billie was as mad at Zutty as she was at the whole South.

On tour, the band members tried their best to put a protective mantle around Billie, but it was impossible for even the most well-meaning and zealous guardian to stop the hostile glances and impudent racist comments that were occasionally unleashed – North or South – by people who saw Billie surrounded by a group of white men.

When the band played a date in St Louis, the promoter who leased the hotel ballroom informed Shaw that he must have a white girl-singer. Shaw made a stand, then decided that this compromise would possibly solve all his problems. He auditioned several girl vocalistes before deciding to sign little known nineteen-year-old Helen Forrest (later to star with Benny Goodman, Harry James, and others).

Billie did her best to make Helen Forrest welcome. Miss Forrest told George Simon (*The Big Bands*, p. 416), 'She was wonderful to me, she was always trying to help. I can remember what she used to tell Artie, "Why don't you let that child sing some more? Go ahead. And make her some more arrangements, too!" She really was a great person!' Shaw took Billie at her word, and began to give Helen Forrest more and more prominence. On ballroom dates Billie accepted this with easy grace, but she naturally felt hurt when she found that she had less and less to do on the band's twice-weekly broadcasts on the Columbia network. She finally came to dread Tuesdays and Saturdays because she was uncertain as to whether she'd be featured during transmission time. Finally it was made obvious to her that she wouldn't be required for radio work and that Helen Forrest would do the singing. Billie still managed to smile her way through this disappointment; Shaw himself never did quite understand how upset she was. Years later he summed up his reactions 'The bigger our success the more dissatisfaction there seemed to be in the band. Billie Holiday who got along fine with Helen Forrest began to resent her' (*Down Beat,* 29 June 1951, p. 3).

The situation wasn't helped by the fact that the photography used on the front cover of the *Metronome* magazine's issue dated September 1938 showed the full Shaw Orchestra, with one girl singer seated in front – the girl was obviously white.

Music-publishers were at the root of the decision to 'rest' Billie from the radio programmes. Their song-pluggers (or contact-men as they were then called) carefully graded their potential hit songs, and they were only willing to allocate exclusive material to Shaw if he promised not to allow Billie to sing their songs on the radio. For them, Billie's style didn't stick closely enough to the written melody. Their dictum was: less artistry equals more sheet-music sales (at that time a bigger source of income to music publishers than the royalties from record sales). Shaw absolutely detested these pressures, but his management were in total agreement with the Tin Pan Alley dictum and described Billie in print as being 'too artistic'.

Shaw might be criticised for ever allowing himself to be diverted. However one of the main reasons for his disenchantment with Billie concerned record-making. In the spring of 1938, Shaw had changed record companies. He left Brunswick and signed an exclusive contract with Victor, which originally involved him recording for their Bluebird label. When Billie first began working with Shaw she indicated to him that she was free to record with his band, however as Shaw later pointed out 'she failed to mention that she was under contract to Brunswick and didn't have the right to record for anybody but Brunswick. She re-signed with Brunswick after promising she wouldn't.' (*Down Beat* 1939.) This explains why Lady only ever made one side with Shaw ('Any Old Time', recorded 24 July 1938) – the record was issued on Bluebird but later withdrawn after breach-of-contract complaints by Brunswick. Subsequently Shaw had no choice but to use Helen Forrest on the next recording (made in September 1938), and it would have been plain bad band-leading if he hadn't given the tunes that he had recorded any radio exploitation.

The inevitable crunch came eight months after Billie had joined Shaw. The band had finally won a booking at the Lincoln Hotel in New York; they began their residency there on 26 October 1938. An incident that occurred soon after the opening ended Billie's days with the band. John Best remembers 'The hotel's owner and manager, Maria Kramer, told Billie not to enter the Blue Room through the main entrance but to come through the kitchen with the rest of the band. This upset her, and as I recall was the direct cause of her leaving the band, as Artie sided with Mrs Kramer.'

A few weeks later, in January 1939, Billie told Bill Chase of the black newspaper the *New York Amsterdam News*, 'Gee, it's funny, we were really a bit hit all over the South and never ran into the color question until we opened at the Lincoln Hotel here in New York City. I was billed next to Artie himself, but was never allowed to visit the bar or the dining room, as did the other members of the band. Not only was I made to enter and leave the hotel through the kitchen but had to remain alone in a little dark room all evening until I was called on to do my numbers. And these numbers became fewer and fewer as time went on. One night, John Hall offered to buy me a drink at the bar, but when I told him that I wasn't allowed to drink there he gave me five dollars and told me to go outside to a bar that wouldn't refuse me because of my color. Gee, he was swell.' (Big deal, say I, but people who knew Billie say that was exactly the type of comment she was likely to make during those early years).

In another 1939 interview, Lady elaborated on her final days with Shaw. 'The hotel management told me I had to use the back door. That was all right. But I had to ride up and down in frieght elevators, and every night Artie made me stay upstairs ... I would stay up there, all by myself, reading everything I could get my hands on, from ten o'clock to nearly two in the morning, going downstairs to sing just one or two numbers. Then one night we had an airshot (a radio broadcast not emanating from a studio) and Artie said he couldn't let me sing. I simply got enough of Artie's snooty, know-it-all mannerisms and the outrageous behaviour of his managers and left the band. With Basie I got seventy dollars a week, with Artie I got sixty-five dollars.' Billie added, 'The real trouble was this, Shaw wanted me to sign a five-year contract, and when I refused, it burned him.' Billie also claimed that Shaw had failed to pay her for the one song that she had recorded with his orchestra – a charge that Shaw immediately refuted. The December 1938 issue of *Down Beat* plumped for the non-signature of the long-term contract as being the severing blow in the Shaw–Holiday tie-up, but in the same month Leonard Feather wrote in the *Melody Maker*: 'It is now said that Holiday left Shaw because (a) His new radio sponsors, the "Old Gold" cigarette people, refused to use her on the air – maybe because Billie smokes a different kind of cigarette and (b) she was made to enter the Lincoln Hotel, where the band plays, by the back door.'

The Holiday–Shaw split became national news, and the late Walter Winchell remarked in his widely-read column that it was ironical that the hotel concerned should be named after Lincoln.

*Down Beat* commented on the extensive publicity that the affair had received: 'Negro press throughout the U.S. gave the Billie Holiday split with Artie Shaw wide space in news columns. Billie was tagged "the last survivor of coloured singers with ofay bands." Shaw made headlines by denying prejudice caused her dismissal. Billie, meanwhile, is not complaining as she rounds up her own band for a Greenwich Village spot.'

The 'Village spot' was a new club soon to be named Cafe Society, situated in Sheridan Square where West 4th merges with Washington Place. Billie's booking at the club proved to be the turning point in her career; it was rough justice that the publicity from the Shaw shindig greatly helped her to establish herself. Soon after leaving Shaw, Billie took great delight in guesting on a radio programme with his ace rival Benny Goodman.

Billie's summary of the whole Shaw episode (printed by *Down Beat* late in 1939) temporarily re-activated the controversy surrounding her dismissal. Artie Shaw, answering through a third party (Les Zimmerman) complained that he had been wronged by Billie's article, and said that his Jesus Christ comment was 'a casual remark'. *Down Beat*'s footnote (which closed the debate) was, 'In other words, it's Artie Shaw's word against Billie Holiday's.'

Billie's rancour didn't last long, she soon forgave Shaw, and although they were never again close friends she always spoke well of him, describing him as 'a good cat deep down'. In a letter to an English fan, Charles Saunders (mailed on 10 March 1940), she wrote, 'Artie deserved it because of his treatment of me, still don't say he not a good musician because he is good, one of the best, and I bet he will come back bigger than ever' (referring to the first of Shaw's retirements from the music business). Shaw, for his part, took a lot longer to mellow; however, in later years he was always quick to defend Billie, and on being asked to appear on Billie's 'Comeback Story' (televised in October 1953), he instantly and willingly complied – unlike some of Billie's other colleagues from earlier years.

In 1973, Artie Shaw gave B.B.C. producer Steve Allen an affectionate summary of his memories of Billie, 'My band was obviously a rather strange place for her to be, our music wasn't like any of the music she sang with ... it worked, but it worked in a very strange way, and oddly enough a lot of

B Holiday
286 w 114 st
apt 2 E
n y

Dear mr Sanders
I recived your letter and was glade
to know I have a new friend and
I have aplenty on new Record
on the market to day in my
own right and I hope to see
you all soon as I am getting
a manager now and I hope
he send me there and
when I get there I hope
to make evry one like me
and I expect to come very
soon write again soon
from B Holiday .
let me know if you want
a picture .

*Posted New York, 30 August 1939*

Miss Billie Holiday
286 W 142nd St apt 2E
New York

Dear Charles

I dont know wthern I sent you a picture
but I am sure I did but if I didn't
let me know again please and
the please you gone Artie he
dervserted it because he treatened
me still dont say he not a good
musian because he is good one app the
Best and I Bet he will come Back Bigger
then Ever now you know Charles Every
Body will take advage app you if my
Can because you just goo to watch
everybody now all but it want be
a next time Because I will watch
out next time Well Charles write
me agan soon
        from B Holiday

*Posted New York, 10 March 1940*

people didn't like it. R.C.A. for example. When she left my band ... it was a mutual agreement. She was under contract to me and I offered to finance her act and buy her gowns and arrangements. We remained good friends to the day of her death, but she had developed a sense of total resignation to the fact that the large audience was not going to recognise her abilities. She had a certain amount of inner pride, she was a very strong person, but as a singer I think she was completely resigned, at the time, that she would never have a mass audience. Later, when she tried to get one and couldn't, I think that was indirectly part of why she took drugs to ease the pain.'

Cafe Society (Downtown) was the first club venture for Barney Josephson, then a thirty-six-year-old ex-shoe manufacturer whose parents had been immigrants from Latvia. The club was later to have a twin – Cafe Society (Uptown). The Downtown branch had room for 220 customers, its slogan was 'The wrong place for the right people'. Admission charges were $2.00 for weeknights and $2.50 at weekends, beer was sixty-five cents a glass and hard liquor seventy cents – you could, if needs be, nurse one drink all night without the staff having apoplexy. More novel than the tariff was the rule that black and white customers could sit together anywhere within the club.

Whitney Balliett, in his book *Ecstasy at the Onion,* eloquently summed up Josephson's modus operandi: 'His intent was simple and revolutionary; to present first-rate but generally unknown Negro and white talent to integrated audiences in honest attractive surroundings.'

Once again, John Hammond had been the instigator of a new phase of Billie's career; it was Hammond who recommended Billie to Josephson, who admits the debt. 'Whatever I learned, I learned from Hammond.'

In general Billie and Josephson enjoyed an easy-going relationship. The club-owner told writer Derek Jewell, 'Don't misunderstand me. We had our rows. To her I was a white man boss – and no white man was to be trusted. She wasn't a bad girl. She had to stand so much she got moulded wrong.

She was good-looking but never a beauty. She never had a really big voice — it was small, like a bell that rang and went a mile.'

After a few minor setbacks, the club became fully operational in January 1939. The opening bill featured Billie Holiday, trumpeter Frankie Newton and his Band, and the boogie-woogie pianists, Albert Ammons and Meade Lux Lewis (who were later joined by Pete Johnson). Billie was accompanied by 'Sonny' White, the pianist in Newton's Band. Ellerton 'Sonny' White from Panama, was then just twenty-one years old, he enjoyed working with Billie and the professional relationship between the two soon developed into personal closeness. In a November 1939 *Down Beat* interview, Billie said that Sonny was one of the three men that she had loved: 'One was Marion Scott, when I was a kid. He works for the post office now. The other was Freddie Green, Basie's guitar man. But Freddy's first wife is dead, and he has two children and somehow it didn't work out. The third was Sonny White, the pianist, like me, he lives with his mother and our plans for marriage didn't jell.'

Billie's friends were uncertain about her genuineness in wanting to marry and settle down, or rather they were doubtful that any one man could keep her happy for long at this time in her life; others saw her unrestrained sexual activities as a symptom of a restlessness that would have been dispelled by the security of marriage. Trombonist Benny Morton, a life-long teetotaller, said he saw a quieter side of Billie than most other musicians since she never had to prove her drinking capacity to him. Conversely, another musician said that he was always impressed by the fact that Billie ate and drank like a man.

Some knew Billie as a straight-forward, lusty heterosexual, but others are positive that she occasionally indulged in lesbianism. Friends who had known Billie since the early 1930s emphatically deny stories that she ever worked in a New York brothel, but two people who knew her well are adamant that prostitution played a part in her life, before, and after, she moved to New York. One of them, seemingly without malice, was convinced that Billie's tasks in a Baltimore brothel (which she mentioned in her autobiography) were more carnal than menial, an opinion not shattered by writer Millard Lampell's diligent research in Baltimore which led him to a girl who had worked in the whorehouse with Billie. But, whatever Billie's habits were, she enjoyed the admiration and respect of every musician who ever worked with her.

# CHAPTER FOUR

Frank Newton's Band enjoyed working at the Cafe Society, there was a good group spirit, and excellent rapport with Billie. John Williams, bassist with the band, said 'Billie and Newton would kid each other about the Band. It was Frankie's band but Billie would say, "this is my band," and would go to Barney the owner and say, "Newton don't need a raise but give my band one." Her dressing room door was always open to us and I've never known her to hurting anyone but herself. She had the "World on a String", being beautiful, having a hell of a figure, personality plus, and a style of her own that no one could steal. She was always the same and would never say "you fellows didn't play my music right, so that's why I didn't go over big." Lady Day was a beautiful woman and it's a shame Hot Pants were not in style, for the Boys really missed something.'

Occasionally the band and Billie did 'outside gigs', working at private parties and receptions away from the Cafe Society. Kenneth Hollon, who played tenor-sax in the band told writer Johnny Simmen of one such booking — 'We had a society date to play in the Sixties street area, and Billie and I went by car. Since we arrived at the address too early we stayed in the car until it would be the time to get to the place. Billie was smoking pot, I didn't know too much about reefers at that time. Billie said, "This stuff is good. It comes from Dakar, Senegal, Africa. Try one." Billie showed me how to inhale, hold it in and then exhale what was left. I followed all her instructions to the last detail. When we arrived at the place where we were to play I got out of the car but could hardly pick up my heels. We went inside and everything was going round and round including my head. I made an attempt to set up my stand for the music, but somehow I couldn't do it. All this time, Frankie Newton was watching me, noticing how strangely I was acting. Finally, I was ready to play the first tune. I felt so good that I just tried to play the tune from memory. I thought I was knocking everybody out (I sure was knocking myself out) but when we finished our first number Frankie came over to me and said: "What the hell did you think you were doing?" I replied, "Playing my horn man, what else?" Frankie said, "You think you're raising hell?" I answered, "Yeah man that's what I'm doing," but he didn't think so. "Well you ain't," he said. When he said this, right then I got tickled and all I could do was laugh! I couldn't play another thing. I stayed high for four or five days. I ate like a pig, drank gallons of water, but nothing helped. Never since that night have I ever touched another reefer. There's no doubt that the stuff Billie gave me that night was the real MacCoy.' Hollon, like others who knew Billie at this time, said, 'I never saw her drink or shoot dope, all she did was smoke weed.'

Barney Josephson's strictly enforced rule was that there must be no smoking of marijuana in his clubs. He told Whitney Balliett, 'When Billie Holiday was with me, she'd get in a cab between shows and drive through Central Park smoking. One night she came back and I could tell by her eyes that she was really high. She finished her next number and I guess she didn't like the way the audience reacted.' Because of the heat from the spotlights, Billie like many other female night-club artistes wore no underwear on stage. She didn't criticise the audience verbally for their indifference;

instead, she turned her back on them, bent over, and flipped up her gown to give the crowd a full view of her rear, she then strutted back to her dressing-room. This was an isolated incident; usually, Billie's performances were received in rapt silence.

But appreciation from a dedicated audience, and stimulation from marijuana, were not enough to dispel the bouts of melancholia that Billie got. An inkling of her occasional despair can be felt in a letter that she wrote in June 1939 to English bass-player Jack Surridge: 'Nothing anyone would say could make me feel any worse than I do, but I guess it will all come out alright in the end.'

Billie was the victim of the educational restrictions that were imposed on many of those who dwelt in black ghettos; she never got beyond the fifth grade during her school-days in Baltimore, and as she grew older, she became increasingly aware of the limitations of her education. One musician revealed how he became aware of how she felt. 'At Cafe Society, Frankie Newton, who could be a very serious guy, would get some listeners round him, and he'd talk about pretty deep subjects like "the economics of Marcus Garvey's return to Africa scheme", or "The Soviet Five Year Plan". If Billie ever heard any part of the discussions she'd say, "I don't want to fill my head with any of that shit." Years later, it came to me that she didn't understand much of what Frank was talking about, and the worse part of it was, she really wanted to, because if any one of the musicians sat down and explained something to her she'd really be as attentive as a kid being read to out of a story book. I guess it was sad in its own way. This woman's talent and her looks, and yet in some ways she really had the mind of a twelve-year-old – but she was as sharp as you like, and had a great deal of what we call "mother wit". She lived more than a lifetime by the time she was twenty-one, and I guess the whole book was thrown at her before she ever got to New York. She could spot a hustler three blocks away, but crazy as it sounds, she was naive about so many things.'

Songwriter Johnny Mercer described his reaction to Billie:

'She was an impressive-looking woman, who always reminded me of a Polynesian beauty, but there was something about her that made you feel that she needed help.' Ernie Anderson, publicist, promoter, and jazz-lover, who knew Lady during the 1930s and 1940s, described the 'little girl' quality: 'People thought that I had a great "in" with Billie, particularly after she did the Carnegie Hall concert for me. We got along fine, but the real secret was that I used to always take her a well-wrapped bundle of comics. She loved reading them, in fact, I think that's all she ever read, but because of the sophisticated image, it would have been out of the question that she should be seen buying them.'

Besides reading comics, Billie also played cards during her spare time at Cafe Society – the club had three shows a night, at 9 pm, midnight and 2 am. She would often visit the bandroom and play hearts or blackjack with the musicians. Overall, Cafe Society was probably the happiest booking of Billie's life, it did wonders for her confidence on-stage, enabling her to project a more sophisticated act. Barney Josephson encouraged and advised Billie; later he was to do the same thing for Lena Horne, who said, 'It was Barney who encouraged us, as artists, to express our individuality in our performances. It was Barney who decided that all guests were to be seated and served without discrimination.' (*Lena,* p. 192.)

It was at the Cafe Society that Billie began to feature 'Strange Fruit', the song that was to become irrevocably linked with her. The liberal atmosphere of the club, with its clientele of 'New Dealers', and the humanitarian principles of its owner made it a receptive setting for the presentation of the song's dramatic anti-lynching lyrics.

Poet Lewis Allen, then working as a schoolteacher, approached Barney Josephson and Robert Gordon (who helped organise the floor-shows) with a set of lyrics that he had adapted from his own poetry; they recommended that Allen should meet Billie and offer the song to her. At first, Lady was slow to understand the song's imagery, but her bewilderment decreased as Allen patiently emphasised the cadences, and their significance. After a few readings, Billie was 'into' the song, but was unconvinced that the material was suitable for her. Her incredibly gifted interpretations of lyrics had enhanced many songs, but these songs, for all the varying skills of their composers and lyricists, had only dealt with the problems of love, unrequited or otherwise, skies blue and June moons. Here, Billie was being asked to provide a musical commentary on an issue raw enough to be unmentionable in urban New York.

Billie's hesitancy showed that although she often proudly said, 'I'm a race woman,' she was uncertain about accepting the onus of delivering this early protest song. She told Lewis Allen that she would have to think it over. Within minutes of his leaving the club she had made up her mind; as Frankie Newton's Band came off stage she greeted them with the words, 'Some guy's brought me hell of a damn song that I'm going to do.'

Her decision to feature 'Strange Fruit' was to be the factor that changed her career. The overt brandishing of an anti-racialism banner was certainly not the sole reason for Billie's choice; being the great artist that she was, her intuition told her that here was a lyric into which she could pour much of the pent-up dramatic feelings that sometimes engulfed her. The material and the message were powerful enough to allow her to project the qualities of a great actress without appearing absurd. Overnight, she changed from being a marvellously talented club singer to 'La Grande Chanteuse' – fortunately, this change in presentation didn't diminish the jazz content of her work.

Leonard Feather visited the Cafe Society in April 1939, just before Billie first recorded 'Strange Fruit'; he described the night to *Melody Maker* readers: 'Frankie Newton leads the regular band in this pleasant room which had modern decorations, and many brilliant murals to help the atmosphere. During the show the M.C. announced Billie Holiday who stood in a small jet of light, turned on her most wistful expression for the mike, and sang a number written specially for her, "Strange Fruit", a grim and moving piece

69

about lynching down South. To-day she is recording this for a special Commodore Music Shop session.'

The Commodore Music Shop that Feather mentioned was owned by Milt Gabler. From there Gabler ran his own record label which catered exclusively for jazz fans. He had known Billie ever since she visited his original shop on 42nd Street in 1936; in 1938, he opened a branch at 45 West 52nd Street, and from there he would often go downtown to hear Billie at Cafe Society; he had said 'There was no sense in going home without hearing Lady. When she was out of town it was no town to me. Billie was my constant love, I don't mean the physical kind, we had a great thing for each other, and she respected me. When she was on stage in the spotlight she was absolutely regal. It was something, the way she held her head up high, the way she phrased each word, and got to the heart of the story in a song, and to top it all, she knew where the beat was.'

It was through Gabler's admiration and enterprise that Billie managed to record 'Strange Fruit'. Her guarded acceptance of the song was soon followed by a spate of passionate fervour for every stanza in the song, she felt that everyone in the world should hear the words. The big drawback to this was that the Columbia Record Company, to whom she was contracted, weren't willing to issue a recording of the song. However, they were not against its message and gave their permission when Billie and Milt Gabler asked if they could record the song for Commodore. This decision surprised and delighted Gabler, he said 'Billie and I were grateful to Columbia for allowing her to record this important song for my label.'

On Billie's first session for Commodore she recorded four tunes: 'Strange Fruit', 'Yesterdays', 'I Got a Right to Sing the Blues' and a twelve-bar blues, 'Fine and Mellow'.

In a 1973 *Down Beat* interview Gabler explained why he particularly wanted Billie to record a twelve-bar blues: 'Her 1936 "Billie's Blues" was (and still is) a favorite of mine. Billie didn't sing the blues like Bessie Smith or Ma Rainey. She was more like *today*.

'The night before the session. I went down to Cafe Society to get things set with the band and Billie. I told her I wanted a blues, so we sat down at a little "deuce" table just outside her dressing-room door and started to write down blues verses for the still untitled song.' In this extemporised lyric session Milt Gabler came up with a line that provided the title for the composition: 'Fine and Mellow'.

Everything went well at the recording, both for Billie and the accompanying band led by Frankie Newton, with Sonny White on piano. After the session Billie felt on top of the world and impetuously told the *Melody Maker* correspondent an item of news that was dutifully printed in the 20 May issue: 'Billie Holiday, still singing at Cafe Society, announces that she will shortly be married to her piano accompanist, Sonny White.'

The marriage never took place, Sonny was supporting his widowed mother, and Billie was doing likewise; the economic and domestic problems of setting up an instant home for four were insuperable – the romance ended in a fairly fast-burning fizzle.

Billie was still a long way from being 'in the money', she was one of life's spenders and rarely saved any of her earnings. In the late 1930s, when she was averaging seventy-five dollars a week she always bought Coty perfumes and expensive bath oils; once she splashed two weeks' salary on matching shoes and handbag made in green crocodile. Her wage at Cafe Society was not colossal but the booking brought her into contact with promoters, film stars, agents, show-bookers, and news columnists. She loved the feel of hob-nobbing, but never let it interfere with, or affect, her own social circle. Many of her old friends dropped into the club, including Lester Young. One dawn in the summer of 1939, after deciding that there was still time for more fun, she accompanied Lester up to Puss Johnson's Tavern on St Nicholas Avenue in Harlem, where a big after-hours jam session had been planned. This was the era of the jam session – the informal assemblies where jazz musicians could improvise for as long as they liked on any material they

*Jam Session: l. to r. – J. C. Higginbotham, John Kirby, Rex Stewart, Billie Holiday, Harry Lim, Cozy Cole, Eddie Condon, Max Kaminsky and Hot Lips Page*

chose.

The gathering planned for Johnson's bar was something special. Coleman Hawkins, then the undisputed champion of jazz tenor-saxophone playing, had recently returned to the U.S.A. after five years in Europe. During his absence, several younger men were put foward as contenders for his crown, principally Lester Young, Leon 'Chu' Berry, Ben Webster and Dick Wilson. It seems significant that Hawkins, after looking down the short list, arranged that one of his first tasks was to be blowing in the same place and at the same time as Lester Young. He let it be known that he would attend the jam session at Puss Johnson's Tavern; Lester Young, who had planned to go before receiving this news, was undeterred.

The meeting of the twin colussi of jazz tenor playing had all the drama of a gun-fighting duel, the result however, was less conclusive. There could scarcely be any winning or losing, since both men played in such dissimilar styles. Nowadays, with hundreds of recorded examples of both men's work readily available there is still dispute as to which man was the greater jazz player.

In a summary of the session, *Down Beat* passed on the views of the Fats Waller Band (who were at the Tavern as listeners); they thought that Hawkins came out on top, and they also reported that Lester had said he'd had enough after an hour's blowing.

Billie was working in Chicago by the time the magazine appeared, and after reading the report her reaction was swift and decisive. She immediately contacted the main *Down Beat* office in Chicago and emphatically refuted the suggestion that Coleman Hawkins had 'carved' Lester. *Down Beat* published her comments that the report was 'unfair', and that 'Young really cut the Hawk, and most everyone there who saw them tangle agrees on that.'

By this time, 'Strange Fruit', and its coupling 'Fine and Mellow', had been released. None of the reviewers was ecstatic, however 'Gordon Wright' (a nom-de-plume for George T. Simon) wrote in *Metronome*: 'A record that's going to cause tremendous controversy is Billie's "Strange Fruit", an anti-lynching song, which she sings with immense feeling, and which also has effective passages by trumpeter Frankie Newton and pianist Sonny White. Its reverse "Fine and Mellow" is good blues.' 'Barrelhouse Dan' in *Down Beat* was much less enthusiastic: 'Perhaps I expected too much of "Strange Fruit", the ballyhooed Allen-Sacher tune, which, via gory wordage, and hardly any melody, expounds an anti-lynching campaign [sic]. At least I'm sure it's not for Billie, as for example, "Fine and Mellow" is.'

Considering the record was issued by a small company, at the relatively high price of one dollar, it sold very well indeed. Its release gained enormous publicity for Billie, but despite the wide press coverage she still felt that she was no nearer receiving acceptance from the general public. As soon as the tumult of acclaim had subsided she felt that she was as far as ever from the glamorous fame for which she was striving. Late in 1939, she told Dave Dexter (then associate editor of *Down Beat*), that she would quit the singing game if she failed to gain national prominence – 'with the public as well as musicians and jazz fans,' by the time she was 26 (1941). She admitted that she was aware of the great respect that musicians had for her, but said that she was discouraged 'after nine years of hard work' and felt 'at a loss as to why the public at large had failed to respond to her.'

The publication of this interview was the first inkling of one dilemma that was to shadow the rest of Billie's life. She was worshipped by jazz musicians of every school, she was envied and copied by almost every girl vocaliste of the day, writers showered her with praise, but to the masses she was practically a nobody. She yearned to see the glint of recognition in everyone's eyes, she longed to be pestered by autograph hunters, instead, she was virtually ignored.

Ella Fitzgerald, who had shyly asked Billie for her autograph a few years before, was, by 1939, well on her way to international stardom, her record of 'Tisket a Tasket' having sold a quarter of a million. Billie's first real talks with Ella had taken place in 1938; then, Ella had often visited the Roseland State Ballroom in Boston to hear Billie sing with Artie Shaw's band. At that time, Ella was the featured singer with the band led by drummer Chick Webb. She too, had had a very hard childhood; the change in her fortunes had occurred after her successes at amateur nights, first at the Harlem Opera House and then at the Apollo. As a result, she signed with Chick Webb's Band, remaining with that leader until his untimely death in June 1939. Billie did not feel jealous of Ella's success and her subsequent popular adulation; she learned to shrug off any comparisons and poll-placings. However, she felt keen disappointment in 1939 when the leading journalists of the Associated Negro Press voted Ella their favourite female vocalist and chose Maxine Sullivan in second place.

Billie's initial run at Cafe Society lasted for almost nine months. Long after it had ended, Billie saw how important it had been in terms of publicity and prestige, but in August 1939 she could merely reflect that she was getting little more than she was at the beginning of the residency. However, Milt

Gabler said in 1973, 'I never heard of Barney Josephson retiring with a bundle, in fact, he is back in the business running "The Cookery" in Greenwich Village.'

In September 1939, Billie moved to Chicago to play a series of dates at the Off Beat Room (which was the downstairs section of the Three Deuces Club). At the Off Beat (which was partly owned by two *Down Beat* writers, Carl Conns and Glenn Burrs), Billie worked for a week with the newly formed Muggsy Spanier's Ragtimers, she then did two weeks with a band led by cornettist Jimmy McPartland. This temporary partnership was a happy one. McPartland recalls: 'Billie was in the floor show, the band was Joe Rushton (clarinet), Floyd Bean (piano), Harry Jaeger (drums), Joe Masek (tenor-sax), and Pat Patterson (bass). It was not long after she had recorded "Strange Fruit", and we played it for her, in fact, we backed her for the whole show. Billie loved the way we played, and she would show her thanks by kissing me.' *Down Beat* published a photograph of a young, up-and-coming Frank Sinatra sitting in rapt attention at the club listening to Billie sing.

After leaving Chicago, Billie returned to New York, where she played more dates at Cafe Society, before doing stints at 'Kelly's Stables' and at 'Ernie's'. Early in 1940, she returned to 'Kelly's' for what proved to be a long, and successful stay – alongside Roy Eldridge's Band. Roy, who had known Billie since before she ever came to New York, was surprised and delighted by the impressive stage presence that Billie had developed; he said of the stay at Kelly's, 'She seemed to have such rapport with the people. By then I'd been recording with Billie for years, and I'd seen her in clubs way before that – but at Kelly's I saw she was a star.' The bill did good business for the club (which was then managed by two ex-saxophonists, Ralph Watkins and Irving Alexander), so much so, that Joe Glaser took an advertisement in *Down Beat*, drawing attention to the fact that two of his artists – Billie and Roy – were in their 18th week at the club. Thereafter, Billie played the club on and off for several years. Ralph Watkins said, 'She was one of our sure fire attractions.'

Meanwhile, the success of Cafe Society (Downtown) enabled Barney Josephson to open a second club, Cafe Society (Uptown) which opened at 128 E. 58th Street in September 1940. Billie continued to appear at the Downtown branch, and accepted a return booking there for a show due to commence on 1 October 1940 – the bill also featured Art Tatum, Sister Rosetta Tharpe, and a new sextet led by white pianist Joe Sullivan, containing black and white musicians. However, Billie failed to show up on opening night. *Down Beat*, reported that 'Josephson immediately decided to cancel her contract, declaring he could get along without her very well.' The magazine also mentioned Billie's reluctance to be predictable: 'Her temperament troubles have been the talk of the trade for years.' *Music and Rhythm* also spoke of her 'undependability', and The *New Yorker* categorised Billie as 'moody'.

Billie's reaction to demands for punctuality and reliability were, from her earliest days, casual – to say the least. Leonard Feather succinctly summed-up her early attitude when he said 'Billie preferred balling to taking care of business.' In the years before she received star-billing her non-appearance would irk, and inconvenience, both the club-owner and the band, who usually had to play Billie's sets as well as their own. The audience might heave sighs of disappointment when told that Billie would not be appearing, but rarely did anyone make an issue of her absence. Usually, Billie would bounce back the next night, brighter than ever, and all would be forgiven. However, attitudes hardened when club-owners began advertising Lady Day's appearance in the press; then, a missed show reflected not only on the artist, but also on the reliability of the club.

Billie's change in presentation did bring her stardom, but it also brought attendant problems. The glamorous role of the dramatic songstress suited the image that Billie had chosen for herself; paradoxically she had always detested repetition and regimentation. This meant that the disciplined act that she had fashioned was, if the mood was not right, agony for her to perform. There were many occasions when 'the show must go on' edict of the old stage trouper seemed to her a slogan for torture.

In the spring of 1941, Barney Josephson booked Carnegie Hall to present two shows featuring artists who worked for him at his Cafe Society clubs; Billie then working at Kelly's Stables was ineligible. Lena Horne, who was appearing for Barney at his Downtown branch, was on the bill. Lena, who had previously worked with bands led by Noble Sissle and Charlie Barnet, was beginning to do great business in the night clubs, a prelude to her successes in films and in the theatre. As a token of her admiration for Billie she sang 'Fine and Mellow' on the concert. At first, Billie didn't appreciate the compliment at all; she brooded, and pooh-poohed anyone who tried to console her – Lena felt the vibrations on the grape-vine and called into Kelly's to ask if Lady minded her using the song. It was the perfect gesture and one that endeared Lena to Lady (the whole issue may have well brought back memories of the contretemps over Ethel Waters's material that had occurred years before). Lady assured Lena that she didn't mind at all, and thereafter Lady always said of Lena 'That gal really knows her business.'

Billie was never short of admirers; during 1939 and 1940 she had strings of men-friends, many of them willing to make permanent rather than temporary arrangements with her. However, she wouldn't let anyone get too serious with her for quite a while after she and Sonny White broke up. Although she and Lester Young were still dear friends, they saw less and less of each other, Lester having moved out of the family apartment to re-marry. Billie generally preferred the company of musicians, but very occasionally she went out with a fan – a well-known Scandinavian jazz aficionado hinted that his night with Billie ended with more than a good-night kiss on the front-porch.

Billie had an unveiled preference for strikingly handsome men; if she liked the look of a man she'd make no bones about letting him know how much he appealed to her. She had boundless admiration for Buck Clayton's good looks, and had no hesitation in praising them in her autobiography. For a while she dated another musician who was also renowned for his looks, the late Dick Wilson, tenor-saxist with Andy Kirk's Band. She also liked Pha Terrell, Kirk's vocalist; two close friends of hers were Ben Webster and drummer Sid Catlett – years later she wryly remarked 'They don't call him "Big Sid" because he's six foot three you know.'

But in 1941, whilst Billie was playing a residency at 'The Famous Door' in New York, she started going out regularly with the man she said was, 'the most beautiful man I'd laid eyes on since Buck Clayton' – he was Jimmy Monroe, brother of her former employer Clark Monroe. She had known Jimmy from years before, when she had worked at his brother's club 'The Uptown House', but it took years for a romance to get under way. Neither Billie's mother nor her agent, Joe Glaser, liked Jimmy Monroe, they both told Billie that he would be a bad influence. This made him all the more interesting to Lady, and her interest soon developed into total fascination. On 25 August 1941, at the end of a six-week run at 'The Famous Door', she and Jimmy Monroe drove to Elkton in Maryland for a register-office wedding. It was Billie's first marriage, and her husband's second – previously the 30-year-old Monroe had been married to the film-star and vocaliste Nina Mae McKinney.

Immediately after the ceremony, Billie and her husband left for Chicago where Billie spent part of her honeymoon making guest appearances with Lionel Hampton's newly formed big band, then playing at the Hotel Sherman.

From Chicago, the couple moved on to California, for Billie's first-ever appearance on the West Coast. She was booked indefinitely at a new club in Los Angeles called 'The Cafe Society'. The club was billed as 'A West Coast edition of New York City's Cafe Society', but Barney Josephson had no connection whatsoever with the California enterprise and he soon took action against the club's owners. One of the club's owners was Jerry Colonna, who had formerly been a successful trombonist before making a name for himself as a screen and radio comedian. Billie had known Colonna since the mid-1930s; many of his show-business friends visited the club and this delighted Billie. She was only singing short sets with the resident band led by trumpeter Al Golden and this allowed her plenty of time for socialising. As an ardent movie fan, Lady loved movieland gossip and envied Hollywood fashions. If she saw a star wearing wide-brimmed hats in a film then they were a must for her, if Kay Francis was seen draped with silver-fox furs then Billie would soon need to be swathed in similar pelts.

During the late 1930s Ginger Rogers was reported as saying that she wished her mouth had been shaped like Billie's; the publication of this comment meant more to Billie than all the praise that music critics had ever given her. At this new club, she met several of her movie idols and loved the experience, the briefest chat with a famous film star could put her into a happy mood. But, her joy at this particular club was short-lived; it opened on 1 October 1941, and closed three weeks later. Billie hadn't saved a cent from the 175 dollars a week that she had been paid, her husband too was temporarily short of funds; neither had the price of two rail fares. Monroe decided to stay on the Coast to follow-up business possibilities, Billie began the long journey back to New York completely broke.

Billie recouped by playing familiar clubs in New York for a few months, she then did a residency at the Club Congo in Detroit before appearing at the opening of a new, racially-mixed, club in Cleveland called the Boogie Woogie. The booking was for a month, but disappointing business caused the last two weeks to be cancelled. Billie always had a staunch following in Harlem, but these were early days for the black populations of other cities to regard her as a favourite. For the Cleveland dates she was accompanied on piano by Lannie Scott; she still hadn't raked together enough money to enjoy the luxury of signing a permanent accompanist. Planning such a signing was important because Joe Glaser was trying to establish Billie as a travelling cabaret artiste as opposed to someone who only triangled club-dates in New York, Los Angeles and Chicago. Glaser's policy dictum was that you could usually make more money in four separate weeks in four different cities than you could by playing a month in the same venue. His boast to artists who hadn't signed with him was that he could triple their salary immediately; he often managed to do this, but his methods could be exhausting in that the distance travelled by his 'acts' between engagements meant nothing more to him than a telephone call to fix the venues. To his credit he was a hard and skilful negotiator. Gradually, he changed from supervising agency bookings to personal management — his real forte. His stable of stars was always impressive; his Christmas 1942 trade advertisement listed many of the bandleaders he represented. They included Louis Armstrong, Les Brown, Lionel Hampton, Red Norvo and Andy Kirk. However, Billie was one of his first solo artistes, and for a long time he didn't know quite how he should promote her talents. During the 1940s he billed her, somewhat quaintly, as 'The Queen of Song'. Joe Glaser was prone to issuing press statements about Billie's career without consulting her — or any party involved. Once he announced that there was a strong possibility that Billie and Earl Hines would be available for bookings as a double-act, something that neither Billie nor Earl knew anything about. Needless to say, this plan never materialised, but a lot of Glaser's schemes for Billie did come off, and her income rose steadily during the first years of World War II.

But money meant little to Billie at this time, it was easy come, easy go. Given the chance she'd always opt for good times rather than good bread. When Milt Gabler began running a series of Sunday afternoon jam sessions early in 1941, Billie was among the first to join in; she would sing song after song for a fraction of the money that a normal club appearance would bring.

In May 1942 Billie returned to California to open at Billy Berg's Trouville Club in West Hollywood. The band there was co-led by Lady's old friend Lester Young, and his brother Lee. Lester, who had left Count Basie in December

*With Lester Young*

1940, was playing alongside another tenor-saxist Hubert 'Bumps' Myers, 'Red' Mack was on trumpet, Lee Young on drums, and 'Red' Callender on double-bass. The group's one white member was pianist Jimmie Rowles. Rowles, who was later to work with Lady Day on many occasions, first met her at the Trouville. He vividly remembers his first impressions: 'Lady was very feminine, good natured, salty, loving. She was young, and one of the most beautiful girls I had ever seen. She was nut brown, with hair dyed red, and she looked great. She was looked up to – one of the guys – no holding back with language, she loved dirty jokes like we do. I couldn't say enough good about her.'

Billie and Jimmie Rowles became life-long friends, but at their first meeting, Billie was decidedly uncertain about the pianist. Years later, in the 1950s, she spoke of her initial wariness. The occasion was at a recording session; the tape-recorder was left running, Rowles sat listening at the piano whilst Billie talked to bassist Art Shapiro, 'He was a

81

gray (Basie Band slang for a white person), I said (to Lester Young), I want to hear him right away, I don't dig him, and Lester says, "I don't know ... this cat can blow." '

Billie was relatively happy at the Trouville; she liked the Californian climate, the money was steady, the accompaniment perfect. Movie stars often visited the club, and Billie was able to renew acquaintances with Martha Raye, John Garfield and Don Ameche; occasionally she sat down for drinks with Bette Davis, Lana Turner and Merle Oberon. She was flattered when Orson Welles showed a keen interest in her career. At the time, Welles was planning a documentary film on the history of jazz, tentatively called *It's All True* (the project never materialised). Welles took Billie to see him work in his radio-theatre series; years later, she recalled Welles playing scenes from *Citizen Kane* before the film had been 'shot'. She was mistaken, she hadn't known Welles in New York, and the film was generally released before her first trip to Hollywood.

During her stay at the Trouville, Billie met up with a twenty-three-year-old Californian who was to become one of the leading impresarios in the jazz world. Norman Granz's very first promotions occurred at that club, and he recalled the circumstances to writer Sinclair Traill: 'I put a proposition to Billy Berg, who then ran a club called the Trouville ... I suggested to Berg that instead of getting a substitute band for his seventh day (the "rest" day insisted on by the musicians' union) I'd provide the music, if he'd agree to the following terms: to have a seated audience, with no dancing; to pay the musicians a fair wage, to charge a reasonable admission fee, to use only the musicians advertised as performers on any particular day, and lastly, and most important, to admit colored patrons on a non-segregated basis — a thing he had never done before. These impromptu sessions were a great success. I was also able to persuade Berg to extend the non-segregation to seven nights a week.'

Billie stayed at the Trouville for two months before singer-dancer Marie Bryant came in to take her place. Once again, Lady had gone through all the money that she had earned, but there was vague talk about recording sessions so she decided to bide her time in California and take advantage of the many party invitations that regularly came her way.

Despite the social whirl in which Billie found herself involved she never got 'big-time' with the musicians that she knew, and was genuinely delighted to see old friends. Trombonist Trummy Young, who had first met Billie in 1937 at Clark Monroe's Uptown House in New York, was in California in 1942; he has good reason for remembering meeting up with Lady at that time. 'Billie and I were in California together, both out of work. We were so poor we couldn't pay our room rent. I had this melody I used to play with Earl Hines' Band, something I made up, it never was arranged or copyrighted. I went to Jimmy Mundy who I'd worked with originally in Tommy Miles' Band in 1930, and got him to arrange the song – at the time he was writing for Paul Whiteman. The tune didn't even have a title; one night Johnny Mercer and his wife heard the Paul Whiteman band play the tune. Johnny's wife named it "Travellin' Light", and Johnny wrote the lyrics.'

The tune and the lyrics ideally suited Lady Day, and Paul Whiteman was keen that she recorded it with his orchestra, The session took place in June 1942, and Billie was paid a straight fee of seventy-five dollars.

When the record was originally issued, there was no mention of the fact that Trummy Young composed the tune, the label credited Jimmy Mundy. Young explains: 'I raised a little hell, and they gave me seventy-five dollars, and later, Johnny Mercer, who is from my home town Savannah, Georgia, got my name put on the tune.' Trummy recalls that the record-date itself was reason enough for revelry, 'Billie and I went out and spent all the money celebrating, and her mother had to send us the bus fare from California to New York. Can you imagine riding a bus for 3,000 miles?'

# CHAPTER FIVE

    It's impossible to pinpoint the exact month when Billie used hard drugs for the first time. She herself said that she had been married to Jimmy Monroe – a man of wide-ranging habits – for a year before she 'got wise to something else that was happening. Jimmy smoked something strange.' Billie's mother, accustomed to the smell of the marihuana that her daughter had smoked since teenage years, was quickly alerted by the sweet pungent drift of smoke from an opium pipe. After Monroe had made himself ill through over-dosage, Sadie gave him his marching orders. Billie joined in the ensuing fracas and when Monroe packed his bags and left 99th Street Billie went with him.

    The couple made their home on 104th Street; rows were frequent, and although Sadie had been giving her daughter the 'I told you so' routine since the day she had married Monroe, Lady felt miserable that her mother wasn't with her. She convinced herself that the real barrier between her and her husband was hard drugs, and decided that everything would be fine if they shared the same 'habit', but the couple's secluded opium-sessions didn't bring them any closer. In her autobiography Billie philosophically surveyed the debris and said 'Jimmy was no more the cause of my doing what I did than my mother was.'

Each addict's reason for taking their initial dose of hard drugs differs. Billie said that the time of her first fix she felt that her marriage was breaking up. Not long before, she had had a serious row with her mother, her basic insecurity coupled with these events seemed to her reason enough to look for solace in narcotics. It was not as though she were suddenly thrown over the precipice of addiction. From her earliest days in New York she had known many drug-takers, but despite seeing the tragedies that addiction brings, she gambled that the pleasure would mean more than the pain. But it was not simple hedonism, it was a decision of despair, the despair that she would never get the widespread appreciation that seemed to come easily to others; the domestic squabbles had only acted as a trigger. Billie had said in 1939 that she would quit the music-business by 1941 unless she gained national prominence. 1941 came and went, and it was plain to Billie that aside from being able to ask for slightly higher fees she was as far as ever from being a celebrity; it was equally obvious to her that singing was her life. As Carmen McRae once said 'Singing is the only place she can express herself the way she'd like to be all the time. Only way she's happy is through a song. I don't think she expresses herself as she would want to when you meet her in person. The only time she's at ease and at rest with herself is when she sings.'

Leaving aside 'hell on earth', no description of drug addiction seems more concise and explicit than the World Health Organisation's 1950 edict:

'Drug addiction is a state of periodic intoxication, detrimental to the individual and society, produced by the repeated consumption of a drug (natural or synthetic). Its chaacteristics include:

1. An overpowering desire or compulsion to continue taking the drug and obtain it by any means.

2. A tendency to increase the dose.

3. A psychic (psychological and sometimes physical)

dependence on the effects of the drug.'

Though close personal surveillance would soon reveal the changing behaviour pattern of a person recently addicted to drugs, it was some while after Jimmy Monroe and Billie had separated that musicians who worked with Billie became aware of her addiction problems. This was because, amazingly enough, she never reached a stage of absolute dependence on opium.

Few addicts can feel certain that they will always be able to take their fixes in comfortable surroundings. For Billie on tour, the secluded ritual of smoking opium in a pipe was impracticable, and hazardous law-wise. She also found that the smoke affected her throat so much that it took her ages to 'warm-up' for a performance; another deterrent was that the sweet, sickly taste of the smoke made her prone to vomiting. These factors induced her to almost gain control over her cravings, but this partial resistance to opium gave her the tragically false impression that she could use any hard drugs with the same controlled restraint.

Her eventual choice of poison was heroin – the number four variety, a white crystalline by-product of opium. This can be taken orally, or sniffed into the nostrils, but the most common method of usage is by injections from a hypodermic syringe. The effect is practically instantaneous, and whilst the addict is high he or she feels that every problem, large or small, can be disregarded. When the effects wear off the problems seem more overwhelming than ever, and then the treadmill of fixes starts.

On 15 August 1942, Billie began a three month stay at Joe Sherman's Garrick Showbar in Chicago, working alongside a sextet led by trumpeter Henry 'Red' Allen. Joe Sherman wasn't noted for an encyclopaedic knowledge of jazz, and *Down Beat* went as far as to say that he had booked Billie under the impression that she was a man (*Down Beat,* 15 November 1942). However, Joe had a fine ear for the sound of a cash register, and the Red Allen–Billie booking brought him good business.

Audiences saw a Billie who was becoming more and more

poised. On stage she was free of extravagant gestures, she swayed her body slightly, crooked her right arm and kept time by moving it in a restrained circular motion snapping her fingers in tempo; the audience rarely took their eyes off her. Off stage, she was liable to be more unpredictable than ever. Now, her first instinct when faced with trouble was to run, and this reflex landed her in jail for a brief spell during her Garrick Showbar booking.

The car in which she was being driven to the club was in a street-corner collision with an ambulance; no one was badly hurt, but both Billie's knees were gashed. Instead of getting first-aid from the ambulance's crew, she decided to seek attention elsewhere; she got back into the car and was driven off. A police car with sirens screaming soon overtook the car, and the law-men, incredulous at Billie's explanation for the sudden departure from the scene of the accident, took her into custody. Fortunately, club-owner Joe Sherman was soon located and he quickly arranged bail – later the charge of failing to report the accident was dropped.

Billie's work at the Garrick Showbar was reviewed by Dixon Gayer in *Down Beat*. Gayer commented on the contrast between Billie on and off stage. 'Billie Holiday is a dual personality. She is unpredictable, laughing and gay, aptly named Billie ... off stage. On stage, her manner and her feelings change completely, to form a new, dignified, sincere, sentimental person. A person who has given rise to such names as La Holiday, and now, most appropriate, Lady Day.' (Actually, 'Lady Day' had been used in print by the *Amsterdam News* in January 1939.) 'La Holiday is an artist with tears in her eyes as she sings "Strange Fruit". Billie is carefree, temperamental, a domineering personality. They are both swell people.'

Billie ended 1942 in Chicago, playing a week at the Regal Theater. The booking was a huge success and *Down Beat* reported that Lady Day and Lionel Hampton's Band 'tore the roof off the Regal Theater on New Year's Eve'. Hampton's explanation of the inspiration that Lady gave was simple, 'Boy, when she sang, she just kicked the band off and

made it fly. She and Louis Armstrong both did that.'

In January 1943, Billie returned to New York and began another stint at Kelly's Stables; a typical bill at the club would be Lady Day, Coleman Hawkins and his small group and Henry 'Red' Allen's Sextet. Business was consistently good whilst Billie appeared at the club, but trade at several other 52nd Street clubs was poor, and *Down Beat* announced in its 1 March 1943 issue, 'the Street is long dead'.

After two months at Kelly's, Billie suddenly left New York, regardless of contract or commitment, and took a train to Los Angeles. The reckless streak in her character had surfaced again. Jimmy Monroe was then living in California, and Billie felt that she had to link-up with him, to try and re-establish her marriage. A permanent reconciliation seemed out of the question and Lady soon returned to New York and began working at the Onyx. She stayed there for most of the year, except for a series of theatre dates that she did with Teddy McRae's Band.

For part of the Onyx booking, Lady again shared billing with Roy Eldridge's Band, later Dizzy Gillespie's small group worked at the club. Dizzy has many memories of the Onyx residency. In 1973 he said, 'I still get people who come up to me and talk about the Onyx Club – service-men who came there on leave, and couples who celebrated war-time weddings there. For a time, Billie was part of the Onyx, she had such a dynamic personality, such a great stylist, the moment you heard that voice you knew it was Billie Holiday. She influenced almost every singer.' Dizzy's contemporary Billy Eckstine had similar praise 'no one could outstyle Billie on a song.' Occasionally Dizzy's band backed Billie, but usually the accompaniment was provided by trios led by Al Casey, or Cozy Cole. Pianist Johnny Guarnieri, who then played in Cozy Cole's Trio gave his reminiscences of the Onyx to Arnold Shaw. 'During this gig I also accompanied Billie Holiday. The first night she handed me some tattered lead-sheets, and said "Give me four bars." I played four bars. But she didn't come in. Figuring she hadn't heard me, or just missed her cue, I started over again. Suddenly I felt a tap on

89

the back of my head and I heard her say "Don't worry 'bout me — I'll be there." She added that she liked to come in behind the beat, as I discovered, and that I didn't have to bother to make her look good.

'Looking back, I would say that few performers had such solid judgment about tempi as she did, particularly when it came to doing certain tunes in a very slow tempo. Most performers who try the slow-tempo bit do it for effect, not because it's right for the tune. Billie Holiday was the greatest tempo singer that ever lived.' (*The Street That Never Slept*, pp. 303-4.)

During Billie's stay at the Onyx, she linked up with a pianist, Joe Springer, who became her personal accompanist for the next two years. They first met at the Onyx whilst Springer was working in Oscar Pettiford's quintet; apart from his sets with Pettiford, he also played for Billie's three shows a night. When the booking ended, Billie asked Springer if he would like to work with her at the next residency she had — at the Downbeat Club — he accepted the 'gig', and from 1944 until 1946 he played for most of Billie's club dates in New York. To this day, he speaks in awe of what he describes as Billie's 'phenomenal musicianship'. He has never forgotten one particular incident that highlighted Lady's incredible sense of time. 'At one of the 52nd Street clubs we were doing the third and final show of the evening. I had learned to slow the tempos of her songs for the final show, because by then B.H. was usually quite stoned. She smoked pot, drank whiskey, and maybe took other things, and as the night wore on her reflexes were slowed down. On this particular night the third show rolled around and B.H. could barely stand up.

'I had never seen her so far gone. She clutched the microphone with both hands and used that to prop herself up. I started the tempo somewhat slower, I couldn't make too drastic a change or else it would ruin the tune. Billie came in O.K. with just a slight slurring of speech, she normally sang a bit behind the beat, and at first nothing was amiss. However, as the song progressed she fell further behind the beat, until she was several bars behind.

'I began to worry. Had she lost her place? This was unthinkable if she were sober or even mildly high. A good accompanist will follow the artiste no matter what errors she may make. If she were to go off tempo I would have to go along with her. It would have been unprofessional for me to cue her in with the melody.

'She lagged further behind and now it became difficult for me to keep *my* place. I was convinced that B.H. was completely oblivious to the music. I was just on the verge of switching to her place when the unexpected happened. Billie skipped a dozen or so words and meshed perfectly with the music. Part of Billie's befuddled brain kept track of the music even though her vocalizing was like an old-time phonograph that needed to be wound up.'

Not many of Joe Springer's evenings with Billie were that taut and anxious. One night, Billie and he were scheduled to play a benefit at the Apollo Theater; a police escort was sent for — Springer remembers Billie being 'gassed' at this twist, 'As we whizzed through red lights with sirens screaming, B.H. exclaimed, a childish grin on her face, "This gives me a big charge." '

In general, Billie got consistently good reviews during her stay at the Onyx, the only criticism was *Down Beat*'s comment that 'Billie is not singing her best, nor does she sing often enough.' Club owners were finding it increasingly difficult to get Billie to adhere to a fixed time schedule. After she temporarily transferred from the Onyx to the nearby Yacht Club at 55 West 52nd Street, the headaches started for Monte Kay, then producing the shows there. Kay, who has since gained international fame as the producer of television's 'Flip Wilson Show', found that Billie invariably wanted to go home after the first show of the night to take care of her problems. Kay told Arnold Shaw, 'I was too naive to know what they were, and I confess that I tended to think of her as anti-social. Once she was home, however, she was lost unless I went and brought her back. I'd get to the apartment and start pacing the floor while she was ostensibly getting ready. I'd have to keep reminding her of show time. It was painful, that's all I can say.' However, of Billie's singing at the club, Kay says, 'She was singing at the top of her talent and no one could top that.'

Trummy Young, who led his own band at the Yacht Club in 1944, loved working with Billie, 'She really didn't make the kind of money a star of her stature should have commanded. On 52nd Street she got a thousand dollars a week – peanuts for her. Everyone thought she wouldn't be at work because of her conduct, but she never missed one night, she packed that little club every night and when she sang it was so quiet you could literally hear a rat pissing on cotton. She was beautiful.'

Frank Sinatra, who said in 1958, 'Billie Holiday was, and still remains, the greatest single musical influence on me. Lady Day is unquestionably the most important influence on American popular singing in the last 20 years,' often went to the Onyx to hear her. One night, as Sinatra and his manager Hank Sanicola sat listening, two men moved into a position which blocked their view of the small stage. Sinatra asked them if they would mind moving, only to be asked sarcastically if he thought that they were Sinatra fans. Sinatra was up in a flash and the questioner got his answer in the shape of a black-eye.

Violence like this rarely flared-up inside the 52nd Street clubs, but on one wartime evening even the hardened club-bouncers held their breath as Billie smashed the top from a beer-bottle and threatened a naval officer who was loutish enough to call her a 'nigger'. The sailor was quickly ushered out of the club, but it took ages for the tears of rage to stop flowing down Billie's face.

The usage of this wounding word symbolised to Billie all the opportunities that she felt had been denied to her on racial grounds. Not long after the incident she was strolling along 52nd Street with pianist Joe Springer. He recalls, 'A black acquaintance walked by and inquired cheerily "How are you doing, Lady Day?" Her answer took me aback, "Well, you know, I'm still a nigger." '

Billie knew many forms of disappointment, and annual popularity polls in particular rarely brought joy to her, although she did come first in the *Metronome* poll in 1946, throughout her life she never won a *Down Beat* poll. Gradually, she learned to ignore the possibility of success in this field. She only ever made one public utterance on the subject, that was in 1947, when she said 'I never won the *Down Beat* poll, guess I never will now.'

Jazzmen hardened to the anomalies of popularity polls often got cynical amusement out of the annual results, but top placing for Billie would have brought her great satisfaction: a confirmation that she was, at last, getting widespread public acclaim.

In 1943, *Esquire* magazine organised its own jazz poll; it was a poll with a difference, in that the voting was restricted only to established jazz critics (the general public being completely excluded). The placings were, as a result, both meritorious and well-deserved: Billie was the clear winner in the Vocalists' section. (She got 23 votes, Mildred Bailey got 15, and Ella Fitzgerald 4.) Billie was delighted to take part in the award winners' concert held at New York's Metropolitan Hall in January 1944. It was her first major concert appearance and thankfully recordings were made of the historic occasion.

Throughout Billie's bookings at The Onyx Club, she took leave to do theatre work, at Loew's in New York, and at The Regal in Chicago where she did great business at the box office. Several critics didn't like the transition from club to theatre work, and in the spring of 1944, when Lady moved from the Onyx to the Ruban Bleu on the East Side of New York City, *Down Beat* commented that Billie was 'where she belongs, in an intimate club. Lady Day is at her best in an informal atmosphere.'

Lady was slow to settle into this new booking; the addiction to narcotics was having its effect on her personality and outlook, more and more she harboured suspicions about the significance of trivial incidents, then she would suddenly emerge from a spell of brooding with a diatribe. On her opening night at the Ruban Bleu, pianist Julius Monk quoted her as saying 'There's a society bitch that plays harp, says

93

she won't share a dressing room with me.' The harpist, Daphne Hellman, was absolutely astonished to hear of this, since she and the rest of the musicians were thrilled to be working and sharing with Lady. Later, she and Lady became friends; she recalls 'Billie was nervous and unhappy at first – missed her second show opening night, disliked playing on the "East Side" after west side jazz spots. She was crying backstage for three nights over the loss of a cherished dog, and life was not smooth for her then, despite her impeccable performances. Ever present was her hard-faced manfriend-attendant-drug supplier.'

The idea of having a dog for a pet had first struck Billie after she got to trust her friend Irene Wilson's dalmatian. During the 1940s Billie was rarely seen without her boxer 'Mister', and in later years she was greatly attached to her Chihuahua 'Pepi'. Lena Horne has commented on the importance that these pets had for Billie: 'Her life was so tragic and so corrupted by other people – by white people and by her own people. There was no place for her to go, except, finally, into that little private world of dope. She was just too sensitive to survive. The thing I remember talking to her about most were her dogs; her animals were really her only trusted friends.'

The dog that Daphne Hellman referred to was a mongrel named 'Rajah Ravoy' which had been given to Billie some years before – Billie couldn't look after it because of touring commitments and she left the dog with her mother at the 99th Street apartment. She renewed her close attachment to the dog when she moved back home after realising that her marriage with Jimmy Monroe wasn't for keeps. But there was no permanence about the move back to mother; Billie had met up with trumpeter Joe Guy, then 25 years old. Joseph Luke Guy had arrived in New York in the early 1940s from his home town of Birmingham, Alabama. He often played at Minton's Club (said to be the cradle of modern jazz) and worked regularly with bands led by Teddy Hill, Coleman Hawkins, Cootie Williams and Lucky Millinder. It was whilst he was with Millinder that Billie first met him – the courtship had grim undertones; an eternal triangle existed, the third partner being heroin.

Because Billie was forced to spend huge amounts on obtaining drugs she couldn't ignore the big money that she could make in theatre work. Her successes at the Regal in Chicago meant that she could almost name her own figure for return bookings. In July 1944, she worked there again, soon after playing two weeks at the re-opened Grand Terrace – the venue was different from the site of her pre-war debacle, but the man who ran the show, Ed Fox, was the same. Billie swallowed her pride and took the fee.

Both *Down Beat* and *Bandleader* magazines announced that Billie would head for Hollywood, after she had finished her Chicago bookings, to make a film for Warner Brothers. Unfortunately nothing materialised. It was rumoured that the 'scouts' who were checking on Billie's career could detect a pattern of events sinister enough for them to give the 'thumbs down' sign when contracts were mooted. Lady took advantage of the respite, she made several trips to the dentist and had some teeth out and new bridge-work fitted.

In August 1944, Billie took up residency at the Down Beat Club in New York, sharing the stand with a combo led by vibraharp player Red Norvo, and a band co-led by Paul and Dud Bascomb; she had lost a lot of weight, and although *Down Beat* magazine courteously said she looked stream-lined, the effect hadn't been achieved by conscientious dieting – Billie had a problem.

Billie began recording for Decca in 1944; this greatly pleased her old friend Milt Gabler who had joined that company in late 1941. Her October 1944 debut for the company showed a bold departure from the instrumental accompaniment that was usually featured on her records; she asked for, and got, a backing group that featured violins. In those days, a jazz vocaliste recording with strings was a rarity. Suitably *Down Beat* called the session 'a surprise date'. The first song that she recorded with the 'new' accompaniment was a song that she was to feature long afterwards, 'Lover Man'.

During the fall of 1944, Billie agreed to play a season at the Spotlite Club, 56 West 52nd Street (the former site of the Famous Door Club). However, Lady failed to appear for a heavily publicised opening night. Pianist Joe Springer remembers the incident well, 'She didn't even call the club. I don't know how she explained this to the management, but she told me "Opening nights bug me something awful." ' The club's manager, Clark Monroe, soon forgave Billie and she played to good business. Billie was still technically Monroe's sister-in-law; his brother Jimmy was engaged in business on the West Coast, and it was mooted that Billie should meet up with him when she next went out there for a concert and club dates. But it wasn't to be: before Billie left for California, Clark received word that his brother had been sentenced to nine months in prison for smuggling marijuana between Mexico and California.

Billie left the Spotlite and travelled to Los Angeles to take part in the January 1945 *Esquire* magazine's 'Critics' Award Concert'.

Besides Billie, the concert featured Duke Ellington's Orchestra, Art Tatum, and Anita O'Day; Billie obliged the enthusiast enthusiastic audience with an 'I Cover the Waterfront' encore. A month later (on 18 February) Billie again appeared in concert, this time at the Philharmonic Hall in Los Angeles. The impresario was Norman Granz, then just starting the concert promotions that were to make him world famous. The bill consisted of an all-star band, led by Gene Krupa (featuring tenorist Illinois Jacquet), the Coleman Hawkins Trio, Kid Ory's Band, Anita O'Day and Billie, who sang 'Fine and Mellow' and 'Squeeze Me' accompanied by Eddie Heywood on piano, Gene Krupa on drums and Beverley Beer on bass.

Whilst on the Coast, Lady Day took a booking at the New Plantation Club, located in the suburbs far south of Los Angeles. The booking was not a happy one. During the latter stages of World War II, a midnight drinking curfew was imposed in the Los Angeles area, principally to reduce the number of inebriated servicemen who returned to their bases at dawn. The curfew affected everyone, and attendances at all night clubs in Los Angeles fell sharply, particularly those situated a distance from the city centre. Few people came to see Billie at 'The Plantation', and instead of reasoning out the situation she immediately assumed that audiences had forgotten her, and that her friends from the film colony knew that she was 'hooked' on hard drugs and were staying away. She had been restricting her intake of heroin to about three capsules a day, but the worry and anxiety of the situation caused her to step up the dosage. She feverishly ran through the supplies she was carrying only to realise that she was without contacts to obtain more. In her autobiography she described the agony of this enforced withdrawal, 'Suddenly I was alone and on my own. I had never realised what that would mean. I had to get it myself and didn't know where to begin. I cried until I was sick, exactly the way I had seen Jimmy sick at Mom's apartment ... Sick as I was, and alone as I was, I headed back to New York.'

Billie's mother's apartment was only a temporary haven. Once again, Lady's choice of men friends exasperated Sadie; Billie's agent Joe Glaser also disliked Joe Guy. Glaser, who always had a string of informants ready to give him the background to anyone remotely connected with his business, certainly knew of the young trumpeter's habits. He forewarned Billie that she was courting disaster, but she stubbornly defended Joe Guy.

Trummy Young, who knew Billie and Joe Guy well, said of Billie's loyalty, 'She just couldn't do enough for the men she loved, or even her friends. She spent a large portion of the money she earned on heroin, but she also spent a lot on down-and-out friends. Keep in mind, during her time the relationship between black performers and their managers was not an honest one. The managers robbed them blind, and this happened with practically all the best ones. Billie was, with all her weaknesses, an honest person.'

Singer Babs Gonzales also stressed Billie's great generosity 'She fed everybody in New York for about four years – with no sweat! Any musician could go there and eat and get

money for the subway or to go to the movies – every day
they could do that. And if she was out of town she would
leave some money with her mother. And every day you
would find those who didn't have no bread, they would be up
at Lady's house in the Bronx – and everything was cool.'

Because of Joe Guy's own playing commitments, the
couple couldn't be perpetually in each other's company. Billie
left New York to play a short season at another Plantation
Club – this time in St Louis, Missouri. The booking lasted for
one show only, by reason of a storming row that Billie had
with the club's management.

At the club, which catered for black and white customers,
Billie met up with a white man friend whom she hadn't seen

since she had appeared with Artie Shaw's Band at the Hotel Chase in St Louis, fifteen years before, he suggested they celebrate the reunion by going out for a meal.

The club's house-rule was that entertainers were not to leave by the front exit – a ruling that other clubs occasionally insisted on – their theory being that patrons about to enter might turn and leave if they saw the star of the show leaving the club. The Plantation insisted that the dressing-room exits were to be used; this wasn't made clear to Billie (who would certainly have been aware that some clubs in St Louis then had 'Jim Crow' restrictions). When she was asked not to leave by the front door she assumed that the request was being made because she was leaving with a white man.

The *Melody Maker* reporting the incident, said, 'Billie hotly protested, her escort was forcibly ejected, but Billie triumphantly followed him out. Returning for her second show, she claims she was again insulted and warned not to forget herself. Whereupon she promptly forgot the show and returned to New York.'

Billie returned to the Spotlite Club in New York, again drawing capacity crowds, then in the springtime of 1945 she and Joe Guy travelled out to California. Whilst on the Coast, Lady announced that she had secured a divorce in Mexico and married Guy. Whether the couple were ever legally married has never been established. It's uncertain if Guy was ever divorced from his first wife; and in a 1947 court hearing, Billie was described as still being married to James N. Monroe.

The couple moved back to New York and on 22 May 1945 Billie opened at Mike Westerman's 'Downbeat' Club. It was rumoured on 52nd Street that Billie's addiction problems would cause her to cancel all bookings temporarily, it was said that she'd made herself ill by taking 'bad stuff' (poor quality drugs) whilst travelling from California. But Lady made the bookings on time, and *Down Beat* magazine reported 'Billie dispelled the gossips by being on hand for her opening at the Downbeat, where she shares billing with Coleman Hawkins.'

However in this instance, Billie found opening night easier than the rest of the run; routines were almost out of control as she became more and more enmeshed with her addiction problems. By July, *Down Beat* reported 'Billie is worrying her associates again', and a month later they printed 'Billie Holiday was under contract, but not appearing regularly.' Soon afterwards Billie ceased to work at the Downbeat; she and Joe Guy began organising a big sixteen-piece touring band.

The organisation of a big touring band requires a big outlay of capital: arrangements, uniforms, and attractive music-stands have to be paid for, a coach has to be bought or hired, a road-manager and a band valet are virtually essential, and the services of a publicity man are needed. The finances involved in such a project are usually too great for individuals, and most bands are sponsored by corporations, or occasionally by other bandleaders who advance their former sidemen enough funds to start a new band – knowing that part-ownership means they have two horses in the race.

Billie and Joe Guy were almost innocents regarding the problems of running a big touring band – Guy had played in several big bands but had never been active in their administration. Organising a big band was the easiest way in the world to say goodbye to 35,000 dollars, which was what Billie later estimated the venture cost her. But during these big band days, Billie suffered an even greater loss – her mother died. Billie said she had a premonition about her mother's death whilst the band were playing in Washington, she mentioned it to Joe Guy, but he told her that she was crazy. The sad news reached her next morning.

Billie immediately returned to New York, where Joe Glaser had made the funeral arrangements, he also forewarned promoters that Billie would probably abandon her working schedule temporarily. To everyone's surprise, Billie decided to try to work her way out of her sadness, she returned to Washington and finished the week. Billie and her mother had a very close relationship, despite their occasional tempestuous rows. Sadie never admitted to being more than

38: she was however 49 when she died. Her early life had been very hard indeed. In later years, with Billie's help, and the small profit from her catering projects, things were more comfortable. But the financial security didn't bring peace of mind. The more famous Billie became, the more her mother worried and fretted over her daughter's misdemeanours. Billie was rueful when she reflected on this, 'Wherever Mom was going it couldn't be worse than what she'd known.'

The news of her mother's death numbed Billie, and it was months before the full impact of the bereavement hit her. She said that she just could not cry at the time. The tears came later, and long afterwards she would try to hide the choke in her voice as she told old friends 'Duchess is gone now you know.'

After Billie had finished a short series of theatre dates with Don Redman's Band she hit the road with her own unit in late August 1945. The band's playing schedule included Chicago and Detroit, but most of the dates were in the South; by September the band had started a long string of dates through Virginia, South Carolina and Georgia. Trombonist Floyd 'Stumpy' Brady, who was with the band, recalls, 'I had a wonderful time travelling with Lady Day, the wonderful Lady of Song who used to stop the band-bus and lead her boxer dog "Mister" around for his walk — everyone in the band used to get mad, bar me.'

Discipline was not greatly in evidence, and the band's departure from point to point was always delayed whilst musicians were pulled from bar or bed. Guy wasn't a born leader, and when it came to a showdown it was usually Billie who made the decisions. Floyd Brady gives an example of Billie taking care of business: 'Lady Day always had me at the microphone for "Don't Blame Me" and "Laura". One night in a small town in Georgia (after we had been drinking together) she called me up front to play "Laura"; being so high, I missed the top note in the release. That was it — she told the valet to tell me to take off the band uniform.' Thus ended Floyd's days with the band. He no longer drinks and can look back now and describe it as a pretty wild orchestra.

Another trombonist, Clyde Bernhardt, remembers being asked to join the band for a booking at the Apollo Theater, 'At the time, I was playing steadily with Dud and Paul Bascomb. Billie heard Joe Guy talking to me, she butted in and said to me "Don't you like my band?" I said "yes", then she said "Well why in the hell don't you join the damn band if you like it? Don't bullshit man, just shit or get off the pot." I began to laugh, then she began to laugh, and said to me "Now, what in the hell is funny?" She was really something. I liked to talk to her when she was in a good mood, and she would talk her trash. One night she told her boxer dog "Mister" to go on stage in her place, because she didn't feel like singing that show. "Mister" looked at her and barked lightly; she said to him "Yes take your ass out on that stage and sing the next show for me." '

But Billie could be business-like and efficient if the mood was right. Bob Haggart, whose studio orchestra backed Billie on recordings in 1945 and 1947, had to meet her for preliminary discussions on routines and keys before he began writing the arrangement for the sessions. 'The first meeting I had with Billie Holiday was at the club on 52nd Street where she was appearing. I believe it was Kelly's Stables. I went to her dressing room at the club and introduced myself, "I'm Bob Haggart, bass player, I'll be doing the date at Decca for Milt Gabler, so I've come by to get your keys and talk over the tunes." She was very cordial and friendly, and put me completely at ease immediately. She had all four song copies in front of her (for the tunes we planned to record), and knew just what she wanted. Being a rather naive studio musician accustomed to working mostly mornings and afternoons, my sudden exposure to night club life was a bit strange. I must admit I was shocked to notice needle marks on both of Billie's arms. I had heard she was on hard drugs (on and off). I met her when she was feeling good, and I must say she was marvellous to me.'

Work for Billie's Big Band proved scarce, and she spent most of the winter of 1945 at the Downbeat Club alongside Sid Catlett's Band. By the end of the year her band, as a regular unit, had virtually ceased to exist. There were insufficient bookings to guarantee keeping 'key' men on a payroll. Billie and Joe Guy switched to a small band format – Guy playing trumpet with a four-piece rhythm section. The lineup worked well together, and Billie decided to use this backing for her solo concert debut.

On 16 February 1946, Billie appeared at the New York Town Hall for what was her first solo concert; she was accompanied by Joe Guy on trumpet, Joe Springer on piano, Tiny Grimes on guitar, Lloyd Trotman on bass, and Eddie Nicholson on drums. The concert was a success – musically and financially – and although it lasted for only an hour and ten minutes, the overflow audience felt that they had had their money's worth in hearing Lady sing 18 songs. John Hammond writing in the magazine *Hollywood Notes* said, 'She sang with far more apparent pleasure and ease than on West 52nd Street. It was a triumph long overdue.' Leonard Feather in the March 1946 *Metronome* said, 'Lady Day was in wonderful voice; her dignified bearing and her wonderful poise helped to keep the large, quiet, intelligent audience enthralled.'

Billie's dignified bearing didn't stop her being a woman of direct action when she felt the occasion called for it. In the spring of 1946 she heard that singer Josh White, who had recorded 'Strange Fruit', was featuring the song in his act at Billie's old stamping ground Cafe Society. Billie had known Josh casually since they met at a wartime party given by photographer Gjon Mili. Josh had shared Billie's one and only excursion into active politics, when in May 1944 she appeared at the Golden Gate Auditorium in New York for a rally held under the auspices of the Associated Communist Clubs of Harlem, nevertheless, she showed no hesitation in storming into the night club to sort him out. Josh White recalled the incident in a 1959 *Melody Maker* interview, 'For a time, she wanted to cut my throat for using that song which was written for her. One night she called by the Cafe to bawl me out. We talked and finally came downstairs peaceably

103

together, and to everyone's surprise had a nice little dancing session.

'I loved her interpretation of the song, but I wanted to do Strange Fruit my way. I explained how I felt to Billie, and I think she saw the point. After that, she often came in the Cafe — more often than not for the late show around 2.30 in the morning — sometimes she was real late and wouldn't even come in. She'd drive down to 2 Sheridan Square and sit outside listening to the car radio with her big boxer dog "Mister". Then, we would drive around the after-hours spots, the key clubs, the drinking places like Alex's. We became the best of friends.

'Billie was accused of being temperamental, hot-tempered and wild. She had her weaknesses, also more than her share of troubles and finally they wrecked her health. But at heart, Billie was a good girl. She had more thought for humanity and was more race-conscious than people thought.'

Billie resumed working at the Downbeat Club and began to settle into a routine; living with her habit was hard, working with it was harder, but slowly she began to adjust. She took leave from the club to make a short tour, then she returned there for a further two months; during this period, she was one of the guest stars in a 'Jazz At The Philharmonic' production that Norman Granz had organised at Carnegie Hall. Granz agreed that Billie could choose her own accompanying group; she used her own rhythm section, plus Joe Guy and, despite Coleman Hawkins, George Auld and Illinois Jacquet being on the bill, she felt that the only tenor-sax player who would exactly suit her needs was Lester Young, who made the group into a sextet. Billie sang four old favourites, 'Billie's Blues', 'All of Me', 'Them There Eyes' and 'He's Funny That Way' and was given a tremendous reception.

In September 1946, Billie left New York and travelled to Hollywood for what was to be her only appearance in a major film.

# CHAPTER SIX

Billie Holiday's solitary major film appearance was in a Majestic–United Artists production entitled *New Orleans* (produced by Jules Levey, directed by Arthur Lubin). Besides the film's stars, Arturo de Cordova, Dorothy Patrick, and Irene Rich, the cast boasted an impressive array of talent from the jazz world: Billie Holiday, Louis Armstrong, Kid Ory, Barney Bigard, Meade Lux Lewis, Red Norvo and Woody Herman's Orchestra. Those jazz fans who read the preliminary sales message that '*New Orleans* is the story of the odyssey of jazz' were in for a disappointment.

The film, which was shot at the Hal Roach Studios in Culver City, used many of the clichés that Hollywood reserved for its treatment of jazz, and the casting followed the then long-established practice of only allocating menial roles to Negroes acting in films.; Louis Armstrong was a butler, and Billie a maid.

A promotional pamphlet gave the plot in a nutshell: 'Lovely lyric soprano, Dorothy Patrick, a young Crescent City society girl, is captivated by a Louisiana gambler, Arturo de Cordova, who instils in her his love for the "new" music [jazz]. Their romance falls foul of Dorothy's mother, Irene Rich, who sees her daughter's career threatened, and uses her wealth to drive De Cordova from town.'

Naturally, all ends happily. Cordova makes a lady out of jazz by presenting her in a concert hall, and there, by a felicitous coincidence he is reunited with Miss Patrick. En route to this preposterous finale jazz fans are treated to some fine playing by Louis Armstrong – seen leading his Original New Orleans Jass Band – and some magnificent singing by Billie.

The film exemplifies Hollywood's oft-repeated ending for a jazz movie. The ingredients are: a big concert hall, an orchestra (the bigger the better) grappling with a spectacular jazz theme, and many close-ups of bunioned aristocratic feet twitching in unco-ordinated rhythms.

Both Louis and Billie were naturals at film acting, and Billie's easily discernible skills apparently irked the film's leading lady. Billie said 'After the star looked at a few days' rushes she decided I was stealing scenes from her.'

*From the film* New Orleans – *Louis Armstrong, Billie, Barney Bigard*

Certainly, relationships on the set were often less than cordial. The routine of getting up at six am each morning was new to Billie, and as she was also playing club dates during the weeks she was filming, time for resting was very short. As a result, Billie's attendance and punctuality tended to be somewhat irregular; this naturally irritated some of the cast. However, the musicians were not dismayed by any delays caused by Billie's non-appearances. Barney Bigard was one of several who viewed the situation calmly, as he later explained, 'As far as we were concerned the hold-ups were no problem since we soon ran into overtime pay.'

But despite Billie's gruelling schedule of club work in the evenings and film work at dawn there are no signs of exhaustion in her performance. When the cameras started rolling she seemed serenely happy, for in many ways, appearing in a big film was the fulfillment of many of her dreams; in order to achieve that ambition she was prepared to swallow her pride and play the part of a singing maid. It certainly wasn't type-casting for Billie: years before she'd vowed to her father's friend Clyde Bernhardt, 'I'll never be a maid for white folks,' and she candidly told one interviewer 'I wouldn't lift a suitcase for anyone in the world.'

Originally she was looking forward to the filming, and told Leonard Feather, 'I'll be playing a maid, but she's really a cute maid' (*From Satchmo to Miles*, p. 77).

Had Joe Glaser been on hand, many of the problems that developed on the set could have been nipped in the bud, for he was agent to both the main musical stars (Louis and Billie). But he was in New York (his usual base) during the filming, and Billie was continually making long-distance calls trying to let him know of her grievances. By now, Glaser felt that he was only ever called on to sort out Billie's problems when they were insuperable, he was tired of arguing with her; earlier that year he told Ralph Watkins, owner of Kelly's Stables, 'Talk to Billie yourself. Whatever she agrees to is okay with me' – an unexpected line from someone who could be a ruthless negotiator.

Glaser was certainly a complex man. He found it inspiring

(and it must be said, profitable) to secure better-paid engagements for the many black artists he represented. He encouraged his stars to come to him with their problems, and afterwards he would talk paternally about their visits, yet he could still refer to them as 'my schwarzers'. Billie would have no truck with that sort of expression, and Glaser was never indiscreet enough to use it in her presence. Glaser's relationship with Lady Day was straightforward in comparison to his long association with Louis Armstrong. Glaser, who died in 1969, left Armstrong a considerable amount of shares and capital; Louis, during his last years, often referred to Glaser as the best friend he ever had, and vigorously denied the suggestion that Glaser had reaped most of the benefits of their long tie-up. Glaser had the power to sign Louis' contracts, but for all the power that this gave him, he couldn't go too far in pushing the great trumpet player into roles that he didn't want. On one occasion, a Hollywood mogul approached Glaser for Louis' services in a proposed musical version of *Uncle Tom's Cabin*. Glaser told the enquirer to go and contact Louis direct. The man's visit to Louis' dressing-room was one of the shortest on record, and he certainly went out of the door a lot faster than he entered.

Billie's friend Hazel Scott was very selective in her acceptance of film parts; in the late 1940s she was quoted as saying, 'I have turned down four singing-maid roles in movies during the past year.' Miss Scott's film contract had stringent clauses to ensure that there were no loopholes through which racialism could seep. Billie had no such safeguards against Hollywood's colour phobia, and she felt a big sense of disappointment and frustration when she finally saw the completed film; years later she said, 'I never made another movie, and I'm in no hurry.'

Early in 1947, *New Orleans* was premiered in many cities throughout the U.S.A. Reviews were luke-warm; many critics by-passed both the plot and the performances of the 'stars' to concentrate on praising Billie and Louis Armstrong. However, very few of the writers commented on the fact that two of America's greatest musical performers were cast as servants. Leonard Feather was a notable exception: in *Metronome* of April 1947 he pointed out, 'Socially, Mr Levey bent over backwards to avoid offending the South. Billie Holiday is (of course) a maid, Louis Armstrong talks to his horn, no Negro shakes hands with a white man, and the cast racial overtones of the story are carefully muted. Billie Holiday sings "Goodbye to Storyville". "The Blues are Brewin" and shares with Louis the fair pop song which runs through the film, "Do You Know What It Means to Miss New Orleans?". But until Hollywood stops pussyfooting on the race question, and makes a picture with the attitude that it doesn't give a damn whether the South shows it or not, there will not be any real movie about jazz.'

Despite the film's shortcomings, it did present Billie's talents to a wider audience than she had ever reached before, and for the first time in her career, she was getting regular mentions in the national press. But this added publicity didn't bring a bonanza, a recession in night-club trade was well under way, and Billie like most other performers suffered.

She returned to New York to resume work at the Downbeat Club, where pianist Eddie Heywood's Band was playing. Billie and Heywood had recorded together on many occasions since 1941, they had also shared club-dates, on which Heywood's band accompanied Billie as well as playing their own sets. However, by 1946 the sextet had achieved considerable fame, having appeared in a couple of movies, and been featured on many radio programmes. As a result of a big selling version of 'Begin The Beguine', Heywood was, for a time, more well-known than Billie. Heywood and his management thought it unwise that he accompany Billie at the Downbeat. A few harsh words were exchanged between Billie and Heywood, and thereafter the pianist ceased to back Billie, but as it happened the change did Billie no harm since it enabled her to meet-up with an accompanist who was to work with her regularly until mid-1949. In late 1946, Bobby Tucker who had recently finished his Army service, was working as Mildred Bailey's accompanist. The circumstances under which he left Mildred to join Billie were unusual.

On the opening night of Billie's return to 'The Downbeat', Bobby Tucker happened to be strolling along 52nd Street; his long-time friend clarinetist Tony Scott spotted him, and asked if he was free to play an immediate engagement with Billie. Bobby, who has been Billy Eckstine's pianist for over 20 years, recently recalled, 'I just happened to be passing by. Full house – show in ten minutes – no music – no pianist. Somebody had goofed. Since we were next-door neighbours in Morristown, New Jersey, Tony Scott and I grew up on Benny Goodman and Teddy Wilson records – it was incidental that the singer on a lot of my favorite sides was Lady Day. Tony introduced me to Lady and she picked a show. All of the tunes I had been playing for fun, and now, for the first time the singer herself was involved. From that first show (she hired me in the middle of it) till she died, we were the best of friends.'

Tony Scott remembers questioning Lady Day as to whether Bobby Tucker was suitable. 'I kept asking "was she satisfied?", and she kept saying "I'll let you know." At the end of the week in the Downbeat Club, she said, "He's a Bitch." When she went to jail for a year Bobby refused work with Ella Fitzgerald, Sarah Vaughan, and Dinah Washington so as not to drag Lady.'

Billie was greatly touched by Tucker's loyalty, and years later she spoke of him as her 'faithful accompanist.' Tucker wrote regularly to her whilst she was in Alderson Reformatory, and whilst there Billie knitted elaborate cable-stitch sweaters for Bobby and his son. Tucker still corrects anyone who speaks of his two spells of working with Billie: 'There was only one. We never considered the nine months she spent in prison as a cause for terminating the relationship.'

Attendances at all New York night-clubs dropped drastically during early 1947, and this recession caused several clubs to revise their scales of pay. The Downbeat was forced to reduce Billie's salary (and that of Art Tatum, who was also working at the club) by twenty per cent – stringent economies directed towards two of the biggest earners that

110

52nd Street ever had. But despite the reduced wage bill, the club plunged deeper into financial difficulties and soon New York's emblem of the failure of a small business, a padlocked door, meant that another club had closed.

Billie had occasionally experienced the occupational hazard of having a contract to appear at a club which no longer existed. However, this foreclosure was to have a decisive effect on her life. The free time that had suddenly become available became a factor in her making the decision to attempt a 'cure' for her heroin addiction. Joe Glaser seized the intitiative and presented Billie with a 'now-or-never' ultimatum that she seek treatment.

*Down Beat* magazine euphemistically wrote that Billie was undergoing 'a general check-up,' but it was an open secret on 52nd Street that Billie was going into a clinic to try and kick her habit. Joe Glaser organised her admittance to a New York clinic, then kept in close contact to see what progress had been made. The cost of the three-week stay was put at 2,000 dollars. After Billie was released she travelled to the

*Recuperating after a 'cure'*

home of Bobby Tucker's mother in Morristown, New Jersey and relaxed there.

The sanitorium's expensive 'cold turkey' treatment (enforced and absolute withdrawal from hard drugs) was intended to shock Lady's system into permanent rejection of heroin. Unfortunately, it was only temporarily successful; effective for only as long as Billie stayed away from the musical scene. As soon as she re-entered the world of first-night nerves and performance tensions she was an easy target for the drug-pushers.

She resumed 'shooting' with a vengeance, almost as though she sensed that time was running out for her. It was, for by now the agents of the Federal Narcotics Bureau were biding their time waiting for the right occasion to swoop on Billie and arrest her.

Lady always felt that the Federal agents were in cohorts with someone on the staff of the sanitorium, and that she had been informed on after taking 'the cure'. She stressed, with a deal of bitterness, that no one had ever trailed her before she stayed at the clinic. However, the reason for her stay at the clinic was common knowledge among many of the performers and operators of New York's clubland, and her hospitalisation coincided with re-organisations of the New York Police Department's Narcotic Squad and the Federal Bureau of Narcotics. A rivalry was said to have existed between these two departments and this meant that each organisation followed every lead with extra diligence. It was inevitable that the club and bar-room gossip rife on 52nd Street would reach the attentive ears of the law. Within weeks of leaving the clinic, Billie was arrested.

In May 1947, Billie played a week's theatre booking in Philadelphia, sharing the bill with Louis Armstrong's Big Band. After the last show on Friday 16 May, Bobby Tucker and Billie's young road-manager Jimmy Ascendio followed their customary routine and returned to the Attucks Hotel. As usual, Billie stayed on in the theatre dressing-room to remove her make-up. After she had finished, she was driven back to the hotel by a chauffeur.

There are two greatly varied reports of what happened when Billie returned to the Attucks Hotel – both were told by Billie – one in her autobiography, the other in an interview that *Down Beat* published soon after the incident (in their issue dated 4 June 1947).

In *Lady Sings The Blues,* Billie tells of her premonition that the police would raid the Attucks Hotel; she also gives a dramatic account of her runaway ride, and how she escaped from police bullets by driving a car for the first time in her life. She recounts that the chauffeur and her boxer dog were the passengers on her wild drive back to Camden, New Jersey. However, her account of the incident, published soon after it occurred, was very different.

'You know what actually happened? I was coming back to the hotel and we noticed a lot of people around it, and my driver Bill said it looked like it had been raided. I told him he was crazy, but we parked by the side of the hotel, and he went up there to see what was going on. He saw some agents and came running back to the car. Evidentally he had one offense against him for something and they had told him he would lose his car if he did anything else. Well, he started the car like it was a jackrabbit and we tore by a couple of policemen on the sidewalk.

'I heard a couple of sounds like shots and I ask him and he said "yes they were shots," but that he was afraid to stop, he didn't know what was going on. So we came back to New York City.'

The aftermath of the police raid was that Bobby Tucker was taken into custody – lawyers quickly secured his unconditional release, as Billie said at the time, 'Bobby Tucker? The strongest thing he ever had in his life was a Camel cigarette. Believe me he is the most innocent thing that ever was' (*Down Beat,* 4 June 1947). Bobby travelled back to New York to open with Billie at the Club 18 (formerly The Onyx). During the first week at the club, Billie and her manager Joe Glaser had a show-down. Joe Glaser strongly advised Billie to 'come clean' and return to Philadelphia to face the police – he felt confident that he could use his influence to get the authorities to waive a prison sentence, and substitute instead a compulsory entry into a rehabilitation centre where Billie would undergo a cure at Government expense. However, Glaser's big proviso on co-operation was that Billie should keep away from Joe Guy. Billie made no effort to conceal the rift that existed between Guy and Glaser; in a *Down Beat* interview she said 'My manager hates him (Guy), says he's responsible for everything that has happened to me. Don't you believe it. I'm grown-up. I knew what I was doing. Joe may have done things he shouldn't, but I did them of my own accord too. And I never tried to influence anybody. Joe didn't make it any easier for me at times – but then I haven't been any easy gal either.'

Detectives kept Billie and Joe Guy under close surveillance; for a few days they watched and waited, then they suddenly swooped on the couple's room at the Hotel Grampion in New York and arrested them. Guy was held in custody whilst efforts were made to hustle up the 3,000 dollars required for his bail.

Billie was released on bail of a thousand dollars, and she continued to work at New York's Club 18 awaiting the date of her trial. During the interim, she gave a long interview to Mike Levin of *Down Beat* which appeared on that magazine's front page under the headline 'Don't Blame Show Biz'. As preliminary to the main story, the magazine reflected Joe Glaser's optimism: *'Down Beat* learned from an unimpeachable source that, in all probability, charges would not be pressed against her, she would be allowed to finish out her run at Club 18, New York City, and other work presently contracted and then would probably go to Lexington, Kentucky, for medical treatment of some months' duration.'

However, things did not work out that smoothly. Detectives continued to track Billie's every movement, she felt sure that she would get no peace at all before her case was heard so she agreed to Joe Glaser's suggestion that she contact the Philadelphia authorities and request that her trial be convened at the earliest possible time.

Billie telephoned Assistant U.S. Attorney Joseph Hildenberger on the morning of Tuesday 27 May and told him that she wanted to get the case over as soon as possible. Hildenberger made arrangements with Judge J. Cullen Ganey for the trial to begin that very morning. Despite being driven at full speed to Philadelphia by one of Joe Glaser's top road-managers, Lady arrived an hour late for the scheduled time of her trial.

The trial had to be postponed until 4 p.m., and at that time a tired and fraught Billie appeared before Judge Ganey in the Philadelphia Federal Court and was charged with violation of Section 174 of the U. S. Narcotics Act: 'That she did recieve, conceal and facilitate the transportation and concealment of drugs.' Billie pleaded guilty, and as she was without an attorney to represent her she addressed the judge herself, telling him that she was broke, and willing to enter a state hospital to be cured of her addiction. She told Judge Ganey that Joe Guy had started her on the habit, and that she and her husband James N. Monroe had been separated for three years.

In his summary, Judge Ganey told Billie that he was dissatisfied with the way she had observed her parole – Joe Glaser had acted as a guarantor when paying the thousand-dollar bail, but he had done so on condition that Billie kept away from Joe Guy. After telling Billie that she must co-operate with Federal Agents in their efforts to track down the suppliers of drugs, the Judge then questioned her about general aspects of her career. Assistant Attorney Hildenberger provided background detail in telling the court that Billie was the victim of 'the worst type of parasite you can imagine! They followed her around charging her a hundred dollars for dosages of narcotics costing five dollars.' In court it was said that Joe Guy 'posed as the singer's husband and obtained most of the dope she used.' Billie later estimated that she spent an average of 500 dollars a week on heroin during the mid-1940s.

The outcome of the case was not the one that had been optimistically forecast: Billie was sentenced to a year and a day in the Federal Reformatory for Women at Alderson, West Virginia.

The duration of the sentence was not the most troublesome aspect of the verdict. Billie could have been eligible for parole after serving eight months; however, the fact that she had been sentenced meant that it would be impossible for her to work again in New York clubs that served liquor, by reason of the New York Police Regulation which forbade the issuance of a cabaret working card to anyone convicted of a felony (this regulation remained in force until Mayor John Lindsay repealed it in September 1967).

Billie was not surprised by the way that the newspapers reacted to the court's verdict. Press coverage dwelt on the sensational aspects of the case; one leading radio station banned Billie's records from the air because of her 'notoriety'. Billie's pre-prison statement was direct 'Don't forget ... I just want to be straight with people, not have their sympathies.'

A few hours after being sentenced, Billie, in the custody of two white matrons, began the train journey to the Alderson Reformatory. To prevent the withdrawal symptoms of sickness and diarrhoea occurring on the train-ride, Billie was given a shot of heroin.

The addiction cure began soon after she reached Alderson. The agonies of her previous treatment in the sophisticated New York clinic were cushioned by gifts, telephone calls and contact with the outside world. At Alderson there were no such diversions, and Billie found the torment of the first 19 days almost unbearable. She said, 'But after a while it passes like everything else, after you've been through hell.'

In 1947, Alderson had segregated accommodation, a little under half of the inmates were black, and although all the 650 girls worked together, black and white ate at different times, and slept in separated dormitories. Initially, Billie was given no preferential treatment, and after her four-week quarantine she began working in turn at picking vegetables, tending the pigs, and scrubbing and scraping in the kitchens. She said 'I started out as a Cinderella, washing dishes and peeling potatoes, after that it was a little easier, but still rugged in contrast to my former life.' She became a permanent room orderly for one of the 'cottages' in which the inmates were housed. There she lit the stoves, cleaned the windows, polished the floors, and prepared light meals for the fifty women who lived in the building. A minority of the inmates were ex-junkies, the rest were a compound of thieves, prostitutes and forgers.

In September 1947, Billie's routine was interrupted; she was taken back to Philadelphia to appear as a witness at Joe Guy's trial. Guy, then 27, faced the same charges that Billie had been convicted of in the previous May, 'transporting and concealing drugs'. Like Billie, he stood trial in the District Courthouse.

Although Billie was ostensibly appearing as a Government witness, it was her evidence that saved Joe Guy from prison. She testified that she alone used the drug, and that the 16 capsules of heroin (which were found in her stockings), and the two hypodermic needles, were not given to her by Guy. After 51 minutes of deliberation, the jury returned a verdict of 'Not Guilty'. Billie was not in court to hear the verdict; as the jury retired she was ushered out of court and taken back, in custody, to Alderson. Soon afterwards, the authorities there issued a statement saying that she was 'responding well to the cure, and had gained ten pounds since her confinement.'

Billie was generally co-operative with both the white and the black staff at the Reformatory and in October 1947 she was allocated her own individual room. There was absolutely no possibility of her being able to obtain hard drugs inside the reformatory; the only illicit trading there concerned the buying, swopping and selling of each girl's sixty-a-week cigarette ration. Nevertheless, the authorities, uncertains as to whether Billie's craving for heroin had gone completely, delayed giving their approval to a premature release; the early parole confidently predicted by the musical trade press was not forthcoming.

Several of Billie's friends gathered funds for a post-Thankgiving gift basket, but they were unable to get the

Alderson authorities to accept the hamper on Billie's behalf. The reformatory also kept to the rules in allocating Billie only three letters a day; the hundreds of messages that arrived from fans were given to Billie at the end of her sentence; she was allowed telephone calls, provided they concerned her rehabilitation.

In New York, a benefit concert for Billie was held at Carnegie Hall on 29 November 1947. Guitarist Oscar Moore (then working in the King Cole Trio) had originated the idea of a benefit, and he mentioned it to impresario Norman Granz who began working wholeheartedly to organise the show. The Nat King Cole Trio and Granz's own all-star package 'Jazz At The Philharmonic' were willing to waive fees and play the concert for nothing. However, to avoid unfavourable reaction from the American Federation of Musicians, they agreed to accept basic union scale. The A.F. of M. raised no objections, but Billie's manager Joe Glaser did. Five days before the concert, Glaser notified the press that the concert was completely unauthorised, and said that he had in his possession a letter from Billie Holiday saying that she neither wanted nor needed a concert. (*Down Beat,* 17 December 1947, p. 6).

Norman Granz candidly admitted that his relationship with Glaser hadn't been good, but pointed out that he was organising the concert to benefit Billie. The publicity that attended this squabble did nothing to boost ticket sales. Not long before the concert, Nat King Cole's Trio discovered they were to be banned from appearing, since their contract with the Paramount Theater had a barring-clause which prevented them playing any other concert in New York City within a six-week period. Nevertheless, the show went on, but the hall was only two-thirds full, which meant a net profit of 514 dollars. Joe Glaser refused to accept the money, and Granz passed the sum total on to charities.

On 16 March 1948, Billie was released on parole from Alderson, having served nine and a half months of her year-and-a-day sentence. She travelled by train from West Virginia to Newark in New Jersey, and from there she made the short journey to the farm that Bobby Tucker's mother owned in Morristown; this was Billie's parole address and there she began readjusting to outside life. Rehearsals with Bobby Tucker at the piano began almost at once, Billie was full of nervous excitement wondering how people would react to the 'Welcome Home' concert that Ernie Anderson was promoting at Carnegie Hall on 27 March.

One of the first things that Billie did after leaving Alderson was to appoint herself a new manager, Ed Fishman. Fishman, a veteran in the entertainments world, had begun his career promoting in Pennsylvania during the 1920s; he often telephoned Billie whilst she was in Alderson, outlining the plans that he had for re-shaping her career, Billie went along with the idea that a new manager would help her (and the club-owners who booked her) forget the past. Remembering the stormy scenes that she had with Joe Glaser just before her trial, Billie decided to put all her business affairs in Fishman's hands.

The issue was soon complicated by Joe Glaser's insistence that he was still legally Billie's manager. His original intention of taking action against Billie to establish this point soon proved unnecessary for Billie quickly regretted having got involved with Ed Fishman, and she was quite willing to re-appoint Glaser.

These ramifications meant that no one in the entertainment world was at all certain who represented Billie. Ernie Anderson, about to promote Billie's Carnegie Hall Concert, avoided confusion by pre-paying both managerial candidates for Billie's services. He recounts, 'I had to be certain that Billie would appear, and if I'd have signed with only one manager, the other could, I suppose, have placed an injunction preventing Billie from appearing at the concert.' He speaks ruefully when remembering the negotiations, 'I paid Fishman $2,500 and Joe Glaser a thousand.'

Six weeks after Billie's release, the dispute between Glaser and Fishman came up before the American Guild of Variety Artists, who ruled that Joe Glaser's company, The Associated Booking Corporation, were Billie's representatives.

Fishman made his exit, and although he had only represented Billie for a matter of weeks, it took two years, and a court action, before he silenced his claims for breach of contract.

But neither money matters nor managerial problems were foremost in Billie's mind in March 1948 as she prepared for the most crucial engagment that she had ever played. She was deeply worried about her forthcoming concert at Carnegie Hall, and the public's reaction to her 'come-back.' Before she had gone to serve her time in Alderson she told *Down Beat* 'Sure I know about Gene Krupa' (the famous drummer who successfully overcame a drugs scandal), 'but don't forget he's white and I'm a Negro. I've got two strikes against me and don't you forget it.'

Billie need not have fretted about Carnegie Hall, the reception that greeted her was described by *Down Beat* as 'one of the most thunderous ovations even given a performance in this, or any other, concert hall,' and *Metronome* echoed the enthusiasm in saying that Lady Day came back in 'a blaze of glory'.

Disc-jockey Fred Robbins introduced Billie at the midnight concert. She was obviously overjoyed by the reception but chose not to make a speech, instead, she went straight into 'I Cover the Waterfront'. Everyone agreed that Billie looked fitter – and lovelier – than she had looked for years; she had put on almost 20 pounds and was radiating enthusiasm. Jack Egan in *Down Beat* summed up the mood of the audience (21 April 1948, p. 1): 'Whether or not her voice is quite as perfect as a year ago didn't matter a whit to the 3,000 disciples.' The ten months' lay-off certainly hadn't impaired Billie's vocal stamina, she sang 21 songs, then amazed the audience with six encores. Originally it was planned that her accompanying group, Bobby Tucker on piano, Denzil Best on drums, John Levy on bass, and Remo Palmieri on guitar, should warm-up the second-half of the show by playing a number before Billie re-appeared. But Lady was impatient to get back on-stage, and as soon as the fifteen-minute interval was over she went on to re-start the show with a song that she had written in collaboration with Andy Razaf, called 'Don't Explain'.

The concert, which was a complete sell-out, is remembered by pianist Bobby Tucker as 'the musical treat of my life'. The audience shrieked for, and got, six encores. This acclaim quickly dispelled Billie's fears about the public's reaction to her release from prison; however, she was still uncertain how people in the music business would greet her return.

Ernie Anderson, who promoted the Carnegie success, said, 'Actually, some of Billie's colleagues in the music world stayed well away from her for quite a while. They didn't want the stigma of drug-taking on them even by association.'

The side of Billie's nature that looked for insults began working overtime. On a backstage visit to a show she felt that she had been snubbed by Sarah Vaughan; Sarah, notably short-sighted, emphatically denies that such a situation ever occurred. She told Max Jones in 1973, 'I would never have deliberately ignored Lady, never. The chances are that I was walking in a dim light and without my glasses on I wouldn't bet on recognising anyone.' Indirectly, Billie supports Sarah's explanation: in an *Ebony* magazine article published in 1949, she talks of the weeks that followed her release from Alderson, 'On one occaion I suffered with laryngitis so badly that my good friend Sarah Vaughan came to my dressing room and insisted that I take a rest; she offered to appear for me. This she did for two days.'

As expected, the Police Department refused to issue Billie with a cabaret card, so she was precluded from working in New York night clubs; she now had the option of going out again on tour (which she didn't feel ready for), or of taking theatre work in New York. A few weeks after the 'Welcome Home' concert she headed a 'Holiday on Broadway' presentation at the Manfield Theater, New York. The show which featured Slam Stewart's Trio, Cozy Cole, and the organ–piano duo of Bob Wyatt and Billy Taylor received good reviews, but the unusual venue (the theatre had never before presented jazz) meant that the staging of the show was risky. The gamble didn't come off, and the show folded after five days. Producer Al Wilde had tentative plans to present the show in other cities, but nothing materialised, and Billie was left as unsure as ever as to what would happen next.

Her uncertainty was dispelled when John H. Levy entered her life. Levy, together with Dicky Wells (not the trombonist), and Al Martin, managed the Ebony Club at 1678 Broadway. Levy convinced Billie that she could work at his club without any action being taken by the New York police, and, more important, he somehow got the police to ignore the fact that Billie was working at his club.

Billie sang at the Ebony undisturbed, and with great success. Gradually she got more and more confident, and soon said that she felt ready to take on bookings outside of New York; she temporarily left the club to play dates at Frank Paulumbo's in Philadelphia and at the Blue Note in Chicago.

Her return to the Ebony brought enormous business to the club; by now, she was the 'in figure' with a vociferous crowd of New York sophisticates, whose interest was stimulated by the publicity concerning her past misdemeanours. They had sensed that Billie, by law, should not be appearing at the club, and this added to the thrill of hearing her.

Joe Glaser was only too well aware that Billie was unlikely to appear at any other club, but the fact didn't thrill him; he could see that the cabaret card embargo would soon restrict his managerial income. He suggested to Billie that she change her image from a night-club singer to that of a concert artiste, his strategy doubtless affected by the sharp rise that had occurred in Louis Armstrong's earnings since he had begun concentrating on concert dates in the previous year.

Billie was co-operative and agreed to play a season at the Strand Theater in New York, sharing the bill with Count Basie's Orchestra. The Strand, like many other theatres in the U.S., featured films and stage-shows. Billie, the Basie Band, Strump and Strumpy, and the Two Zephyrs were the added attractions for the showing of the film *Key Largo*. The season began on 16 July 1948, and lasted for almost six weeks; it was to be the longest theatre residency of Billie's career.

Business was usually good, but whether the theatre was full or not, Billie always got an ovation. She was consistently in fine voice, and seemed to be settling into her return to theatre work. On the surface all seemed well, but later, Billie was to describe the Strand run as the unhappiest time of her life. She gave some indication of her sadness to Barry Ulanov, then writing for *Metronome,* who visited her at the Strand. Billie speaking of the audiences there said, 'They come to see me get all fouled up; they want to see me fall flat on my can.' She went on to emphasise her determination to stay away from heroin, 'When I was on it, I was on it! I wouldn't stop for anybody, anywhere, ever. Now I'm off it, and I won't have it, and that's the end of it.' Billie also harked back to her lack of education, 'John Levy and Bobby Tucker wouldn't believe I only went as far as the fifth grade. They asked me all sorts of questions, history and geography. They made me count. They insisted I was too smart. They asked me what I was trying to pull.' All the old miseries were crowding in on Billie, and she told Ulanov, 'I'm tired of fighting.' One aspect of her unhappiness was connected with the love-affair that she was having with John Levy. She had fallen for Levy soon after beginning work at the Club Ebony, and once again her choice of men was disastrous. A friend of Billie's remarked, 'Billie always liked men's company, and any passing affairs that she had were really due to her physical feelings, she could really take care of business. No, certainly not a nympho, just a real appetite for living, but when it came to getting involved with a guy, well, her choice always seemed weird. A certain type of guy really appealed to her, it was like a pretty chick in high school – if anyone warns her to stay away from so-and-so they're pushing her starting button. If there was one guy in a crowded room that was tough, and mean, and meant trouble, then Lady would find him. There were a lot of bruises in Billie's life, and I just didn't understand all that.'

Benny Morton also spoke of the unhappiness that Billie brought upon herself, 'Very few men who were close to Billie were really interested in her. I believe she was deceived by a lot of people, because anyone could butter her up, saying nice things about her, she wanted to hear these things, because no grown-up seemed to love her when she was growing up.' Another old friend, trumpeter Max Kaminsky, said, 'Billie had a dual nature – the good, sweet side, and the wild side. I knew about the wild part of her life, but we never spoke about it.'

Initially, John Levy spent thousands of his own money on Billie. He rented an expensive apartment in Queens for her, he bought her exquisite gowns, he gave her the first mink coat she ever had; she liked the look of a pea-green Cadillac, and soon afterwards that too was hers. But all of this apparently boundless generosity turned out to be little more than the act of a business-man investing in a prospect that would bring rich returns.

Soon, Billie found that Levy was controlling every aspect of her finances, and although her fee for a week at the Strand Theater was $3,500 she had to plead for pocket money, and even the most trivial purchase had to be accounted for. Levy, who died in 1956, had few close friends, and it has been difficult to find anyone who reminisces affectionately about him. But he, and his partners, held the key to Billie's club appearances in New York. Billie, by herself, could not get the police to waive the rules; somehow, the Club Ebony owners managed to do just that.

The possibilities are that either Levy and his cohorts were influential enough to get the law to turn a blind eye to what was a blantantly advertised contravention of a New York Police Regulation, or the detectives allowed Lady to work at a solitary New York club in the hope that they might spot the drug-pushers and fixers visiting Billie in attempts to get her to resume old habits. Certainly the police not only attended the club, but also kept Billie under close observation even though her parole had ended. Before Billie began her residency at the Strand Theater, they visited her dressing-room at the Club Ebony with a warning that she should 'watch her step'. Billie later said 'I have been caught between the crossfire of Narcotics Agents and drug peddlers and it's been wicked.'

The Club Ebony closed for the summer of 1948; business

resumed in the fall and after Billie had finished her Strand residency she returned there, drawing capacity crowds night after night. The success pattern was repeated when she went to Washington to appear at the Club Bali, but the prolonged taste of success at the Strand was causing Billie to reconsider all her bookings. She announced that she would leave night-club work and concentrate on theatre dates – using her own group and vocal chorus for backings. The scheme was ambitious, but no one was prepared to sponsor it. Certainly not John Levy who was doing splendidly under the existing system, and shrewd Joe Glaser, though keen on more theatre work for Billie, thought it a hazardous idea. Glaser was still unsure whether or not Billie had completely reformed her ways; he felt that he couldn't take the chance by investing big money in the plan in case a misdemeanour by Billie made 20 or more wage-earners redundant – all of whom would be round to his office waving valid union contracts. The idea of a full-time production company was quietly dropped, and Lady Day resumed her pre-Alderson routine, playing night clubs from coast to coast.

Billie travelled with John Levy and pianist Bobby Tucker; for a while, drummer Eddie Nicholson worked alongside Bobby Tucker, then Denzil Best came in on drums. Bassist John Levy (not related to Billie's manager) made the backing unit into a trio. When Denzil Best and John Levy left Billie to join George Shearing's group, Bobby Tucker recruited a drummer and a bassist in the particular city in which Billie had a booking. This proved unsatisfactory, and Bobby Tucker said 'The last few months I worked with Lady, we didn't use bass or dums. It was pretty hard to replace Denzil and John, so we went it alone.'

More often than not, Billie and the group went by road to engagements, using trains only for the longer journeys. Once Billie had settled into her hotel she telephoned any close friends who lived in the district and made plans for shopping expeditions, or visits to local bars or restaurants. Her love of going to the cinema never left her, and she always tried to take in any movie that she had missed in New York.

Occasionally, she played cards or listened to records with the musicians, but more often she relaxed in her own room watching television or listening to the radio. If she was wearing an elaborate hair-style then hours would be spent with its coiffure; at one time when she wore her hair in tight curls she would sit for ages in front of the mirror crimping with an old-fashioned curling iron. She always carried more earrings, bracelets and necklaces than she ever needed, and her preference for neatness showed in the way she carefully arranged everything in her hotel-rooms.

The neatness and other touring routines were similar to Billie's pre-Alderson days, the biggest change was in Lady Day herself. The reformatory experiences had honed away a lot of the laconic humour with which she had formerly shrugged off minor, and occasionally major, irritants. She felt that she had lost much more than a year of her life, she worried whether she had anything to offer the world, she felt sure her voice had harshened. During the 1940s, pianist Bobby Tucker summarised this uncertainty, 'She had the most terrible inferiority complex. She actually does not believe she can sing, that might have something to do with her troubles.'

A doctor who knew Billie well echoed Tucker's feelings. 'She was one of the kindest people I ever knew, and the outward manifestation of harshness and being tough was only a compensatory mechanism for an inferiority complex. Few people really knew Lady because she never allowed herself to get close to people.'

Peggy Lee, who had begun listening regularly to Billie at the Famous Door heard her on many, many occasions during the 1940s, yet there was always a barrier. She said, 'I never knew Lady Day very well, but I knew her well enough to realise her greatness.'

After Alderson, Billie became more sensitive than ever about comments on her appearance; one hostile voice cutting through the babble of a night-club crowd would hit her as hard as a blow to the solar plexus. She hated to arrive at a club and see old publicity photographs on show depicting her as a much younger woman, and in order to demark between the old image and the 'new', Billie stopped wearing a gardenia in her hair. She never resumed regular wearing of the flower, but for years afterwards she would graciously accept a gardenia as a gift, and often she would wear it to avoid hurting the donor's feelings.

In the late 1940s Billie looked magnificent; whenever she was off hard drugs for any length of time she moved easily toward her natural weight, and photographs of the time show a buxom Lady Day looking absolutely beautiful. Physically everything was fine, but often Lady's morale was very low simply because she couldn't cope with the post-withdrawal depressions that easily overwhelmed her, they made her gloomily lethargic and quarrelsome. More often than not these moods manifested themselves on the occasions that Billie dreaded most – opening nights.

Often only the first show of an opening was troubled, but occasionally the mood lasted for the length of the booking. If Lady had a particularly bad opening night then she usually

*With Marian and Jimmy McPartland*

felt that nothing could save the rest of the engagement, and then it would be routine performances throughout the run. Occasionally things were very much worse, and Billie's complete disenchantment reduced the performance to something that was much less than routine.

Early in November 1948, Billie (with pianist Bobby Tucker, bassist John Levy and drummer Dodo Anderson) began a three-week engagement at the Silhouette Club in Chicago. Trouble started during Billie's opening show — she was suffering from a bad cold, and sang short sets. Despite the three-shows-a-night schedule the cold soon cleared up, but by then the damage was done and Billie was thoroughly disillusioned at the prospect of working at the club for the rest of the contracted time. Night after night she turned up late at the club and when she did appear she chose to sing only four songs in each show. Jimmy McPartland's Band were also on the bill and reports published at the time praise the way the Band entertained the audience during the time Billie should have been on stage.

Jimmy McPartland had no ill feelings towards Billie, he always remembers her with admiration and affection; however the club's owner Joe Saletta was distinctly restless. He was paying Billie a salary of $2,850 dollars a week, and in addition Lady was scheduled to receive a bonus consisting of an agreed percentage of the money taken over the bar. Mr. Saletta felt he was being generous enough to expect a full performance from Billie, but nothing that he said or did could change Billie's attitude.

Pat Harris, in reviewing one of Billie's shows at the Silhouette for *Down Beat* magazine was forced to comment 'Billie didn't seem interested in singing. Her presentation was so mechanically stylised as to seem almost a mimic's mockery of what she had done before.' Club owners who were holding signed contracts for forthcoming appearances by Billie waited with trepidation knowing that the magazine report signified that Lady's old enemy, unreliability, was back.

After Chicago, Billie played a follow-up date at Ciro's in

Philadelphia; the engagement passed without major incident, but the drama that marked the next booking (at Billy Berg's in Hollywood) again pitch-forked Billie on to the front pages, and landed her, and her manager John Levy, in custody.

# CHAPTER SEVEN

Lady was pleased to be back in California, she always enjoyed working at Billy Berg's Club. Hollywood's glamour may have been fading by the late 1940s, but to Billie it was still vivid enough.

Opening night at Billy Berg's – 15 December 1948 – went off without a hitch, and Billie and the musicians settled down knowing that business would be especially good during the Christmas holidays. Sure enough, the festive season brought out the crowds, and, as usual, the club was jam-packed on New Year's Eve.

1949 was not many minutes old when Billie, who had finished her first set, walked through the club's kitchen where a group of the owner's friends were celebrating.

Billie complained to John Levy that one of the revellers had tried to get fresh with her as she passed by. Levy charged into the kitchen and demanded an explanation, Henry Martin spoke up and said he had only bumped into Billie as she walked through the room; another guest, John Petiva, joined in the ensuing argument. Insults were traded, tempers spiralled, then Levy picked up a carving knife and lunged at Petiva, but he was so wild and angry that he missed him completely and slashed another one of the crowd, Robert Donovan, in the shoulder. All hell broke loose as Billie began hurling crockery and glasses at the wounded man's friends. Meanwhile, the man who had been stabbed ran from the kitchen and jumped on to the bandstand where Red Norvo's group were playing, the knife-blade still sticking in his shoulder. In a hark-back to a scene that could have taken place in Prohibition Chicago, Norvo shouted to the band to keep playing, as loudly as possible.

The police arrived soon afterwards and the pandemonium subsided. Three people, Robert Donovan, Marion Epstein and Henry Martin had been hurt in the fracas and they were taken to hospital. Neither Billie nor John Levy were injured. Levy was arrested and later released on bail of $2,500. Billie was not charged at the time; she surrendered to the police three days later when a warrant for her arrest was issued. She too was freed on bail of $2,500 after being charged by the District Attorney on three counts of assault with a deadly weapon (*San Francisco Chronicle,* 5 January 1949, p. 9).

On the day of the preliminary hearing – 13 January 1949 – Billie opened to 'standing room only' notices at Joe Tenner's Cafe Society in San Francisco's Fillmore Section. A good proportion of the crowd were attracted to the club by the crime-page publicity that Billie got, but within a fortnight of the opening, Billie was involved in an even more sensational story.

'Billie Holiday is held on opium charge' said page one of the *San Francisco Chronicle* on 23 January 1949. On the previous afternoon, agents of the Federal Bureau of Narcotics had raided Billie's and John Levy's hotel on Taylor Street. There, according to the agent's district superintendent, Colonel George White, a quantity of opium 'worth less than fifty dollars' and a pipe were found in the couple's possession.

When they were charged at San Francisco's Hall of Justice, both Billie and John Levy (described as Billie's husband) vehemently denied any knowledge of the drug. After being released on bail of five hundred dollars each, the couple told reporters that the whole affair was 'a frame-up'.

131

The sensation seekers had a field day, and the Cafe Society Club was packed for every show until Billie's final appearance there on 9 February.

Meanwhile, Billie had retained the services of the celebrated attorney J. W. Ehrlich, who was later to refer to Billie's case in his book *Never Plead Guilty*. Billie was indicted by a grand jury on 11 February; the case against Levy was dismissed since it was claimed that Billie had the opium in her possession at the time of the raid. A successful petition was entered. It pointed out that Billie would suffer serious financial loss if she was unable to play engagements already contracted; the judge agreed to defer the case.

Shortly after Billie was released on bail, John Levy called Dr Herbert B. Henderson, who had known Billie and Levy since the 1930s. Levy told the doctor that he and Billie were being asked to vacate their hotel rooms because of the bad publicity that the arrests had brought. Subsequently other hotels throughout the Bay area refused to accommodate the couple and Dr Henderson decided to invite them to be his house-guests until the engagement at the Cafe Society had ended. The doctor was convinced that Billie was not using hard drugs at this time, he conferred with Jake Ehrlich and told him that he felt Billie was innocent and that he would like to help prove the point.

After the Cafe Society dates had ended Billie remained in California, and Dr Henderson set about establishing Billie's innocence. He referred her to Dr James Hamilton, a psychiatrist who lived nearby, who in turn arranged that Billie be admitted to the Belmont Sanitarium in Belmont, California. Dr Henderson and his wife drove Billie to Belmont, en route, during the thirty-mile journey. They stopped at Mountain View where Billie bought herself a tiny chihuahua dog and asked Dr Henderson (who already owned a chihuahua) to look after it until she was released.

At the sanitarium's Admission Office, Billie was thoroughly searched, even the lining of her mink coat was split to ensure that she was not concealing drugs. The small radio that she was carrying was impounded, in case that was being used to smuggle in narcotics. Billie willingly underwent urine and blood tests; they proved negative, and this established that there was no trace of opium in her body. After two weeks Billie left Belmont.

To avoid being subpoenaed as a witness, John Levy left California immediately after his 11 February acquittal. Nevertheless, Billie decided to go ahead with a tour of Northern California that had been arranged for March 1949. The accompanying group was led by Billie's old friend, vibraharpist Red Norvo; the newest member of the group was a young bassist, Charles Mingus. The tour flopped, and after a bad night at Bakersfield, Billie disregarded her contracts and quit.

She moved east and was re-united with Levy, whose connections with the Ebony Club had ended; the club changed hands, it became the Clique for a short spell and then gained widespread fame as 'Birdland'. In the spring of 1949, another New York Club, the Royal Roost, made Billie a substantial offer (said to be 3,000 dollars a week) providing she could get Police Department clearance to play the engagement. Billie decided to make a formal appeal against the cabaret card ruling; this was turned down by Justice Aaron Levy who shattered Billie by saying that the Police Department 'deserves commendation' for refusing the issuance of a card (*Down Beat,* 6 May 1949).

Throughout her adult life Billie had been surrounded by musicians whose maxim was 'if you're big in New York you're big anywhere'. The judge's ruling made it impossible for her to work in New York clubs; temporarily, she was completely demoralised.

Although she had often toyed with the idea of concentrating solely on theatre work, the great performer instinct within her knew that her perfect working locale was in a New York night club. There, she was on her home ground. In front of the city's audiences her slightest nuance provoked a response, Lady felt that they came closest to understanding her own personal torments. *Down Beat's* summing-up of the judge's ruling was all too prophetic: 'Billie

133

Holiday may have made her last New York night club appearance.' This made bitter reading for Lady Day who still had the California trials to contend with.

At the end of May 1949, Billie returned to face the 'opium possession' trial alone. The Belmont Sanitarium findings were never presented in court; just as Jacob Ehrlich was about to introduce the medical details an objection by the Prosecuting Attorney was sustained. Nevertheless Ehrlich's skilful presentation of Billie's evidence ensured her acquittal. Her version of the incidents leading up to the arrest plainly indicted John Levy, who, she alleged, passed the opium to her seconds before the police entered the hotel room. Billie was adamant that she had not seen the package until Levy handed it to her with instructions that she flush it down the toilet; the jury's verdict meant that they believed that Billie had been framed by Levy.

Ralph Gleason, reporting for *Down Beat* (15 July 1949, p. 3) told the poignant story of how Billie had arrived at the trial with a black eye, which she said had been given to her by John Levy. Billie told Gleason, 'You should see my back, and he even took my silver-blue mink coat — eighteen grand worth of coat. He said he was going to give it to his sister to take care of for me. I got nothing now and I'm scared.' Yet, she was still able to say, 'If he was to walk in the room this minute, I'd melt. He's my man and I love him.' Billie's friends despaired.

Billie also told Gleason, 'I turned my life over to John. He took all my money, I never had any money, we were supposed to get married. On 22 January, John came back from Los Angeles. We had been arguing about money.' Billie went on to describe how Levy had handed her the small package of opium. 'I took it. I didn't know what was in it. I went into my room. John closed the door behind me. Then someone grabbed me and threw me against the wall. I never smoked opium in my life. John told me to throw some trash away. I did it. My man makes me wait on him, not him on me. I never did anything without John telling me, that's all I know.'

But despite the accusations, the tears and the bruises, the couple were soon reconciled. Billie had been tempted to resume her marriage with Jimmy Monroe, a move that Levy had quickly and positively discouraged, soon afterwards, Billie revived her tradition of publicising imaginary matrimony by telling *Ebony* magazine in July 1949, that she and Levy had married in January 1949, on the day following her final divorce from Monroe. In the same interview, which was headlined 'I'm Cured For Good', she also said 'In John Levy, my personal manager, I have a wonderful friend who has stood by me in all my recent trials. I have turned over my entire life to him, and I think he's managing it all right. I don't know how I'd have survived without his help and guidance. He knows what I want.'

Someone who knew the couple well said, 'John Levy could easily be mistaken for white, and with the name of Levy, he was often considered white. This was really a blessing in disguise, as he was able to book Lady Day at many places that it would have been impossible for her to work if she had continued associations with her previous "partners".'

In June 1949, soon after Billie's trial acquittal, she played to capacity crowds at the Million Dollar Theater in Los Angeles; stimulated by the warm reception she felt that things were at last turning out for the best. But the horizon wasn't completely clear, a Californian agent was suing Billie for breach of contract relating to her non-appearance at bookings during the springtime tour of Northern California. However, this was a minor problem for Billie, audiences everywhere were giving her tumultuous welcomes, and her return to the Apollo in New York was given an almost messianic reception. These displays of public affection gave Billie the confidence to be nonchalant, and she summed up her mood in August 1949 by recording an old Bessie Smith favourite 'T'ain't Nobody's Business If I Do'.

Billie's optimism continued as she went from city to city playing to good business everywhere. Levy didn't always travel with Billie, and on one occasion when he was absent she was involved in a misery-making incident in Detroit. She met up with an old friend, trumpeter Chuck Peterson, who had worked with her in Artie Shaw's Band. Peterson, who had gained fame with Tommy Dorsey's Band, was working on the same bill as Billie; he invited her to join him and his friends at a nearby bar. A stranger approached and made insulting remarks about anyone of Billie's colour being allowed into the bar. Peterson quickly bundled the man outside to try and resolve the situation away from Billie's hearing, but in doing so was badly beaten up by the racist.

The incident made Billie sick for the rest of the booking, and she never forgot it, but somehow this traumatic experience became telescoped in her memory; in later years, she always imagined that the incident had taken place in 1938 (whilst she and Peterson were with Artie Shaw's Band), but in reality the scene took place in the fall of 1949.

On several dates in 1949, Billie shared the bill with a new band led by saxist Herbie Fields; they worked with Billie when she played a critical month at the Blue Note in Chicago in December 1949. In Chicago, a year previous, Billie's club dates had been full of problems, and as a result she had been given the most unfavourable reviews of her career. However, this time, there were no hangups and Pat Harris wrote approvingly in the *Down Beat* issue dated 13 January 1950: 'Billie, for whom the Blue Note is reportedly a rather crucial engagement is singing well, and unlike her more recent Chicago appearances, apparently in the songs she's using and their effect on her listeners. The effect is gratifyingly intent, with the house at hushed attention throughout Billie's sets. Looking sleek, relaxed, and comfortable, Billie sang the same way on such new numbers as "Where Are You?", "T'Ain't Nobody's Business" and her own "Now, Baby or Never", in addition to such standards as "Porgy" "The Man I Love", and "Strange Fruit". Despite it being "Nobody's Business", numbers on the order of the first three are almost embarrassingly pertinent in their associations, which might be one reason for Billie singing them with such intensity.'

Trombonist Frank Rosolino, who was in Herbie Fields' Band at the time, remembers that Fields and Billie had an

easy relationship. Billie was affable with Fields' musicians
and they all found her easy to get along with. She made a
special point of introducing them all to her chihuahua.
Chicago in wintertime was not Billie's favourite spot;
commenting on a previous icy trip to the Windy City, she
once told pianist Joe Springer 'I had to have all my clothes
fur-lined, even my douche-bag!'

The Blue Note's owner, Frank Holzfeind, remembered
Billie's visit, 'Billie Holiday came to the Blue Note thoroughly
plastered with every stigma and accusation in the books, so
much so, that I doubted my reason for signing her in the first
place. That first night I just knew she wouldn't show up.' But

show up she did, and Holzfeind saw the audience applaud each of the three shows that Lady did that night, 'I was so befogged, I never heard her sing. At the end of two weeks, Billie had broken all previous attendance records, and I regained the three pounds I'd lost worrying whether she would show up.'

After the Blue Note booking ended, Billie played theatre dates in Chicago and St Louis with Charlie Ventura's Band. The same package did a series of one-night stands through the mid-West, then Billie moved on to the West coast in February 1950 for a two-week engagement at the New Orleans Swing Club, in San Francisco.

Early in 1950, Mike Levin, in a *Down Beat* record review had called Billie 'Lady Yesterday', nevertheless, most of the club-operators were realising that Billie was sure-fire business; all they had to do was let the people know that she was at their club, and then dust off the 'house-full' signs. Lou Landry, owner of the New Orleans Swing Club, publicised Billie's visit with an extensive and expensive advertising campaign. Business was record-breaking and Billie was estimated to have cleared 4,000 dollars a week during the run; she needed every cent of the money for her stay in San Francisco coincided with the hearing of two California Superior Court cases against her. One was a breach-of-contract action brought against her by Ed Fishman (who had briefly been her manager in 1947). Fishman obtained a judgment against Billie for $2,145 after suing for $75,000. The other case concerned the New Year's Day fracas, the outcome there was that Marion Epstein was awarded $1,540 for injuries said to have been received from Billie in the night-club kitchen fight.

Jake Ehrlich, the lawyer who had successfully defended Billie on the 1949 'opium possession' charge, was now pressing for settlement of his fee: this was one of many instances where John Levy had assured Billie that he had paid a bill; later, the creditor would prove to Billie that no payment had been made. Levy had no case when Billie finally confronted him with a pile of unpaid bills. She gradually discovered that she owed money left, right and centre, and although her philosophy had always been easy come, easy go, she was filled with despair at the thought that she had worked steadily for two years and yet had nothing to show for it. Billie was having great problems surmounting the tensions that the rows with Levy, and the money problems, were bringing her, and all the signs seem to indicate that once again she turned to heroin.

Her final break with Levy came during the summer of 1950. In late June, Billie went out on tour with a big band led by trumpeter Gerald Wilson (featuring trombonist Melba Liston). Levy, who had said he would act as guarantor for the musicians' wages, left them high and dry; Billie said later 'He walked out and left me and my goddam band stranded in the Deep South without a dime.'

Lady moved out to California in an effort to recoup. During 1950 she appeared in a Will Cowan-directed short for Universal-International in which she shared billing with Count Basie's sextet and the young entertainer Sugar Chile Robinson. In September 1950 she played a fortnight at the Oasis Bar in Los Angeles, renewing old ties with Lester Young's brother Lee, who was leading a band at the club. After playing the Oasis, Billie moved up to San Francisco to begin a residency at the Long Bar, and once again found that trouble and the Golden Gate Country were synonymous for her.

Shortly after Billie arrived in San Francisco, her chauffeur, alone in Lady's blue Lincoln automobile, was stopped by two non-Narcotics Squad policemen and searched. They found two small packets of heroin. After the authorities had charged the chauffeur with possessing and transporting narcotics, they impounded the vehicle.

Soon afterwards, Billie became involved in the bitter rivalry that existed between two local club-owners, Lou Landry (for whom Billie had worked twice at the Swing Club), and Shirley Corlett, owner of the Long Bar. Both were vying to book Billie, and Landry threatened legal action to

139

prove that he had prior rights under a re-booking clause in Billie's previous contracts.

This amalgamation of problems greatly upset Billie; after missing a couple of shows at the Long Bar, she walked out on the third night without waiting to pick up the thousand dollars in wages that had accrued during her short stay. Once again, she was alone, her manager had gone, her chauffeur had gone, and she had no regular pianist to keep her company. Since Bobby Tucker and Billie had parted company in the summer of 1949, Billie had changed her accompanists with great regularity. The longest serving pianist in the 1949-50 period was Fletcher Henderson's brother Horace, but after working with Billie for several months he left to settle in Denver, Colorado; a girl pianist from Oakland named Memry Midgett also did several months with Billie, but most of the other accompanists stayed for briefer periods – in late 1950 Jack Russin (brother of tenorist Babe Russin) played only a few engagements with Billie before quitting.

Billie left California and moved on to Chicago. In December 1950, she opened at the Hi-Note with a group fronted by Miles Davis; the club was packed for every show and Billie's behaviour was exemplary. At the Long Bar in San Francisco she had rowed with the club's management, she had missed shows and given dispirited performances. In Chicago, everything was perfect. The Hi-Note's manager, Mart Denenberg, highlighted the enigma, 'She's a wonderful person, very easy to get along with, goes on stand on time. I couldn't ask for more.'

The Chicago booking ended on 7 January; soon afterwards Billie met up with Lester Young when they played a week together in Philadelphia. The reunion of these kindred spirits, both of whom were suffering so much, was short-lived, and thereafter it was over three years before they spoke to each other. Billie was addicted to heroin, Lester to alcohol. This sensitive man was easily hurt, and the Jim Crow treatment he received whilst in the Army was the factor that virtually wiped out his confidence. He withdrew into a shell, and emerged to give mono-syllabic answers, typified by his words to an interviewer in 1953, 'Lady Day? Many moons no see. Still nice.' The fact that his style of playing was copied by hundreds of young tenor-saxists brought him neither comfort nor security. He longed to escape from the hurly-burly of one-nighters; when this proved economically impossible he specialised in working in touring package-shows, but still he encountered sadness. He almost cracked when he discovered that one of his own disciples – a white musician who then based his style on one facet of Lester's playing – was getting more for playing the concerts than Lester. He understood that the musician couldn't be blamed for this financial set-up, but he was appalled by the irony of the situation. Lester once told Nat Hentoff, 'No one has come up and said "Thank You".' Lester, like Lady Day, needed regular comforting, but, in the make-up of both of these sad geniuses there seems more than a hint of masochism.

The reason why these two close friends broke-up is difficult to ascribe to any one incident. Lester's laconic exterior gave no clues, but apparently he felt wounded because Billie always used the past tense when referring to him in print during the late 1940s. On several occasions, she said, 'Lester was my favorite tenor player,' and she seemed to emphasise this attitude by choosing not to use him on any of her latter-day recordings. Lester once made a comment to Billie about her managerial matters, and was quickly told to mind his own business. The tenor-player hated trouble of any kind, his usual reaction was to move as far as possible away from the source; magazines spoke of a feud between Billie and Lester, but it seems as though they deliberately avoided each other, each nursing their own hurts.

In the springtime of 1951, Billie heard that Decca would not be renewing her recording contract; soon afterwards she signed a twelve-sides-a-year agreement with Aladdin Records; one of the terms of the new contract was that all her accompaniments were to be provided by other Aladdin artists. Decca seemed unperturbed about Billie's departure and announced via *Down Beat*'s columns that they were building-up a West Coast singer, Kitty White, to take over Billie's place on their label.

Billie played a further series of theatre dates with Herbie Fields' Band before travelling to Boston in late October 1951 to work for a week at George Wein's Storyville Club, accompanied by Buster Harding and a rhythm section. During this booking, Nat Hentoff culled an interview from Billie that was as joyful as any she ever gave. The reason for the abundance of happiness was, according to Billie, her new husband Louis McKay. Hentoff summarised the changes in Billie's attitudes, and commented on her new sense of responsibility and co-operativeness. She made every set on-time and volunteered to work an extra set on several nights for WMEX radio station who had a direct-transmission line installed in the club.

Billie told Hentoff (and the readers of *Down Beat*) that she was thinking of retiring in two or three years, because she 'just wanted to be a housewife and take care of Mr McKay.' She then gave lavish praise to her accompanist Buster Harding. Buster, a veteran of the big band scene and an ace arranger, had only been working with Billie for a short time; she said of him, 'Buster not only plays for me, writes for me — he feels the way I feel. Some nights I'm tired, and I don't feel too good, and I don't want the tempo too fast; he knows and sets exactly the right tempo and mood.'

Stan Getz and his quintet were sharing the bill with Billie at the Storyville Club; Billie expressed admiration for Getz's work, and other 'modern men who swing', adding, 'for me, music if you can't pat your foot to it or hum it, it's not music.' Later, Getz revealed how much the meeting had meant to him, 'I marvelled how strong she was for a person who had taken so many knocks from life, and at her honesty as an artist. When I had the opportunity to work with her I found her to be nothing but sweet and gentle.' Billie and Getz joined forces for some of the radio transmissions and fortuitously some of their collaborations were privately recorded and later issued on LP.

Billie's new husband, Louis McKay, began to take a firm hold on the reins that guided Lady's career. The couple had first met in 1935, when Billie was singing at the Hot-cha Club; then it was only a casual acquaintanceship. Sixteen years later, they met up again whilst Billie was playing dates at the Club Juana in Detroit and within a fortnight Billie had appointed McKay as her personal manager and adviser, and soon afterwards they married. McKay, five years older than Billie, had two children from a previous marriage. Billie's talk of domesticity wasn't reserved only for magazine interviews, most of her close friends knew that she desperately wanted to have a family, but any question of even a temporary withdrawal from singing was out of the question. Lady was still clearing up debts that went back to 1949.

Early in 1952, Lady took Louis McKay's advice and set-up temporary headquarters in California. It was time to face the creditors; the fat fees that could be earned on the West Coast would gradually clear away all the debts. *Down Beat* magazine shrewdly observed, 'One of the reasons so many wires were pulled to get Billie Holiday back to San Francisco, is that she still owes Jake Ehrlich loot for beating that dope rap a few years back.'

The long stay on the West Coast was (by Billie's standards) relatively trouble free. She got a black eye (in a domestic squabble) during her run at the Say When Club in San Francisco, but otherwise all the dates that she played in California passed without major incident. In fact, the only extensive publicity given to Billie during the spring of 1952 concerned her attack on modern jazz. In April, the *Melody Maker* printed an interview that Billie gave whilst she was working at 'Tiffany's' in Hollywood; she said, 'I don't dig all this modern stuff. All this Oop Bop Sh-Bam and Kluga Mop business. Jazz is not what it used to be. For me, Benny Goodman is still the greatest.' Then, the writer pointed out, 'Billie went back on stage backed by a modern Wardell Gray combo, including pianist Hampton Hawes, and drummer Chico Hamilton.'

This was rather an untypical outburst by Billie; usually,

she spoke encouragingly about the work of younger jazzmen. In 1946, when she picked her ideal all-star band for the *Esquire Jazz Book*, she included several musicians who were then known as 'modernists'; her line-up was: Joe Guy (trumpet), Charlie Parker (alto-sax), Vic Dickenson (trombone), Eddie Davis (tenor-sax), Jimmy Hamilton (clarinet), Erroll Garner (piano), Tiny Grimes (guitar), Eddie Nicholson (drums), and John Simmons (bass). Surprisingly, Billie picked two white singers (Perry Como and Jo Stafford) to go with the all-black ensemble.

In 1951, Billie chose her ten favourite records for *Metronome* magazine; they were Dizzy Gillespie's 'Round About Midnight', Ella Fitzgerald's 'Lady Be Good', Erroll Garner's 'Cool Blues', Lester Young's 'These Foolish Things', Gene Ammons' 'My Foolish Heart', Nat Cole's 'Jet', Woody Herman's 'Detour Ahead', Oscar Peterson's 'Tenderly', George Shearing's 'When Your Lover Has Gone', and Louis Armstrong's 'You're Just In Love'. But all these varied styles were for Billie the listener. Billie the singer had some very definite views on the style of her own backings. In 1950, Billie spoke her mind to Leonard Feather during a 'blindfold test'. After hearing Duke Ellington's 'Don't Get Around Much Any More' she said, 'Duke! I always loved this ... I've always wanted a band to play under me like that when I sing; they don't mess around or noodle, they just help you. I've wanted it all my life. I almost got that with Gordon Jenkins on "You're My Thrill", but that was pretty music, this has bounce too. You know, the only ones who can take a solo while I'm singing and still not interfere are Lester and Teddy.'

Billie's year-long contract with Aladdin Records expired in March 1952; she then immediately signed a recording contract with Norman Granz, and in Los Angeles, on 26 March, she cut her first sides for the Mercury label, backed by an all-star unit which included Oscar Peterson on piano.

During the summer of 1952, not long after Billie moved back to the East Coast she went to 'Birdland' to listen to Count Basie's new band playing their opening date there. She shared the audience's delight, but she said that her pleasure was lessened by the recurring thought that she was still precluded from working any New York club.

In October 1952, Billie was due to make her long-awaited tour of Europe. This time, everything seemed definite, and Billie cancelled existing bookings to ready herself for the trip. But to her great disappointment, the whole project was scrapped. For part of the tour, Billie was scheduled to share billing with singer Dick Haymes; however, at that time, Haymes was in deep trouble with the U.S. Bureau of Internal Revenue and he was ordered to remain in the United States until he had sorted out his tax problems. No suitable replacement could be found quickly, so the whole tour was cancelled.

Billie began to appear more regularly on television. In the fall of 1952 she starred in an ABC Spectacular – backed by a string section and a vocal chorus. Jazz fans who saw the show felt dissatisfied with the accompaniment, but Billie thought it 'just perfect'. She once said of her recordings, 'The things I like most I think are the things I've done with strings.'

On television, Lady Day usually appeared cool, suave and relaxed, but this impression was only achieved by tremendous effort, for no matter what successes she achieved, the special occasion was always a huge strain. She still had to conquer her 'first night' nerves and stage-fright. In September 1952, Billie played a return booking at the Storyville Club in Boston, (where Nat Hentoff had obtained an ecstatic interview in the previous October). On opening night this time, Hentoff found Billie very troubled and uncertain.

In his *Down Beat* review he reported, 'Lady Day seems to have chronic opening-night jitters ... Billie was less than perfect musically, besides being hampered by a rather disorganized rhythm section. A widely read Boston columnist caught the show, and his column the next day was hardly a eulogy. The next night, and eleven succeeding nights, Billie was superb ... but the columnist had not returned, and both he, and those who had not found out for themselves, will long associate Billie with inadequacy.'

Billie was hyper-sensitive about audience reaction, and on another occasion at the Storyville Club a group of 'Shriners' (a society which raises money for charities) unwittingly disrupted her show. A party of the fez-wearing fund-raisers were in Boston for a convention, they wandered into the club, not knowing that it specialised in jazz, and probably not even realising who Billie Holiday was. They were affably talkative, and when Billie heard the hum of continual conversation going on in the club she assumed that the crowd was restless and perhaps antagonistic. She looked distressed as she left the stage, and when Paul Nossiter (a musician friend of the club owner) called backstage to say how much he enjoyed the show, he found Billie in tears. She sobbed out, 'Why don't they like me?' Nossiter explained that they were a party of guys out on a convention spree who meant no harm to anyone, but it took ages for Billie to be consoled.

When Billie was distracted on stage she either cried or cursed. The Shriners may have brought on the tears, but an earlier incident raised Billie to full fury. Pianist-singer Rose Murphy told writer Gilbert Gaster of an incident that occurred in San Francisco during the 1940s. Rose and Billie were working independently at the Savoy Club. During Billie's set one of the kitchen staff, a Chinaman, made a great deal of noise by rattling plates. When Billie had finished her set she charged backstage to tell the man that he would have to be quieter in the future. The man understood very little English, he saw that Billie was in a great rage, and this set him off; he went completely berserk and chased everyone, including Billie, round and round the kitchen.

Late in 1952, Billie 'looking more handsome than ever,' sang at Duke Ellington's '25th Anniversary in the Music Business' concert at Carnegie Hall. Duke, who once affectionately described Billie as 'the essence of cool', added his applause to the huge reception that the audience gave the singer. Reviewer Bill Coss said that this was 'the new Billie', and expressed delight that she used 'Fine and Mellow' as an

encore, instead of 'Strange Fruit'. The evening was a great
success for Billie, and no one on the star-studded bill (Stan
Getz's quintet, Ahmad Jamal's trio, Charlie Parker with
strings, and Dizzy Gillespie) received more acclaim.

It seemed almost as though the New York theatre and
concert audiences were trying to compensate Billie for the
disappointments and frustrations caused her by the New
York Police Department's cabaret-card ban. An emotional
reception greeted Lady's appearance at a Stan Kenton
Carnegie Hall concert some months later, and even the
Apollo's audience, renowned for the enthusiasm with which it
greeted its favourites, gave out more than usual whenever

147

Billie appeared there. Frank Schiffman, who ran the theatre for many years, summarised this particular affection, 'Aside from her wonderful talent, Billie herself was a very warm person, she was highly popular at the Apollo. Sometimes you listen to a performer, and every fibre of that performer's body seems to be incorporated in what she is doing. It's not only the voice, you feel that what the person is saying or singing comes from the innermost depths of her being – this was one of Billie's characteristics, and this is the thing which endures in the minds of people who remember her.'

The Apollo always meant a lot to Billie, she never felt like deliberately missing a show there, but in August 1953 she had no option but to cancel out temporarily. Her face was badly swollen; the press said that she had 'an abscessed jaw', but those closer to the scene thought that the swelling could well have been caused by a collision – between Billie's jaw and a male fist.

Vocalist Annie Ross, who had recently returned to America after playing dates in France, got an early morning call from Joe Glaser; he said 'Get ready, you've got a date to play at the Apollo at ten.' Annie, who had never worked at the Apollo before, asked Glaser if he meant that evening. 'No! This morning,' he said. 'You've got to replace someone who can't make the show.' Annie asked who she was replacing and was told that it was Billie Holiday. 'Then I felt really nervous, I had always idolised Billie, ever since my uncle had given me my first record as a child – a Billie 78. I got hold of my accompanist, George Wallington, and went to the theatre. When I got there I realised that Duke Ellington and his Orchestra were also on the bill. I was very nervous and fidgety, and Duke, whom I had known since I was a child, came over to ask me what was wrong. I told him that making the debut was tough enough, but trying to replace Lady Day was making it all the harder. He said, "Have you ever met Lady?" "No," I said, "and I don't want to, I heard she can be very tough if she doesn't like you." "Oh no," said Duke, "you must meet her to find out the truth." He took me to the dressing room, and Lady was sitting looking at her swollen face in the mirror, talking to pianist Carl Drinkard. She was marvellous, and asked me if I had everything I wanted, like the right dress; she said she would loan me anything to help out. I thanked her and went on stage to do the act. The M.C. announced that Billie couldn't make the show, and some of the hard guys, who only came to hear Billie, got up and left. I went on and did my songs, and got a nice reception. I finished with "Twisted", and as I came off I found Billie waiting in the wings, she had been there all the time watching over me. I was so overwhelmed that I started to cry. Billie hugged me, then she started to cry. Duke Ellington came over to see what was going on, and he got us to pull ourselves together by saying, "Now dear ladies, I think you should both take a bow." The two of us went out to face the audience, and got a great big burst of applause. Billie soon recovered, the swelling subsided, and she was able to play the rest of the shows. Thereafter she was always great to me.'

In October 1953, Billie took part in a coast-to-coast television show called, 'The Comeback Story'. Many people who had played a part in Billie's career were invited to appear on the programme, some accepted with alacrity and willingness, some refused point-blank, others turned the offer down because they felt that the appearance fee was not high enough. The show's sponsors were a well-known firm of mattress makers. Billie's story, the third in the series, was certainly the most unusual in the run. A mass audience heard drug addiction being openly discussed, and harsh comments on racial segregation were directed at, and received by, viewers in the South. Neither Benny Goodman, John Hammond, nor Teddy Wilson would appear in the programme, but 'Pods' Hollingsworth the club owner, Artie Shaw, Leonard Feather, song-writer Arthur Herzog and several others did participate. Viewers saw a biographical resumé of Billie's life, with the spell in Alderson Reformatory given due mention; the musical background to the narration came from Billie's records. As the programme neared its conclusion, Billie was asked by George Jessel, the show's compere, to sing a number and she responded with 'God Bless The Child' backed by Carl Drinkard and a trio. Billie looked tired and ill, and the camera shots were restricted to certain angles because Billie's face was again swollen, but before being driven away in her new Cadillac by Louis McKay she smiled happily and thanked her friends for appearing on the show with her.

Louis McKay usually drove Billie to all the engagements that she played in the Eastern States. This arrangement was practical, McKay was a good, fast driver, and the Cadillac afforded Billie comfort and seclusion. However, she was still convinced that Federal Narcotic Bureau agents were continually trailing her; McKay denied this possibility years later when he said 'She was a 25 or 30 year narcotics user' (referring to the sentence that Billie could have been liable for, if convicted), 'and they could have made things really tough for her if they'd wanted to. If people get the idea that the police and the Feds harassed her, then that's wrong.' But Billie's fears of being kept under close scrutiny were real enough to her in late 1953. To avoid giving agents a chance to survey her as she got on and off aeroplanes she asked her husband to drive her out to California for the San Francisco dates that she was due to play in December 1953. McKay had less than four days to make the 3,000-mile journey; his schedule was twenty hours a day driving and four hours' sleep a night.

Fortunately, Billie was not in the least perturbed by the prospects of Transatlantic flights, and early in 1954 she realised one of her biggest ambitions by going to Europe.

Jazz writer Leonard Feather starred her in a package show that he organised and took to Europe. Billed as 'Jazz Club U.S.A.' (the title of Feather's successful 'Voice of America' radio programme), the show featured Billie (accompanied by Carl Drinkard), Red Norvo's Trio, Buddy De Franco's Quintet, and Beryl Booker's Trio. Louis McKay also travelled with the party.

Billie almost didn't make the trip. In applying for a passport she ran into trouble because she couldn't produce a birth certificate — she had never had one. After a fruitless application to the Maryland Division of Vital Records, Billie was advised to contact any living relatives and to ask them to stand surety for her. This was almost impossible, but in the end Mrs. Elizabeth 'Fanny' Holiday (Clarence's second wife) stood as guarantor, and this got Billie her passport.

Billie's passport problems were preliminary twinges of the many headaches that the tour was to bring to Leonard Feather. The scheduled opening was in Stockholm on 11 January 1954. The package made the date on time, just. Because a snowed-up airport prevented landings at Stockholm, the whole party had to leave the plane in Copenhagen and travel by train and ferry to their destination. Feather worked wonders in keeping everyone on even-keel as the temperature fell and tempers rose. The unavoidable changes in the travel arrangements meant that valuable rehearsal time was lost.

Further problems came to light when it was realised that en-route instruments had gone astray, causing the musicians to use borrowed bass and drums. To add to the administrative worries, a contretemps developed as to who Billie wanted to assist Carl Drinkard in accompanying her. The selection was complicated by the fact that some of the musicians didn't want to work with Billie anyway. Finally, bassist Keith 'Red' Mitchell and drummer Elaine Leighton made up the trio.

Things slowly settled down as the package played more dates in Scandinavia before moving on to Germany. Leonard Feather, in a half-way stage report published in the *Melody Maker* on 23 January 1954, said 'We're in good shape now ... but it took a week of headaches to reach this stage' (one of the headaches having been caused by the discovery of a hypodermic-syringe in the star's dressing room — it was never established whether it belonged to Billie or to a Swedish musician who had dropped in for some backstage chat). Feather went on to say, 'Lady Day is looking and singing better than she has in years. She has been bringing out songs like "Strange Fruit", "Don't Explain", "My Man", and

151

"Porgy", and it's a thrill to hear this unique voice back at the pinnacle of its form.' Danish music-critic Harold Grut concurred with Feather on the successes of the tour; he wrote 'She held the audience at Copenhagen's vast KB Hall spellbound.'

Whilst in Paris Billie again met up with Annie Ross; she asked Annie if she would mind going with her on a shopping spree as she wanted to buy some underwear. Annie vividly remembers the outing: 'She looked fantastic, wearing a red ski suit, a red hat and her blue mink coat. We set off down the Champs Elysées to do the shopping, but en route Billie decided it would be a good idea to visit all the bars. At that time she was drinking Pernod with a brandy floater (neat Pernod topped up with brandy). I was well and truly drunk by the end of the marathon but Lady seemed to be absolutely sober. She changed her plans and said she'd like to buy some jewellery; we entered this magnificent store and Billie began looking at tray after tray of brooches and trinkets, but in the end she said she wouldn't be buying anything and out we came. When we settled in the next bar, I started talking about some of the nice things that we had seen. Lady fished her hand in and out of her coat and showed me two gold medallions and a St Christopher, she said "Thought I'd pick up a little something for my daddy." She had pocketed them right in front of my eyes and the eyes of the assistant – she had money enough in her wallet to pay for them a dozen times over, it was just that she really got a big kick out of lifting something from a very high class establishment.'

In Paris, Billie met up with an old friend, pianist Mary Lou Williams, then working in Europe. Through Mary Lou, British singer Beryl Bryden gained an introduction to Billie. Mary Lou, knowing of Beryl's great admiration for Billie, forewarned her that she wouldn't effect the introductions until the moment seemed right – in case Billie was in a restive mood. Fortunately, the vibrations were right from the first meeting and Billie was soon visiting the Trois Mailletz Club where Beryl was singing. Billie made a special point of asking for the words and chord sequence of a number that Beryl

*With Beryl Bryden*

featured, Bessie Smith's success 'Young Woman's Blues'. That night, Billie, Beryl, Mary Lou and a crowd of friends visited the 'Pied de Cochon' restaurant. Billie, dressed in plaid trousers, an expensive sweater and elegant high-heels, looked as suave as any Balmain model; to top the ensemble her new tightly-curled hair style was sprayed at the edges with silver.

In Europe, Billie's sophisticated image occasionally tempted hotel and restaurant staffs to apply the technique usually reserved for rich tourists. The Ladies' toilet attendant at the 'Pied de Cochon' was one such optimist. She told Billie (who was notably generous) that she considered the tip was too small. The attendant didn't get an extra gratuity, but – for free – she learnt some new American phrases as Billie let fly, with both barrels, a selection from her extensive vocabulary of earthy curses.

After three weeks of touring Scandinavia, Germany, Switzerland, Holland, and France, Billie finally arrived in London on Monday 8 February 1954. She was about to begin her first-ever tour of Britain – an event that had been originally planned 18 years before. She travelled with Louis McKay and Carl Drinkard, Leonard Feather joined them a day later, but the rest of the package could not work in Britain due to Musicians' Union and Ministry of Labour rulings which prevented musicians from overseas appearing in Britain until a man-for-man exchange had been arranged with their own country's unions. Billie, being categorised as a variety artiste, did not encounter these restrictions, neither did Carl Drinkard, who was allowed into Britain as Billie's accompanist.

Not long after arriving in London, Billie met press reporters at her hotel in Piccadilly. The representatives of the national press, eager for any sensationalism, slanted most of their questions towards narcotics, and the non-issuance of the New York Cabaret Card. To one questioner she said 'I'm trying to get my police card back. You know I'm not the only one. Some kids been in trouble two or three times are still working. So why pick on me? Somebody's got a hand in it, somewhere, some kind of politics. That's what I'm squawking about.' Louis McKay added that getting back into New York clubs could mean upward of $75,000 a year. Billie said saltily 'It's not just the dough, it's the principle of the thing. To me it's unfair.'

The questioning proceeded relentlessly, but fortunately Max Jones of the *Melody Maker* – one of Billie's life-long fans – was on hand to divert the pressure. Max did a rescue act and began asking Billie about her career; her mood changed instantly and she began talking happily about Louis Armstrong, Bessie Smith and Lester Young. She never forgot Max's sympathetic approach and their friendship lasted until Billie's death.

Lady's short tour of England opened at the Free Trade Hall in Manchester on Friday 12 February 1954. Max Jones reviewing the opening concert for the *Melody Maker* said 'On stage, she looks calm and dignified, but she also looks warm, and sounds warm, and her whole attitude seems spontaneous and very, very hip.' After Billie had sung eight numbers the microphone failed. Lady then delighted the front rows by

154

singing 'My Man' without a mike; she then left the stage.

Her next dates were at the Astoria Ballroom, Nottingham, where she sang two sets each consisting of five songs accompanied by Carl Drinkard and a local rhythm section. After the concert she was driven back, overnight, to London by Max and Betty Jones. The car broke down half-way through the hundred-and-twenty-mile journey, and Billie warmed the winter air with her views on country life; she finally arrived back at her hotel at 5.30 a.m. Less than twelve hours later she was rehearsing with Jack Parnell's Band for the main concert of the tour at London's Royal Albert Hall where she gave a 'splendid performance' for the 6,000 crowd, singing 15 songs and ending with 'Strange Fruit'.

The reception was tumultuous, and everything seemed fine with Lady, but within minutes of returning to her dressing room she became upset, and writer Steve Voce waiting to catch a glimpse of his idol saw her leave the stage-door with tears streaming down her face. But that night she was determined to sing her way out of despondency and she went

*With Louis McKay, Manchester, 1954*

on to the Flamingo Club where she sang for an audience many of whom were musicians who hadn't been able to see the concert.

Before flying back to America on the following Friday she spoke of the healthy work situation. 'We've been offered so many jobs, Paris, Africa, even some Variety in England'; looking across at Louis McKay, she added, 'Daddy hasn't made our plans yet, but we have had a good offer back home.'

Certainly Billie's engagement book was comfortably full – new venues in different cities throughout the U.S. were offering her more money than she had ever received. Despite the high fee that she could now command, Billie was a certainty for the inaugural Newport Jazz Festival held in July 1954. Billie's appearance on Sunday night's presentation (18 July) was described by *Down Beat* as 'the climax of the concert, it was the most relaxed and subtly compelling Lady Day performance in many years'; in *Metronome* Bill Coss said 'The over-30 segment had been waiting mostly for Billie and they were more than compensated.'

Billie was delighted by the overwhelming reception, which she said reminded her of Europe; the occasion was made all the more memorable by a spectacular on-stage reunion between Lester Young and Lady Day. A specially assembled 'all-star' trio consisting of Teddy Wilson on piano, Jo Jones on drums and Milt Hinton on bass accompanied Billie. Buck Clayton on trumpet and Gerry Mulligan on baritone sax made the unit into a quintet. The group soon became a sextet when Lester Young, unannounced, joined them at the end of the first number. *Down Beat* made the reconciliation a front-page news item. Headed 'Feud Is Over' it described how 'Gerry Mulligan lugged his baritone on to the stage and provided some picturesque clusters of sound behind Lady Day. This was enough for Lester. He shuffled on stage and once again was part of a Billie presentation. They later embraced in the dressing room and the feud was over' (*Down Beat*, 25 August 1954).

Teddy Wilson was taciturn in summarising this 're-union

concert'; he said of Billie, 'A very interesting person. I felt that the magic was there, just like in the old days. You can feel her singing, like another instrument' (*Down Beat*, 6 February 1958, p. 34). His attitude showed that he and Billie no longer enjoyed the easy friendship they shared during the mid-1930s. Conceivably Wilson felt that Billie never gave him the credit that was surely due to him. His musical partnership, never quite as obvious as the Lester–Billie rapport, was nevertheless a big factor in the success of Lady's early records. Wilson was the pianist on over 50 of the 60 records that she made between July 1935 and June 1937; the fact that he was the leader and musical director on many of these sides seems to have been ignored on several long-playing re-issues – an omission that he must find irksome. Nevertheless, Wilson has recorded his own 'Tribute to Billie' album.

Throughout the mid-1950s Billie was featured in many jazz concerts and festivals; her principal income still came from night-club engagements, but the boom in large-scale jazz presentations was distinctly to her financial advantage. Rarely a month went by without her being featured in a mammoth concert, but in spite of this frequency she always had an uneasy feeling about facing huge audiences in the open-air; by now she knew that the essence of her art was in establishing closeness between herself and the audience, she felt she worked best in smallish surroundings and often said her ambition was to own a small club, seating about 125 people, where she could work in exactly the way she wanted to.

During this era, package shows got bigger, if not better, and some promoters emerged who hadn't the slightest interest in jazz or artistic presentation. One of them even banned instrumentalists from playing ballads on his shows, feeling that they slowed down the proceedings. Billie continued to sing ballads as and when she chose to, but more and more on concerts she played safe by using the same few numbers for most of her shows.

Billie was happy that she and Lester Young were friends

again, and not long after the Newport success the two worked in a package that was as star-studded as any yet assembled; the cast included Count Basie and his Orchestra, Sarah Vaughan, Charlie Parker and The Modern Jazz Quartet. The show played a string of one-night concert dates (including Carnegie Hall). For most of the tour, Billie was accompanied by a small unit from Basie's Band.

In 1954, Billie's disappointment at never winning a *Down Beat* poll was lessened by that magazine's decision to give her a special award as 'One of the all-time great vocalists in jazz.' The presentation of the trophy, which took place whilst Lady was working in California, greatly pleased her. It was a symbol, albeit a small one, that the press in general were looking at her with a sympathetic eye. *Down Beat* and *Metronome* were always eminently fair to Billie, but she felt bitter about the treatment that she got from several Negro newspapers. At the time of her first drugs trial she said, 'I'm proud I'm a Negro, but you know the funniest thing, the people that are going to be hardest on me will be my own race.' Later she said, 'Certain Negro newspapers forgot their responsibility and dreamed up some pretty fantastic yarns. They made some grim predictions about my future.' Few black publications chose to examine, or comment upon, Billie's singing, and the only time that she was given anything other than passing mentions was when she was in trouble. In this respect, they were exactly similar to their white counterparts.

Most of the contemporary reviews of Billie's work that appeared in music magazines during the 1950s dwelt heavily on her past achievements. Lady disliked any comparisons between her earlier records and her later work – she said emphatically that she was singing better than ever, and that was that. But time, a thousand fixes, and a sea of swallowed brandy took toll of Billie's health: the warning signs were indicating that it was time to ease up. The years of disregard were shearing away Billie's vocal technique. She never lost the art of conveying deep emotions, but by the mid-1950s, her range had narrowed considerably, and her voice had

taken on a troubled quality. Yet on the nights that Lady felt good, nothing could stop her being the greatest jazz vocalist on earth. She looked as glamorous as ever, and when people spoke of her past as her 'golden years', she felt irritated and hurt. She said, 'Always comebacks, but nobody says where I've been'; nothing irked Lady more than wrinkled adults coming up to her to say, 'I've loved your records since I was a child ... so high.'

Lady Day often said that she wanted to forget about the bad old days, but when the occasion was right, and her mood mellowed by just the right amount of alcohol, she loved nothing more than reminiscing. She always stressed that she preferred working with old friends who 'didn't try to drown the song'. Familiar faces on the bandstand helped her to relax, benefiting her performances. Billie's old friend Buck Clayton led the band that accompanied her when she played return dates at the Storyville Club in Boston at Thanksgiving 1954. A *Down Beat* report said she 'sounded better than she has in the last few years.' In the same review, Bob Martin gave the first news that Billie's autobiography was being prepared.

Billie and her collaborator William Dufty (a writer on the *New York Post*) originally planned to call the book *Bitter Crop*, (a line from 'Strange Fruit'), but at the publisher's suggestion it was changed to *Lady Sings The Blues* – a title that Billie found ironical since she had always been irked when referred to as 'a blues singer'. Dufty's wife Maely became a close friend of Billie's, and later acted as a temporary personal manager for her.

A chance meeting in 1954 led to Billie engaging her own personal attorney. Earle Warren Zaidins, now a District Attorney in the State of New York, was then a recently qualified lawyer, living in the Flanders Hotel on W. 47th Street in Manhattan. Billie was temporarily staying at the same hotel. One evening as Earle was exercising his boxer-dog outside the hotel Billie came out with her chihuahua. The couple struck up a conversation about their pets, the chat led to Billie asking Earle what he did for a living; when she learnt that he was a lawyer she asked him to look over a recording contract that had been submitted to her. Later, Earle realised that this was a superfluous request since Billie had a formidable grasp of the legal technicalities of recording contracts. Zaidins, who later became one of America's top show-business lawyers, said in May 1974 that Billie taught him everything he knew about the complexities of recording contracts.

Billie's showing of the contract was a formality, but it did help provide the foundations of a friendship that was to last until Billie's death. Billie's main reason for initially consulting Zaidins was to give him the task of negotiating the amount that was to be paid in 'advance royalties'. Billie's pride made it difficult for her to ask for 'front money', but during the 1950s she always needed it. Zaidins was successful in bargaining for the amount that Billie had optmistically hoped for, and she subsequently appointed him as her personal attorney.

Billie's agent was still Joe Glaser; their relationship with

each other was always unpredictable and variable, but during the mid-1950s there was almost a complete break-off of diplomatic relations. Billie was very keen to re-visit Europe, but Glaser, who was getting Billie ever-increasing fees for her dates in America, vetoed the idea. In direct opposition to Glaser, Lady wrote to an English agent, Jeff Kruger, saying that she intended to play a series of return bookings in Britain. Glaser countered this in a statement published in London by the *Melody Maker* in which he denied that there was any possibility of Billie re-visiting Europe.

Billie began accepting work from the agency run by the late Milt Shaw. By coincidence, Billie's first husband Jimmy Monroe was an employee of Shaw's; Billie and Jimmy had opportunities to exchange affable greetings on several occasions through this tie-up. There was no question of a reconciliation, Louis McKay saw to that by issuing a hefty warning to Monroe.

During the mid-1950s, Billie's schedule of engagements became more and more hectic; occasionally, she had to dovetail concert and cabaret work on the same night, as in August 1955 when she doubled between The Crescendo night club and the Hollywood Bowl. This sudden contrast of venues was too much for Billie to adjust to. *Metronome* magazine commenting on the Hollywood Bowl concert, said, 'Lady Day, without the gutty glamour of her most intimate appearances in dark-filled clubs, stretched elegance far in white regalia ... her particular type of vitality in her famous "Billie's Blues" was ill-placed.'

Concert appearances always presented a dilemma for Billie; whether the large sums of money offered were worth the misery and tensions that they invariably brought to her. But despite the perpetual problems of drug addiction, heavy drinking, domestic squabbles and chronic insecurity, Lady Day could still give a relaxed show if the surroundings were sympathetic. In late 1955, when Billie played yet another booking at the Storyville in Boston, Dom Cerulli wrote in *Down Beat,* 'she held the audience spellbound'. Usually, her club sets consisted of five numbers, with two optional encores; the Storyville programme was typical: 'Willow Weep For Me', 'Nice Work If You Can Get It', 'I Only Have Eyes For You', 'God Bless The Child', and 'I Cover The Waterfront'. Generally she said little on stage, only announcing song-titles and acknowledging her accompanists. Cerulli summarised Billie in 1955 by saying 'The lazy inflections, the languid phrasing was here, a bit darkened by the years, but plaintive as ever. Billie has an edge to her voice which she uses along with her expressive hands to accent a word or phrase. Judging by the buzz of conversation following her set, the old magic is still there.'

The old magic was still there, but so too was the old heroin habit. Lady once said that nobody could claim that their fight with dope was over until they were dead. She knew that she was often under police surveillance, but even the grim prospects of a long return to prison couldn't divert her craving. Hisory repeated itself, and once again she was arrested in Philadelphia on a narcotics charge. In February 1956, Billie was playing a series of bookings at the Showboat Club; early on the morning of the 23rd, police raided the South Philadelphia hotel room that Louis McKay and Billie were sharing. Billie was subsequently charged with possessing narcotics, and Louis McKay was charged with possessing a pistol without a permit. After several hours in custody Billie was released on bail so that she could continue her work at the Showboat, and later that same evening McKay was also released on bail.

No trial date was fixed and the couple were allowed to leave the city. They returned to New York on the morning following their arrest. Back home, Billie decided that she must enter a clinic as soon as possible. This time, there was no 'cold turkey' treatment. Billie was given a whole series of tests, then efforts were made to wean her from heroin by the use of substitute drugs. The treatment was temporarily effective; the doctors told Billie that – with luck and will-power – she could stay away from heroin for two years. Billie was soon back at work playing club-dates and festivals; to help herself fight the urge to resort to the hypodermic

163

syringe she greatly increased her intake of alcohol, often downing two bottles of spirits a day – either gin, vodka or brandy.

At about this time, whilst Billie was playing dates at Bill Gerson's Pep's Bar in Philadelphia, an old friend, pianist Milt Buckner, invited Billie and Louis McKay home for one of his wife's dinner parties. Each person there was on a different drink, and that night Billie's preference was for gin. As the evening passed, the bottle slowly emptied and Billie became more and more relaxed. Soon, the Rabelaisian jocularity that formerly marked her conversations with musician friends re-appeared. The dinner guests became helpless with laughter at Lady Day's stories, one of which concerned a big-band leader with whom she occasionally worked during the 1940s. At first the listeners thought they were hearing a serious dissertation on the great jazzman as Billie began, 'I think his phrasing is so rhythmic I just can't imagine him playing anything that didn't swing. He seems to be perfect at any tempo, and all that showmanship and yelling never limits his invention. But, shit, I wish he wouldn't keep trying to get his hand into my drawers.'

# CHAPTER EIGHT

During the summer of 1956, the first edition of the book *Lady Sings The Blues* was published in the U.S. by Doubleday. Reviews were mixed, but none was overtly critical. Ralph Gleason in *Down Beat* took Billie to task for equating drug addiction with diabetes. Most of the reviewers dwelt on Billie's chronicling of her own teenage experiences as a prostitute. Several of Billie's long-time associates questioned the accuracy of her memory, and John Hammond, Teddy Wilson, and Leonard Feather all gave their versions of incidents involving them that Billie had chosen to describe differently. Billie's account of her life in a New York brothel particularly perplexed those who had known her and her mother since the late 1920s, and those few who had known Billie in Baltimore could hardly reconcile the girl they knew there with the one described in the book. The initial sales of the book were not spectacular, but the attendant publicity meant that Billie would play to packed houses for the brief span of her remaining life.

Soon after the book's publication, Louis McKay decided on a business venture that temporarily brought about a change in Billie's domestic set-up. McKay became the

part-owner of a small club situated at E. 58th Street on the South side of Chicago. Billie sang during the club's opening week, but soon left Chicago to resume touring. In quick succession she sang in Cleveland, Las Vegas, and Hollywood (where she drew the biggest ever opening-night crowd to Jazz City). In the capacity crowd were two staunch admirers and friends of Billie's, Jose Ferrer and Rosemary Clooney; Billie was especially delighted when these two had asked her to be godmother to one of their children.

Louis McKay left someone in charge of his club and travelled with Billie for part of the tour. In Cleveland, Billie met-up with her old friend Irene Wilson. Irene, who became Mrs. Elden Kitchings through remarriage, recalls the re-union. 'The last time I saw Billie was in company with her husband Louis in Cleveland at the House of Jazz.' This was shortly before she was scheduled to appear in Philadelphia and she made a point of convincing me that she had to be clean and that she was ... I recall the meeting vividly because she invited my husband and myself to attend a matinee on Sunday, at which time she autographed her book for me.'

Billie's pianist Carl Drinkard, took a temporary leave of absence just before this particular tour got underway, and Billie began using a succession of pianists usually hired from the city where she was due to perform. However when Lady reached Las Vegas she hired a girl pianist named Corky Hale on a more permanent basis.

Corky, who is also a brilliant harpist, was playing piano with Jerry Gray's Band at The Dunes Hotel in Las Vegas when she first met Lady Day. Billie was booked to work at the hotel, and it was arranged that the pianist with the band would also accompany her. She came to the band-call and asked, 'Who's the pianist?' Corky said somewhat nervously 'I am.' 'Great, here are the parts,' said Lady, handing over the piano music. The run-through went smoothly and from then on, Corky enjoyed accompanying Billie.

Unfortunately, the heavy drinking was affecting Billie's singing, and she often had difficulty in controlling her pitching. Worse still, the huge intake of vodka or gin (which usually began in the morning) was so affecting Billie that by evening she could hardly walk unaided. This meant that Corky had to help her from the dressing room to the stage for each performance.

Billie's programme during these years was pretty well settled and she seldom deviated from the fifteen or so numbers that formed her basic repertoire. She usually opened with 'Them There Eyes', and always included either 'Strange Fruit' or 'God Bless The Child'. She regularly learnt new numbers for her recording sessions, but rarely did any of these tunes find their way into her latter-day programmes. There could be no question of embarking on an experimental repertoire when every ounce of concentration was needed to perform familiar numbers.

Lady and Corky got on well together, and between shows they sat together for long dressing-room conversations. Lady would usually be nursing her chihuahua dog, Pepi, softly stroking its coat and saying over and over again, 'Of course, you know I never had a child.' Some nights a strange charade was re-enacted, whereby Billie put doll's diapers on the two-pound dog. After saying 'My baby looks ill, my baby looks ill' she would begin to feed the tiny pet with a bottle-and-teat.

After the Las Vegas stint had ended, Billie, Louis McKay and Corky Hale all travelled on to the next engagements in Hollywood. Billie played Jazz City for part of August 1956, and throughout the run business was exceptionally good. She seemed more relaxed in California, and was pleased to link up again with one of her dearest friends, Mrs. Doe Mitchell, wife of bassist 'Red' Mitchell. Doe usually 'did' Billie's hair when she visited Los Angeles. Billie regarded this as a luxury since it saved her so much time and trouble. In Las Vegas, hairdressing had been a real problem for Lady since her head had been badly bruised by violent contact with a telephone receiver.

The next booking on Billie's itinerary after Hollywood was Honolulu, Hawaii. Corky Hale, who had other commitments pending, didn't want to make the journey. Billie said she

understood, and to show that there were no hard feelings she gave Corky a signed copy of *Lady Sings The Blues*. Corky's replacement was Chicago pianist Eddie Baker.

Lady always tried to make her accompanists feel at ease; her sensitivity couldn't bear the thought that there might be antagonism on stage. She understood the ways of all jazz musicians, but a special insight was reserved for pianists. In earlier days she used to make a point of journeying to hear a pianist whose work was new to her – partly for pleasure, partly as a way of assessing their suitability as accompanists should she ever need to call on them to work with her. Harpiste Daphne Hellman remembers one such jaunt to hear a young white pianist who had been described as a rival to the great Art Tatum. Billie, like many other great jazz performers, did not believe in long discussions on quotients of musical talent, her summary of the new pianist was concise and definite 'Art Tatum? Art Tatum?? this is SHIT.'

However, if Lady liked a musician's work she accorded him or her every respect. Eddie Baker particularly enjoyed working with Billie, describing it as 'a great experience', but he had existing solo bookings lined-up in his home city of Chicago, and after playing for Billie's engagements at the Waikiki Sands Night Club in Honolulu he returned home.

Although Baker didn't stay long, several of Billie's pianists remained with her for long spells, and all of them retained the greatest admiration for her, as a person and as a superb artist. Carl Drinkard told Max Jones, 'If she likes you she'll do anything in the world for you, but if she doesn't, look out!' Drinkard's successor Mal Waldron always got on well with Billie, but he too was aware that she could be antagonistic, 'She could be very bitchy towards women, she didn't really like them too much in general.' Max Jones' wife, Betty, was an observer when Billie, during her 1954 visit to London, showed how volatile she could be. Billie discovered that a local girl was paying too much attention to Louis McKay. Her reaction was swift and decisive, she bounced the girl against a nearby wall and hissed out an unmistakable warning 'Now you keep out of my Louis's face, or else ...'

Billie's long-time devotion to McKay baffled, and annoyed, several of Billie's close friends, others felt that in view of Billie's irascibility and unpredictability, domestic life with her was probably not all joy for a husband. Pianist Jimmie Rowles thinks that Billie really loved McKay, and Mal Waldron added, 'Billie was very devoted to Louis McKay. I remember once we went to Detroit, and Louis was supposed to get there before the show started. He didn't arrive, and Billie was really worried about him. So she decided to sing "Lover Man ... where can you be?" It sounds corny, but by the time she'd finished there were tears in everybody's eyes. She was deeply attached to Louis.'

For a while, Billie continued to use free-lance accompanists, and on one occasion Tony Scott (known principally as a clarinetist) played piano for her during a two-week stint in Philadelphia.

Sometime in this era, Tony Scott tape-recorded a Billie Holiday rehearsal. He describes the results as three fascinating hours of Lady 'singing, talking, coughing, and cursing'. Billie was in high spirits on this occasion and she greatly amused the assembled musicians with her impersonation of Sophie Tucker singing 'Some of These Days' and 'My Yiddishe Momma'. Neither rendering was ever commercially issued, but Scott did make a copy of the 'Momma' title for a club-owner who featured it on his juke-box. On the tape-recorded session Billie also sang a composition by Scott entitled 'Misery' and capped everything with a rollicking version of 'The Beer Barrel Polka'.

The session showed Lady having her fun in private, and this informality was in stark contrast to the drama that marked many of her latter-day public performances. The most dramatic concert of all was held at Carnegie Hall soon after the 'fun' session. It was entitled 'Lady Sings The Blues,' tying in with the promotion of the recent book.

The concert, which took place on 10 November 1956, played two houses. Carl Drinkard, temporarily back on piano, joined Chico Hamilton (drums), Carson Smith (ba and Kenny Burrell (guitar) in the rhythm section. Fr

show, Coleman Hawkins and Roy Eldridge were the backing horns, for the other 'house' Buck Clayton, Al Cohn, and Tony Scott made up the front line (except for the tune 'Lady Sings The Blues' on which Scott played piano). Changing musicians at the half-way stage wasn't a usual procedure, but then this was no ordinary concert. The most unusual feature of the presentation was that the links between Billie's songs were provided by Gilbert Millstein (a *New York Times* writer) who read four long excerpts from Billie's book.

Some of the packed audience fidgeted as Millstein read, but most of them tolerated the reading in silence saving all their reactions for Billie's singing. Nat Hentoff in *Down Beat* reported, 'The audience was hers before she sang, greeting her and saying goodbye with heavy applause, and at one time the musicians too, applauded. It was a night when Billie was on top, the best jazz singer alive.' Besides praising the excellence of Billie's performance, Hentoff had some pertinent things to say to those who thought that the concert hall was no place for Billie's self revelations. 'What Billie had to say should be said aloud, and precisely in those places where good manners and "taste" have been substituted for the courage to see. How many symphony orchestras, for example, have played Carnegie Hall with not one Negro in the ensemble, and who cried on stage then?'

*Metronome* magazine also chipped in on the cabaret-card injustice. In its review of the concert it said 'This is a woman of vast jazz talent; it would certainly be more befitting her gifts to allow her to work more frequently in the city that first brought her recognition.' But the publicity did nothing to change the Police Department's ruling on the necessity of authorised cabaret cards; Billie announced publicly that she would sue the City of New York to try to bring the affair into the open.

Even if there were no openings in New York City there were plenty elsewhere. In the fall of 1956 Billie played a series of dates in Florida; during one engagement in Miami she was visited by lawyer Earle Warren Zaidins, and his wife Dorothy. They took Billie and Louis McKay into a nearby

171

Chinese restaurant for dinner. The Chinese proprietor called Zaidins aside and said that, for fear of upsetting his Southern clientele, he would have to refuse to serve Billie and her husband. Billie overheard the comment, and said 'Come on, out we go, I don't want to break the ice anywhere, let someone else do the crusading.'

After Miami, Billie spent Christmas 1956 again working at Jazz City in Hollywood. When this booking ended she remained in California; for a while, the big splurge of publicity connected with the publication of her book meant that she could pick and choose her jobs. Jimmie Rowles, who had first played piano for Lady in 1942, occasionally did club-dates in California during this period, as well as playing on several of her record dates; he says, 'The last records we made with her, she had gotten real thin, and didn't have too much energy. Still the same Lady though. Just kind of tired, and tired of being sort of a "curiosity", instead of an attraction to be really listened to. I imagine lots of people came to check out what kind of shape she was in. I resented that, and she did too, very much. I heard her say one night "If they don't get off my back, I'll release the original manuscript, and *everybody* will be in trouble."

Occasionally, Lady worked for club-operators who weren't quite sure what they were booking, they simply felt that Billie Holiday could mean big business; early in 1957 she played a club in Los Angeles where she was billed as 'the sensational comedienne'.

After playing weekend dates at the Harbor Inn in Santa Monica she moved back East, where she heard the good news that her narcotics trial had been 'postponed indefinitely' by the authorities in Philadelphia. For Billie this good news was supplemented by the report that John Levy, her former manager, had died, aged 53, of a cerebral haemorrhage.

During this period, author Studs Terkel, then putting the finishing touches to his book *Giants of Jazz,* met up with Billie at a publisher's party. He sat reminiscing with Billie, whom he had heard often in Chicago during earlier years.

Billie, gradually getting the better of a huge tumbler full of gin and sliced lemon, sank back in her chair, eyes shut, trying to recall the names of friends and foes who lived in Chicago. Terkel tried to speed up the process by reeling out possibilities; when he hit on an appropriate name, Billie could only snap her fingers in agreement. Later, Terkel accompanied Billie to the bar and introduced her to novelist Nelson Algren. Billie asked 'Who is that guy?' Terkel explained that Algren was a famous writer; Lady's reply was sufficiently far-out to startle Terkel; she said 'He can stay, he's okay, he wears glasses.'

Billie began another round of 'playing the cities', appearing in Philadelphia, Detroit and Baltimore. The booking at 'Pep's' in Philadelphia turned out to be an important one, for it was there that she began working with Mal Waldron who was to be her regular accompanist for the rest of her life.

Mal Waldron's link-up with Billie was unexpected. He was at home in New York City when he received an urgent telephone call from Bill Dufty (Billie's co-author), who was helping his wife Maely to manage Billie. Dufty asked Waldron if he could come to Philadelphia to begin working with Billie; the pianist recalls, 'I rushed out and bought as many old Billie records as possible, and began to learn her tunes and her preference in accompaniment styles. The next morning, I set out for Philadelphia ... very nervous, and in awe of the greatest vocalist of my time. Paul Quinichette was in charge of the group, which also included Nelson Boyd on bass. I soon found out why most musicians who knew Billie called her Lady, because even though I didn't please her completely she spoke to me as a big sister and gave me many helpful hints. She also told me that I wasn't playing funky enough, and from that day on, I worked at playing more and more bluesy and earthy for her.'

The musical partnership with Mal Waldron soon became successful, but by then, Billie's health was inconsistent, and often she felt very weak. She could get temporary vitality from alcohol, but on several occasions in 1957 she was too poorly to perform well. One such night was at the 4th Annual

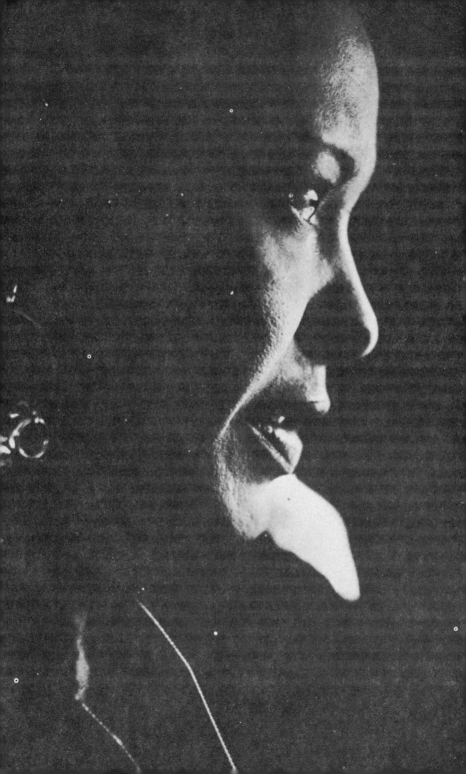

Newport Jazz Festival; Billie appeared with Mal Waldron on piano, Joe Benjamin on bass, and her old Basie Band colleague Jo Jones on drums. The performance seemed listless, and *Down Beat* described the rendering of the six numbers that made up her act as 'soulful recitative'. The set was recorded, and as it transpired, these were to be the last titles that Billie made for Norman Granz's recording company; before the year had ended Billie's contract was transferred to Columbia.

For five years, (from 1952 until 1957), Norman Granz had ensured that Billie recorded regularly, always with top-class accompanists, but although the couple had known one another since the early 1940s, their friendship was always restrained. Billie had a habit of falling out with old friends and acquaintances, then effecting quick reconciliations, but Granz had a reputation for being slow to forgive: a good friend but a bad enemy. He once hinted that he felt that Billie had traded on her unhappy childhood to the point where she automatically assumed that everyone would forgive her of anything because of it.

Time had not mellowed Billie, she was as unpredictable as ever; she never gave up maintaining 'no operator anywhere is going to push me around'. On a $1,500 engagement, if she felt that the promoter was unsympathetic, she'd appear bored and eager to finish the show, but if the mood was right (even in the last years of her life) she would sing for hours for nothing. *Down Beat,* in September 1957, asked 'Who said sitting in was dead? Billie Holiday and Mal Waldron sat in until 4 a.m. at the Five Spot.' Lady could sing at these after-hours sessions without bothering the New York police, and there were no restrictions on her playing a series of summer shows in Central Park during 1957. She continued to play occasional dates at Carnegie Hall, and wryly observed, 'I can play Carnegie, but I can't play the crummiest gin joint in New York.'

In August 1957, Lady made one of her infrequent trips to Canada, this time to play a prestige date at the Shakespeare Festival held in Stratford, Ontario. The *Melody Maker* reported that she was in fine voice, both for the concert and for the follow-up bookings at the Town Tavern in Toronto. She moved on to play dates at 'The Avant Garde' in Hollywood, (alongside her old friend Red Norvo), but the first warning signs of serious illness caused her to cut short her stay; vocalist Lucy Ann Polk was called in to finish the run.

Lady moved back to New York, but Louis McKay remained to make his home in California. Although the couple had lived together for several years, they were only legally married in 1956, after the Philadelphia police raid. The couple's relationship was seldom tranquil during their common-law union; after the legal marriage the stormy scenes became more and more frequent. By the fall of 1957 the estrangement was total, and the couple began living apart.

As Billie's lawyer, Earle Warren Zaidins negotiated a new recording contract with Columbia, part of the agreement stipulated that Billie was to be allowed her request to work with an orchestra directed by Ray Ellis. However, the recording company officials, mindful of Billie's reputation for unpunctuality, inserted a clause whereby Zaidins had to personally guarantee that Billie would appear at the studios by the appropriate time. Billie and Zaidins decided that the first LP should be made at three late-night sessions, accordingly, the lawyer would call for Billie at ten p.m. En route to the session Billie always bought a bottle of Gordon's gin and a pack of Seven-up, and thus armed she would enter the studio in time for a midnight start.

Zaidins remembers that the first tunes recorded at these sessions were the least troublesome. Sadly, Billie couldn't start singing without downing a few drinks at this late stage in her career; by then, she only needed those few tastes to appear quite intoxicated; within an hour of starting the recording session she was struggling to make a satisfactory take. Some of the tunes were totally unfamiliar to Billie, which did nothing to speed the schedule.

Late in 1957, C.B.S. in New York presented one of the most ambitious jazz shows ever televised. A spectacular

177

number of great jazz performers were assembled to take part in Timex's 'Seven Lively Arts' series. Billie appeared, as did Henry 'Red' Allen, Doc Cheatham, Vic Dickenson, Roy Eldridge, Coleman Hawkins, Rex Stewart, Pee Wee Russell, Jo Jones, Ben Webster, Lester Young and many others.

On the show, Lady sang 'Fine and Mellow', and 'My Man', accompanied by eleven of the assembled musicians; by now, her voice was showing the accumulated effect of every twinge of mental and physical pain that she had ever suffered. She looked and sounded frail, and those who had known the plump, giggling twenty-two-year-old Billie Holiday, found difficulty in realising that the gaunt 115-pound Lady Day was the same person. Nevertheless, she was still strikingly photogenic, and once again, the old, old possibility of featuring Lady in a full-length film was mooted. As ever, the project failed to materialise, but plans for making a film based on Billie's life-story seemed to be taking definite shape.

Ever since *Lady Sings The Blues* had been published there had been press mentions of several plans to film the book. It was hinted that an actress was to portray Billie, but that Billie would sing on the soundtrack. Dorothy Dandridge was rumoured to be one of the main candidates for the role, but several other names were mentioned as possibilities. The late Dorothy Kilgallen, (who wrote a widely read column) tipped Ava Gardner for the role; Billie read this snippet, and quite irrationally assumed that this piece of false information had emanated from Annie Ross. Without further ado, Billie stormed into the Upstairs Room, where Annie was then working, and began bawling her out for 'leaking' a story that had no basis in truth. She burst in on Annie and began shouting 'I don't want that bitch to play me – how dare you say such a thing?' Annie, who knew nothing of the film plans, was absolutely stunned by Billie's behaviour; slowly she calmed Billie down and then began piecing together the grabled comments. It didn't take long for Billie to realise that she had made a false accusation, then she was full of remorse. But not everyone had the patience to try and sort out what Billie meant during her vitriolic, obscurely-worded outbursts, and during the last few years of her life, several old friends began keeping out of her way. Leonard Feather has said, 'There was hardly a close friend with whom Billie didn't fall out, at one time or another', and another friend, Max Jones, observed 'The smallest upset would set her storming.'

The original plans for a film biography were slow to take shape, and Billie got more and more disappointed by the delays. However, her morale was always boosted when she discussed a return trip to Europe. Early in 1958 vague possibilities developed into realities and Billie was offered a three-week season at the Olympia in Paris. To tie-in with the bookings in France one concert at London's Royal Festival Hall was arranged for 8 June.

New plans were made for her to record the soundtrack of the film whilst she was in France, thus circumventing any possible hold-ups that an impending Hollywood studio musicians' strike could have caused. Unfortunately, the whole project – tour and film-recordings – was doomed. The Algerian Crisis caused the French Government to temporarily close all concert halls, and as the dates in Paris were to provide the bulk of the revenue for Billie's intended tour, the whole trip had to be abandoned.

Billie had cancelled several bookings in order to be available for the work in Europe, and, at short notice, it was impossible for her to re-claim them. She had earned good money ever since she left Alderson Reformatory in 1948, but little of the ten years' bounty had stayed with her; a temporary cessation of income, as happened when the European dates were cancelled, showed just how low Billie's finances were.

When money was desperately short Billie took almost every date that she was offered; during the mid-1950s through the musicians' grape-vine veteran tenor-saxist Happy Cauldwell heard that Billie was accepting casual gigs. Happy, who has long specialised in providing music for Masonic functions, told writer Johnny Simmen that he approached Billie and asked if she would be willing to sing at one of his New York bookings. Lady readily agreed, but Happy, knowing of the quirk that Billie sometimes showed towards predictability, was on tenterhooks until he saw Lady enter the hall on the night of the engagement. His uneasiness didn't instantly evaporate, for he quickly noticed that Billie had had a lot to drink en route for the booking. He also saw that she had brought her pet chihuahua, and that the dog's slim leather leash was gradually winding its way around Billie's ankles. Happy quickly stepped forward and escorted Billie to the bandstand, unsure whether the next few minutes would lead to a succession of headaches. He need not have worried; as soon as Billie began to sing he realised that she was fully in command of the situation. Happy looked around the crowded hall and saw that the audience were enthralled by Billie's presence – the magical quality was still with her.

reasonably well when she played the New York Town Hall, but for club bookings that she did in Detroit soon afterwards, she had to be accompanied by a trained nurse.

Her old friend Dr Herbert Henderson visited Billie when she played dates at the Black Hawk Club in San Francisco during September 1958. He wrote 'She was ill with cirrhosis of the liver, caused by excessive drinking. Alcohol was resorted to in order that she would have no desire for heroin. She had lost much weight and should have been in a hospital instead of a night club. When I heard her sing – it was pathetic.'

Immediately after the Black Hawk booking Billie took part in the first Monterey Jazz Festival, appearing there for the final evening, Sunday 5 October. She could still be filled with trepidation at the prospect of facing huge audiences (attendances of 15,000 were not uncommon at many of the 1950s open-air jazz festivals). Her reputation ensured that she would be given a warm welcome by the crowd, but still the old 'first-night' fear plagued her. Monterey was a triumph for Lady Day as far as audience reaction, the crowd insisted that she sang three encores; yet, to the reporters and critics present she seemed ill-at-ease throughout her entire set.

Berta Wood reporting for the English magazine *Jazz Journal* highlighted this anomaly; she wrote of Billie's uncertain rush on to the stage and of her general uneasiness. However, the audience seemed not to notice, and at the end 'the tumultuous applause at the end of Billie's set, seemed no less than she used to receive in her greatest days'.

British jazz-writer Albert McCarthy was also at the concert, and he was close enough to hear Billie stage-whisper to Gerry Mulligan, 'I thought Benny Carter was to play with me.' It was her old yearning for familiar faces; she had worked with Mulligan before, but she had known Carter for over twenty years. Benny walked on stage to join Gerry Mulligan and Buddy De Franco in accompanying Billie; Albert McCarthy commented, 'The support she gets from musicians of every school is touching.' However, he struck a sombre note when he reflected on Billie's physical state. 'The

185

tragedy that is hers makes her appearance almost unbearable for me these days – the whole agony is right in the open every time she sings.'

Author Ralph Gleason also reflected on how ill Billie looked, 'At the end of the Black Hawk and Monterey engagements Billie was numbed. She muttered rather than talked, and talked rather than sang. She looked totally wasted, shrunken to the bone. She could even sing off-key. It was painful to see and hear her at that time, even though she could still move an audience.'

On the day following the festival, Ralph Gleason saw Billie as she was preparing to leave for her next engagement, 'I saw her sitting stiffly in the lobby of the San Carlos Hotel in Monterey, the morning after the Festival finale. The jazz musicians tried to ignore her. Finally, in that hoarse whisper that could still (after thirty years of terrifying abuse) send shivers down your spine, she asked, "Where are you boys goin'?" And when no one answered, she answered herself. "They got me openin' in Vegas tonight." '

Louis McKay and Billie were by now irreconcilable, and the *Melody Maker* issue of 18 October 1958 reported that Billie, whilst in California, had filed her divorce decree against McKay – the decree was never finalised.

During the fall of 1958, Billie appointed George Treadwell as her personal manager. Treadwell, an ex-trumpeter, was also Sarah Vaughan's manager (he had continued to manage Sarah even though their marriage had ended in divorce). Treadwell, who died in 1967, didn't remain Billie's manager for long, but he did help finalise negotiations for Billie's return to Europe; the ink on the contracts was scarcely dry before Billie and pianist Mal Waldron were flying the Atlantic.

Billie had been longing to return to Europe, but her 1958 tour had some unhappy moments. In Italy, early in the tour, she encountered one of the biggest failures of her career. She had been booked for a week's run at the Smeraldo Theatre in Milan; the rest of the bill was a typical assortment of variety acts: acrobats, pop singers, comedians and impressionists. Billie's booking only lasted for one night, the booing and hissing that the audience directed at her during the second-house performance 'left the management no alternative but to ask her to forgo the remainder of the week' (*Melody Maker,* 15 November 1958).

Billie in her prime would have found difficulty in riding this blow, being weak and ill she was particularly demoralised. Even so, she was able to joke with Mal Waldron, 'The trouble with these people is that they can't speak English.'

One consolation that emerged from the Smeraldo fiasco was that Billie actually sang at La Scala in Milan. Famous Italian film producer, Mario Fatoria, a devout fan of Billie's, booked one of the smaller halls within the famous opera house, and there, before an audience selected from his friends, he presented a concert 'by invitation only' featuring Billie. Billie was deeply touched by the gesture, and later became godmother to one of Fatoria's children.

In recalling the tour, Mal Waldron said, 'I knew that Billie loved the Europeans, and if she had remained in Europe I believe she would be alive today.

'When we were on tour we used to hire local bass-players and drummers. Sometimes they were good, sometimes they were lousy. But if they were bad, she'd never act up on the stage. She'd wait until we were back in the dressing room before bawling us out.

'She was never demanding of her accompanist. There were no stops and starts, no tricky arrangements. She just wanted you to play jazz and swing behind her.'

Billie's concert bookings in France were well-attended, but fans and critics found the performances disappointing. In Paris, backstage at the Olympia (where she gave several concerts), she was interviewed by Henry Kahn, the *Melody Maker's* Paris correspondent. He wrote, 'Lady Day, or the Princess of Harlem, as they call her in France, looked tired. She sat drinking a glass of Vittel water, and in a meandering voice said, "Since my separation from my husband I do not want to stay in the States. I want to settle in Britain because I love the people. In Britain they do not just call me a singer, they call me an artist and I like that." ' Kahn reported that

Lady Day appeared exhausted after she had finished her eight-tune set. Billie's old Basie Band colleague Jimmy Rushing was also working at the Olympia at the same time (doing the first half of the show), the two singers exchanged friendly greetings but didn't spend much time together.

Billie had no reason to hasten back to America, and after her concerts at Olympia she began working at the Mars Club in Paris. Artistically the residency was a success, and the good reviews began flowing again. Financially, it was less successful for Billie was only playing the job for a percentage of the take. Hazel Scott, who had known Billie for twenty years, was visiting Paris in late 1958, and she went to hear Billie sing at the Mars Club. In 1973, she recalled the night for the magazine *Ebony,* 'On top of all the problems I was having in my own life at the time, I began thinking about what was happening to Lady Day. Brilliant artist, beautiful person, you could pin all the superlatives on her, but there she was, having just been misused again, by somebody who didn't give a damn about her. Having just been given a rough time by the French public because her voice just couldn't do what they wanted it to do on the stage of the Olympia Theatre, there she was singing in a little club for whatever percentage she could get. I started crying pretty loud.' Billie stopped singing, crossed the club and pulled Hazel Scott by the arm to the end of the room. 'She backed me into a corner and in a cold, dry voice said, "No matter what the mother-fuckers do to you, never let 'em see you cry." ' Soon afterwards, Billie, unable to get any suitable offers of work in France or in Britain returned to America.

Mal Waldron continued to play piano for Billie, but by now bookings were sparse. Waldron remembers, 'She used to talk sometimes about the hard life that she'd had, but she never wanted sympathy. Just understanding – what we're all looking for I suppose.

'As the years went by I became very close to Billie and when my first daughter arrived, she was godmother. The scene in church was very amusing, Billie was a little nervous, standing there holding my little daughter Nola in her arms.

'She loved kids. Louis McKay had two by a former marriage and whenever we went to Los Angeles she'd shower them with toys. I remember when she learned my wife was having a baby she wanted to take it from us and keep it for herself.

'She was, for me, the greatest, of course. She was a very warm woman, but also completely candid and down-to-earth. She'd always tell you exactly what she thought of you — she'd say right out if she thought you were beautiful or a bastard.

'Billie was also a first-rate cook and her dinners were milestones in the history of good soul food. She would insist on everything being eaten which was no problem for me as the food was so delicious that I would eat it as if there were no tomorrow.

'I'm sure she'd have loved to settle down, raise a family and cook for them. But she'd had a lot of trouble with her men. I remember once on a 'plane to San Francisco we started putting a tune together. She wanted it to be the story of her life and she was going to put down all men. But it didn't come out that way in the end.

'Faults? Well, of course, she drank too much. She always carried a small bottle of gin with her and somehow it never seemed to get empty though she was drinking all the time. When we played in a dry town she'd be under a terrible strain. She wouldn't stop drinking and she never did really kick the dope habit. But Lady Day had an awful lot to forget. She really wanted to move to Europe and live in England, in London she had no language problems so she was all smiles and very happy.'

In February 1959, Billie did come to London, but only on a brief working visit, she and Mal Waldron flew in on the 22nd and left three days later. The purpose of the visit was a hastily arranged appearance on a television show called *Chelsea at Nine*. Peter Knight's Orchestra backed Billie on two numbers, the other tune was accompanied only by Mal Waldron. On the show, which was televised in March, Billie was visibly ill at ease. After the session she said, 'I was so nervous out there, at first I could have died. Everything is a little different from American TV. I do hope that people like it.' No one who saw the programme could have doubted that Billie was seriously ill.

After returning from Britain, Billie soon reverted to her nightly stay-at-home routine. In March 1959 her despondency was deepened by Lester Young's death. Lester, who had been in poor health for several years, died 24 hours after returning to his New York hotel room after playing club-dates in Paris. His death was described as being due to cardiac failure hastened by alcoholism. He and Billie, once the closest of buddies, had drifted into a non-malevolent friendship; they rarely met, but kept in touch through a mutual friend, Elaine Swain.

Lester's career had run downhill in a way that was almost uncannily similar to the decline in Billie's fortunes. His last years were full of despair: on one of the last visits he made to his doctor he said 'We all have our worries. You have no problems, you're a white man' and in his last interview (with François Postif in Paris) he said 'You fight for your life until death do you part, and then you got it made.' When the interviewer asked about Billie he said 'She's still my Lady Day.'

Billie, together with several past members of Count Basie's Band, attended the funeral service at the Universal Chapel at 52nd and Lexington in Manhattan. Leonard Feather, who escorted Billie to the funeral, noticed how very ill she looked, he also saw her tucking a small bottle of gin into her handbag to tide her through the service.

Annie Ross continued to visit Billie, 'Towards the end, she was quite weak, and poorly a lot of the time, but she still loved to cook for someone. I'd wash her hair for her, and occasionally I'd bath her like a baby. She'd never had a vinegar hair rinse, and she could hardly believe that I was seriously going to pour vinegar over her head, the thought of this really tickled her, and she almost collapsed with laughing.'

By the spring of 1959 Billie was too ill to work regularly; however, she decided to celebrate her 44th birthday in style.

She invited several old friends to her small one-and-a-half-room apartment. Usually she made no special arrangements for her birthday, but symbolically she decided that this 7 April would be party night. Annie Ross, Bill Dufty, Leonard Feather, musicians Jo Jones and Ed Lewis and a few other guests attended. Feather described Billie: 'Looking sharp in leopard-skin blouse and skin-tight toreador pants.' Annie Ross recalls 'Lady really sparkled at that party.' She remembers Lady saying 'This is the first birthday I've really celebrated in fifteen years.'

But most of the gaiety was bravado; after the party, friends tried to persuade her to enter hospital. She flatly refused, and as if inspired by her own defiance, she played an amazingly successful week at the Storyville Club in Boston. Promoter George Wein, who had first booked Billie back in 1951, recalls the engagement, 'I had been in Europe at the time and I arrived on the last day of the engagement, I think it was April 1959. In those days, we had an afternoon session and an evening session. I sat through five performances of Billie Holiday that day, completely mesmerised. She was singing better than I had heard her sing in years. It was as if a miracle had happened. I immediately spoke to her about working the Newport Jazz Festival that July.

'In May, she booked an engagement in Lowell, Massachusetts in a very bad, cheap club. I wanted to go up and see her, but one of my associates had gone and seen her and said "Don't go because she looked so bad, and sounded so bad." I didn't want to destroy my last memory of Billie Holiday, and so didn't see her.'

As the weather turned warmer so Billie began to feel more optimistic; she said that she would soon be playing club dates again. She felt well enough to take part in an all-star concert (with Duke Ellington and Dizzy Gillespie) at Philadelphia's Academy of Art. Two issues after reporting this concert, *Down Beat* published an ominous two-line item in its 11 June issue: 'Doctors have told Billie Holiday to give up liquor or it will only be a matter of time.'

Billie announced that she wanted to emigrate to England,

soon afterwards she said that she would wait until the three years remaining on her apartment-lease had expired. She changed her mind again and told friends she was looking for a house to live in on Long Island. However, the only move that Billie was destined to make was to be her last journey to hospital.

Her condition gradually deteriorated, but to get some badly needed cash she agreed to sing at a concert held on 25 May at the Phoenix Theater in Greenwich Village for 300 dollars (a fraction of her usual concert fee). Leonard Feather, who was sharing master-of-ceremonies duties with Steve Allen, visited Billie in the theatre just prior to the show. His reaction to her appearance is poignantly described in his book *From Satchmo to Miles*. 'I looked into her dressing room to say hello, and saw her seated at the makeup table coughing, spittle running unchecked down her chin.' Billie asked 'What's the matter Leonard? You seen a ghost or something?' Feather found it impossible to hide the sadness he felt in seeing that Billie had lost at least twenty pounds in weight since their previous meeting a few weeks before.

Billie's walk was so unsteady that she had to be assisted to the side of the stage, but when she heard the applause that greeted her introduction she straightened up as though nothing was amiss. After singing two songs Billie was so weak that she had to be helped from the stage. In the wings, she fell into the arms of her old friend Tony Scott. Scott had been scheduled to play clarinet on the concert, but had been prevented from performing by a broken finger. Scott, his wife, and pianist Mal Waldron helped Billie into Scott's car; Waldron could see that Billie was looking very ill, but even he didn't realise that Lady had just finished her final show.

Tony Scott drove Billie to her apartment, she said that all she needed was a good rest, and expressly asked that no one should call for an ambulance. Next day, Leonard Feather and Joe Glaser visited Billie's apartment and tried in vain to get her to go into hospital.

For the rest of the month Billie was under the close care of her personal physician Dr Eric Caminer. A few friends dropped in to see her, and one of them, a young entertainer named Frank Freedom, offered to cook for her during the convalescence.

On the afternoon of 31 May, just as Billie was preparing to eat a light meal of oatmeal and custard prepared by Freedom, she collapsed and sank into a coma. Dr Caminer was contacted and he immediately telephoned for a police ambulance to take Billie to New York's Knickerbocker Hospital.

Frankie Freedom travelled with Billie in the emergency ambulance; after arrival at the hospital Billie lay on a stretcher for more than an hour before she received any medical attention. She was officially admitted at 3.40 p.m. After her case had been diagnosed as 'drug addiction and alcoholism' she was put into another ambulance and taken to a city institution, the Metropolitan Hospital in Harlem.

At 5.30 p.m. Dr Caminer arrived at the Metropolitan Hospital to find his patient on a stretcher in the arrivals' hall, unconscious and unattended. He immediately realised that this was a cardiac crisis, and soon afterwards Billie was placed in an oxygen tent. None of the initial delays were caused by racial discrimination; most of the staff at the Metropolitan are black. They were working under pressure, and at first, none of them were aware of Billie's identity – she was registered on entry as Eleanora McKay.

Initially it appeared that Billie's condition was due to a non-lethal overdose of heroin, and the profusion of needle-scars seemed to confirm this hasty diagnosis. However, on the following Wednesday, the Metropolitan Hospital officials confirmed Dr Caminer's view that Billie's illness had no direct connection with narcotics. After 72 hours in hospital Billie showed no withdrawal symptoms, corroborating William Dufty's view that Billie was not using hard drugs during the last part of her life; an opinion shared by Earle Warren Zaidins.

Billie's illness was diagnosed as a liver ailment complicated by cardiac failure. Miraculously she began to recover, gaining weight each day. A steady stream of visitors came to

Room 6A12 to wish her well, and Louis McKay, her estranged husband, flew in from California.

Earle Warren Zaidins was one of Billie's first visitors, when she was still in the public ward. The ward-sister at the Metropolitan, thinking that Zaidins might be a reporter, told him that he was not to speak to Billie until she acknowledged that she knew him. Billie saw Zaidins walking down the ward and called out 'Hi, Earle, I'm here.' The sister said, 'Do you know this man?', whereupon Billie gave out salty confirmation, 'Course I do, he's my fucking attorney.'

The old optimism and rough-edged humour started to assert themselves again; and Billie began dictating the opening chapters of a new autobiographical book to co-author Bill Dufty, who was a regular visitor.

Then, on Friday 12 June, the police swooped on Billie's hospital room; there, they allegedly found a small tinfoil envelope containing heroin. Subsequently they charged Billie with possession. It was the bitterest blow of all for Billie, she was too ill to be moved from the room so a constant police guard was posted outside the room.

Maely Dufty has subsequently pointed out that it would have been impossible for Lady Day, immobile under the weight of the respiratory equipment, to have reached the spot where the police said they found the drug. Some of Billie's friends felt that the drug may have been planted, others think that it may have been a token offering from someone who mistakenly thought it would temporarily ease Billie's suffering. The police carried out their tasks to the letter of the law, and although they acted in accordance with the statute books, the timing and zealousness of their actions made the affair seem a sordid manoeuvre.

Donald E. Wilkes, a lawyer, went into action, and on Tuesday 16 June, he got Judge Epstein of the New York Supreme Court to sustain a writ of habeas corpus which made it possible for the police to be ordered away from Billie's hospital room.

In a letter to Assistant District Attorney Melvin Glass, (dated 24 June 1959), Don Wilkes summarised the succession of indignities that Billie had undergone in hospital. 'Suffering from a condition so grave that at the time she was considered beyond recovery, she was none the less given a bit of a going over, first by two, and then by three detectives. Her books, flowers, record-player and radio were taken away from her, and in general she was dealt with as if she were a re-incarnation of Ma Barker (a gang-leader of the 1930s), rather than one of the most gifted, brilliant and creative artistes in the history of American music. Then to climax it all, on 21 June, two detectives descended upon her to 'mug' and fingerprint her while she was still in her hospital bed, without permission, knowledge or consent.'

But, despite all this harassment, Billie still didn't give up hope. Although she knew that she would have to face a Grand Jury on narcotics charges as soon as she left hospital, she continued to talk about the future as though nothing were amiss. She held bedside conferences with director Vina Pathak, and writer George Morris, who were planning to film her life-story. A contract for 50,000 dollars for her part in the filming, was left for her to approve – she told William Dufty that she would hold out for double or nothing. She went through a roster of musicians and selected those who she wanted to accompany her on the film soundtrack.

She was responding to the treatment for cirrhosis of the liver, when doctors discovered that a serious kidney infection was replacing the original threat. The stress and strain of the last few months combined to block out any chance of recovery. On Saturday 11 July, her heart began to falter, and once again the emergency oxygen apparatus was wheeled into her room. But the same devil-may-care streak in Billie that had so indelibly marked her life was as strong as ever, to the nurses' anger and consternation she sneaked a cigarette and almost set herself alight smoking it.

Her condition worsened, and Joe Glaser made attempts to transfer her to a private hospital. But Billie was much too ill to be moved, Glaser and his personal physician Dr. Alexander Schiff visited Billie, as did pianist Mal Waldron; Louis McKay went to see her every day.

Early on Wednesday 15 July she received the last rites of the Roman Catholic Church. The treatment that she had received from the staff of the Metropolitan Hospital was faultless, but nothing could save her. She rallied again on the Thursday, and shared her last joke with Bill Dufty, telling him she was going to write another song called 'Bless Your Bones'. Dufty, a constant visitor, was at Lady Day's bedside with the night-nurse when Billie died at 3.10 a.m. on Friday 17 July 1959.

The long, long fight against environmental problems, racism, hand-outs, kick-backs, hustlers, pimps, leeches, pushers, narcotics and booze was over for Lady Day. Yet, even in death she was remembered by many newspapers for her addictions rather than her artistry. However, the *New York Post* printed a moving obituary by Bill Dufty in which he said, 'She was beautiful; no one who saw her exquisite brown head against the hospital pillow would dare talk of her loveliness in bygone days.'

When the hospital staff came to move the body they discovered that Billie had 750 dollars in fifty-dollar notes taped to one of her legs. The money was the advance for a series of autobiographical articles. Billie trusted ready cash, but during the last months of her life precious little of it had come her way – her bank account showed seventy cents credit.

Many old friends went to pay their last respects at the funeral parlour on Lexington Avenue, including people from Baltimore who had known Billie since her childhood. All the funeral expenses were paid by agent Joe Glaser; Father O'Connor (often known as 'the jazz priest') made special arrangements to obtain permission for Billie to be buried close to her mother.

On Tuesday 21 July, dozens of musicians, black and white, attended the service held at St Paul the Apostle Cathedral on 60th and 9th, New York City. The jazzmen deeply mourned Billie's passing, for they, more than others, realised just how rare, and inspiring, her talent had been. During her lifetime, Billie had cursed at, and quarrelled with,

196

most of those who went in procession for the interment at St Raymond's Cemetery in the Bronx, but none bore her a grudge. Throughout most of her life, Billie had been her own worst enemy; the self-destructive daemon within her had finally won.

Billie's financial position just prior to her death had been perilous. Ironically, predictably, her demise brought a resurgence of interest in her recorded work, and by the end of 1959 the accruing royalties were estimated to be 100,000 dollars. Billie's husband Louis McKay was the sole beneficiary.

Lady Day never lacked worshippers, a small army of people had always bought each and every record that she made as soon as it was issued, after her death a new cult grew. But, despite the fervour of the new fans, and the fortune that Billie posthumously presented to her husband, no one bothered to erect a gravestone on the plain two-foot square of earth that sited her burial spot until Mel Mandel, a *Down Beat* advertising manager, brought the matter to the attention of his magazine's readers in May 1960. A year later, Louis McKay announced at a press conference that he was planning to set up a foundation in memory of Billie, which would provide funds for the treatment and rehabilitation of drug addicts; at the same time, it was revealed that plans were being finalised for a film to be made of Billie's life story.

Those particular film plans were soon abandoned, as were three other similar schemes of the 1960s. It wasn't until Berry Gordy and Sidney J. Furie actually began shooting *Lady Sings The Blues* in 1971 that sceptics would admit that a film about Billie Holiday was at last to be made. Some of Billie's devotees had waited 25 years to see a biographical movie about Billie; they expected strict adherence to facts, and they were disappointed, but no one could fault actress-singer Diana Ross, who overcame the banal, and, at times absurd, story-line to give a great dramatic performance.

The film continues to do good business at the box office, and despite its scant coverage of Billie Holiday's actual life-story, it serves a purpose in introducing her name to a world-wide audience. Only those who are completely incurious could leave the cinema without wondering what the real Billie Holiday sang like; the enormous increase in the sales of Billie's records is proof that they have found out.

# PART TWO

## BILLIE HOLIDAY ON RECORD

found it didn't work with me, because I didn't have a big voice ... so anyway, between the two of them, I sort of got Billie Holiday.' But a clinical analysis of all the phrases that Billie ever sang on record would not reveal the thinnest streak of plagiarism, there is no obvious copying of either of her mentors. Billie's singing style was hers, and hers alone, she was one of the great originals of jazz.

But not all of Billie's records were masterpieces; had she disappeared without trace immediately after her 1933 recording debut it's conceivable that her name would only have excited students of nostalgia.

When John Hammond organised Billie's first recording session, he appointed Benny Goodman as the musical director of the session. Deane Kincaide produced the orchestrations, and Johnny Mercer was commissioned by guitarist Dick McDonough to write the lyrics for 'Riffin' The Scotch', one of the two tunes recorded. Billie knew Benny Goodman very well, she also knew of Johnny Mercer's skills having long featured his 1931 song 'Would You For A Big Red Apple?' in her club act; Deane Kincaide was one of the most respected arrangers of the 1930s, yet something was amiss. In retrospect, it's easy to see what went wrong.

During the early part of Billie's career, she sang with the very minimum number of accompanists, usually only a pianist worked with her – at most a quartet. But the band that accompanied her record debut was a nine-piece unit using specially written arrangements. The scores were skilful and slick, they were tailor-made, but too tightly fitted for Billie's comfort. The band's exact course is plotted throughout; there are short interludes that allow the soloists to improvise, but little latitude is allowed for creating excitement. On 'Your Mother's Son-in-Law' the band plays an introductory chorus in G minor, they then change key to E minor for Billie's vocal chorus before modulating to A minor for a rideout in which Billie rejoins the ensemble for the last eight bars. These key changes would not present any problems to someone with Billie's immense natural musicianship, nevertheless they were part of an accompaniment style that she had probably never encountered before. One can imagine her relaxation disappearing during rehearsal. Her inborn dislike of the big occasion would also, inevitably, bring some strain; the result is that Billie's debut is merely professional, and not in the least sensational. She appears more relaxed on the simply arranged 'Riffin' The Scotch', but here, she is given only one sixteen-bar chorus to perform on. Small wonder that the jazz lovers of the world didn't jump up and demand more.

Bessie Smith's recording career ended three days before Billie's began. John Hammond was the man who organised both dates. His original plan was that Billie should begin her recording career accompanied only by a pianist – just as Bessie had done ten years before. Bessie too had originally suffered from recording-studio nerves. With only one accompanist involved, the problems of repeated attempts at the same tune seemed less frustrating, particularly if the singer worked regularly with the pianist. Dot Hill, or Bobby Henderson, would have suited Billie admirably, but not long before the initial session it was discovered that neither of the pianists were in the musicians' union. John Hammond eventually got Henderson into the A.F. of M. but he failed to show up on the day that Hammond had originally booked the studio. Henderson later told Hammond that he had been on his way to the session when he'd been arrested for spitting on the subway.

After the Benny Goodman sessions almost two years passed before Billie made any further recordings, but during that period she took part in a short two-reeler film entitled *Symphony in Black,* in which she was accompanied by Duke Ellington's Orchestra. Billie's brief musical contribution to the film is a long-playing record, it consists of one twelve-bar blues chorus on 'Saddest Tale'. The snippet lasts for barely half a minute, but it is very revealing, in that it shows how little Billie's interpretation of the blues changed throughout her entire career.

Very few of Billie's recordings featured the twelve-bar blues format, and the occasional examples of her recorded

203

blues singing have led to arguments as to whether she was a great blues singer or merely a good one. She herself disliked being called a blues singer, and one can admire her perception for she wasn't a blues singer at all, in the classic tradition of Ma Rainey, Bessie Smith and Clara Smith. The paradox is that Billie imparted a blues feeling to almost every song that she ever recorded.

Usually, Billie adopted a recitative approach to the twelve-bar blues. Her concepts were original, but not particularly tuneful or expansive. The blues seemed to offer Billie little incentive to use her gift of melodic invention; it wouldn't sound incongruous to juxtapose a blues performance from a Billie concert date in the 1950s alongside the blues she sang in *Symphony in Black*.

Billie realised early on, that the twelve-bar blues, per se, were not her metier, accordingly they formed a minimal part of her repertoire. It's true that two of her most famous compositions were blues, but they both came into being at the suggestion of recording managers rather than through any planning on Billie's part, ('Billie's Blues' was created at Bernie Hanighen's suggestion in 1936, and 'Fine and Mellow' was instigated by Milt Gabler in 1939). Billie always said that she liked both of those recordings, but then, she always felt it a matter of prestige to be thought of as a composer; in private correspondence and in interviews she pointedly and proudly mentioned her own tunes. And, though Billie was generous to a fault she would certainly have been aware that the more popular her compositions became the more royalties she would receive. In her autobiography she said she knew nothing whatsoever about royalties until 1942; however, in 1938, during one of the first interviews she ever gave, she told Leonard Feather that she had just received her first royalty cheque — a tiny initial payment of eleven dollars for composing 'Billie's Blues'. Billie would never jeopardise her performances by including unsuitable material for the sake of pride, or pennies, but it is a matter for conjecture whether she would have regularly featured any blues in her act had she not recorded 'Billie's Blues', 'Fine and Mellow', and 'I

Love My Man'. None of the blues that she recorded in later years ever found a regular place in her repertoire.

Billie's supreme gifts were never evident when she sang the blues, but they were immediately obvious when she performed standard material. By her re-phrasing of a melody line, and superbly timed delivery of lyrics she could reveal a depth of expression that few had previously imagined existed in popular music. On the series of recordings that Billie made with Teddy Wilson (commencing in July 1935) this was consistently apparent. Billie's 'real' recording career began with Teddy Wilson.

None of the four tunes that Billie recorded on her first session with Wilson could be called 'class' songs, only one of them was considered worthy of even minimal exploitation by a music publisher. This solitary 'plug' was 'I Wished on The Moon'. The main task of the initial recording session was to wax a successful version of that song, accordingly it was scheduled first.

In a very short space of time, Billie and Wilson's studio band had produced a minor masterpiece. Wilson plays a piano introduction, then shares the first chorus with clarinetist Benny Goodman, prior to changing key for Billie's vocal chorus. Billie, sounding admirably relaxed from the first note, emphasises the words in the 15th and 16th bars, breaking up the timing beautifully, perfectly illustrating an aspect of her talent whereby she shifted a stress in pronunciation in a way that created an ingenious syncopation of the original melody.

This attribute is also clearly apparent on the fast 'What a Little Moonlight Can Do' from the same date, she mouths the syllables 'Ohh ... Ohh ... Ohh' just as a master jazz player might phrase a solo. The fact that this song (initially an unimportant part of a British film called *Roadhouse Nights*) is remembered today is solely because Billie breathed lasting life into the opus by her unforgettable interpretation. John Hammond recalled that at the time of the recording, the American publisher of the song called the tune 'a dog', giving it Tin Pan Alley's lowest rating. Another tune from the same session, 'Miss Brown To You', also lacked any sort of merit mark, but again Billie completely mask's the song's shortcomings. The relaxed feeling of the record is exemplified by Goodman's playing of the melody during the first chorus. The fact that the lyrics are incongruous, they being directed at another girl, causes no problems. Billie sings them marvellously, and adds to the informal mood of the session by calling out words of encouragement to Wilson during his piano solo.

By the time the group recorded the last title of the day ('A Sunbonnet Blue'), Benny Goodman had left the studio; however, the overall effect of the accompaniment isn't diminished, since Roy Eldridge, in great form, and tenor-saxist Ben Webster play some very exciting music.

The musical success of these first four sides made them prototypes for dozens of succeeding Wilson–Holiday records. Subsequently, the pattern of memorised (or 'head') arrangements varied little: the first chorus was an instrumental, the second was sung, the band then played a concluding chorus (or half-chorus) ride-out. A full chorus wasn't always possible, since the duration of all of these records was governed by the three minutes available for each ten inch 78 rpm recording.

The band-singer-band playing order routine was the standard practice of the day, the vocal refrain being – in theory – very much the subsidiary part of any recording. Teddy Wilson explained the attitude that prevailed during the 1930s to writer Don DeMichael, 'On my dates, Billie would usually sing only one chorus, and very seldom would it be the first. The horns would introduce the first chorus, and she'd sing the second. In a dance band then, the girl singer would seldom do the first chorus. The band would play awhile, and then the singer would sing a chorus. The band was the main thing, not the vocalist.'

Four weeks after their first recording date together, Wilson and Billie Holiday returned to the studios to record three more tunes. Wilson has explained how he departed from the procedure adopted at the first session, this time he wrote out arrangements for the trumpet and three reed line-up. He soon realised that this lessened the excitement, and it was some while before he used written arrangements again when backing Billie. Wilson's playing on this follow-up session is particularly brilliant, but Billie, perhaps lacking the inspiration that more spontaneous backings gave her, is fractionally less impressive. On 'I'm Painting The Town Red' she uses a vocal device that she occasionally resorted to when the overall performance seemed to require stimulation; she deliberately sings closer to the melody than usual but attempts to add dramatic impact by ending each stanza with a sort of sighing glissando. This mannerism has often proved effective for lesser artists than Billie, but when she uses it, it seems to detract from the intensity of her performance. It was a trick she rarely used after 1937.

Four of the musicians who played on the first Wilson–Holiday session were also on the second date. Roy Eldridge is again in good form, and drummer Cozy Cole's brush-work on 'What a Night ...' is highly effective. The least satisfying of the three songs recorded is 'It's Too Hot For Words', a run-of-the-mill melody with trite lyrics. However, Billie completely ignores these limitations and gives a fine performance.

The fact that Billie could work wonders in transforming insignificant tunes into memorable songs worked against her in the sense that even when she was well established she was rarely given first option on tunes that song-pluggers held high hopes for. She was in reality a publisher's dream, since by the magnaminity of her talents she could turn a very ordinary tune into a melody that people would respond to decades later. She interpreted lyrics more compellingly than even the most egocentric originator might have thought possible, and with her intuitive talent for melody she could create a layer of feeling that even surprised the composer. Again and again during the 1930s she triumphs over mediocre material, as on her third session with Wilson where she takes all the pain out of 'Twenty Four Hours a Day'. Wilson assembled several all-star musicians for this date including Roy Eldridge, Chu

Berry, Benny Morton, Cozy Cole and John Kirby. No written arrangements were used this time, though here and there the musicians worked out organised endings for some of the tunes, as on 'Yankee Doodle ...' where the concluding musical riff is an embryo version of Chu Berry's subsequently popular composition 'Christopher Columbus'.

Teddy Wilson selected his musicians from various touring bands, and this made it difficult for him to re-assemble the same men for consecutive sessions; only Cozy Cole was able to be present on the third and the fourth Wilson–Holiday recordings but, by way of consolation, Johnny Hodges, Duke Ellington's famous alto-sax player was brought into the group for several recordings during 1935 and 1937; his ravishingly beautiful interpretation of 'I Cried For You' (recorded in June 1936) is a perfect preliminary for Billie's vocal chorus. This particular tune was the first standard tune that Billie ever recorded (it having been a favourite throughout the early 1930s). Significantly, it outsold her previous releases. Billie could make an ordinary song into a good one, but usually she turned in a great performance when she was singing a good song.

Ten days after the 'I Cried For You' session Billie made the first recordings that were issued under her own name. Billie Holiday and her Orchestra made their record debut in July 1936. The personnel of the pick-up group (selected by the composer Bernie Hanighen, who was then a recording director for the American Recording Company) was all white, except for drummer Cozy Cole. It was virtually an all-star line-up, with Bunny Berigan on trumpet, Artie Shaw on clarinet, Dick McDonough on guitar, Arthur 'Pete' Peterson on bass, and Joe Bushkin on piano. This was the date that saw the birth of 'Billie's Blues': neither the band, nor Billie, were happy with the tune that was scheduled to be that fourth and last title of the day, and at Hanighen's suggestion an impromptu blues was substituted. Billie later said that the lyrics were a compilation of lines that she had been singing since childhood. Berigan, always impressive when playing the blues, contributes an impassioned solo, but Artie Shaw (who could play brilliantly) sounds insipid here, and failed to convey the emotion that he said he experienced at the session. On the next Billie session (in September 1936) Shaw was replaced by the talented Bob Crosby sideman Irving Fazola. Berigan is again present, and displays sensitivity in his mellow cup-muted playing. The stand-out title from the four tunes recorded is 'A Fine Romance' — which Billie chose as one of her favourites when she summarised the recordings she made during the 1930s. Her vocal on that title is a rare blend of musicianship and sardonic humour, her diction — as ever — is impeccable, and the elegant pauses that she inserts between stanzas serve to enhance Dorothy Fields' fine lyrics without changing one word.

Billie's variations applied to the phrasing of a song, not to the alteration of its lyrics. She often changed an existing tune by singing an alternative note within that song's harmonies; she could also give the original melody a whole new set of time values, but she very rarely altered a single word.

Billie, flexible and inventive, had no set method of working, her theoretical knowledge of music was rudimentary, and she once said that she could only sing a song the way that she felt it. Sometimes, she sang the tune almost straight, as on 'The Way You Look Tonight'; conversely on 'I Can't Give You Anything But Love' she never goes near the original melody. Both of these songs were recorded under Teddy Wilson's name (in October and November 1936). Two months later, Wilson and other musicians who had played on the November session (including Jonah Jones, Ben Webster, Allen Reuss, Cozy Cole and John Kirby) took part in a session under Billie's name.

This date produced the usual quota of four titles, but two versions of one of the tunes 'I've Got My Love To Keep Me Warm' were issued. These two 'takes' are very similar; once Billie had established her own interpretation of a song she seldom looked immediately for further variatons. Her personal life at the time of this particular recording was chock-full of uncertainty, but she let nothing affect her performance whilst she was in the recording studio. During the years 1936-39 she recorded dozens of second takes, they show that Billie had developed a very impressive consistency.

Teddy Wilson once explained why further recordings of the same song were attempted after one satisfactory performance had already been waxed, 'In those days, we always did at least two takes, because they were recording on a delicate wax, and they had to have two in case one was spoiled. You could ruin the wax with a toothpick. We preferred to get three good takes, just as insurance.'

The same procedure applied to sessions under Billie's name. In quality and format Billie's recordings were similar to those issued under Teddy Wilson's name; the main difference was that on Billie's dates she sang the first chorus of the song, and returned to conclude the record, whereas on Wilson's dates the band invariably played the last chorus.

Most of the Wilson–Holiday sessions were well recorded, but on several of the 1935-36 sessions there seems to have been difficulty in finding a good balance for the guitar. There was no such problem on the session that took place on 25 January 1937 when Freddie Greene, indisputably the best rhythm guitarist in the world, was present. But it wasn't Greene's inimitable work that made the occasion one of the most important in the history of jazz, the significance of the date is that it marks the first recording shared by Billie and tenor-saxophonist Lester Young (then working in Count Basie's Orchestra). This initial amalgamation of two enormously talented artists – sharing an almost telepathic understanding – was enhanced by the presence of a third sympatico, trumpeter Buck Clayton (also with Count Basie). John Hammond, who organised the session, said, 'There was an interplay between Lester, Buck and Billie that was unique. I don't believe we've ever got this kind of interplay in the years since Billie's prime.' Trombonist Benny Morton has also spoken of the amazing unity of conception that these three shared, 'Lester, Buck and Billie were a better match than the other horns. The sound of Billie's voice was unusual when matched with other girl vocalists, and so was the sound of Lester's horn different from any other tenor-player, they were right for each other.'

Lester Young did not have a decisive effect in shaping Billie's vocal style, there is little discernible difference in her singing in 1936 (before she ever heard Lester) or recordings made in 1938. Nevertheless, Lester was all important for Billie, because his kindred example consolidated her determination to retain an individual style. Her artistic loneliness was over; she had, at last, met a musician whose approach was almost identical in concept to her own. It's conceivable that Billie, without Lester's example and encouragement, could well have been swayed by those who urged her to sing in a more commercial style. Worse still, she might well have carried out her threat to quit the music business.

Not that Lester was a pillar of unwavering resolve. He too occasionally needed encouragement, and Billie sometimes had to re-impart the confidence that she had received from him. She spoke of Lester's early problems, 'You know everyone when he first started thought, this man, his tone is too thin ... Lester used to go out of his mind getting reeds, you know, to sound big like Chu Berry, I told him, "It doesn't matter because you have a beautiful tone. After a while everybody's going to be copying you." And so it came to be.'

# CHAPTER TWO

The mutual admiration that existed between Billie and Lester made them perfect musical partners. In a four-bar introduction (as on 'He's Funny That Way' or 'Mean To Me') Lester could set a mood that exactly suited Billie, and his sensitive fill-ins could sustain the exact nuance of that mood.

The ratio of great recorded performances was highest when she was accompanied by musicians from Count Basie's Band; Basie himself didn't take part in any of the recordings because he was contracted to a rival company. On the first of the Billie–Lester sessions, the pianist (and leader) was Teddy Wilson. Initially the three men from Basie's rhythm section were a little unsettled by Wilson's presence; drummer Jo Jones said, 'Teddy's style didn't fit in too well with us, and we'd have to bully him to get what we wanted. He could deliver though, when he had to.' None of this fidgetiness within the rhythm section is apparent to the listener, the accompaniment seems ideal.

By the time the next session was due to be recorded the Basie men were out of New York on tour, and a different personnel, hand-picked from various bands, was assembled.

Henry 'Red' Allen was on trumpet, and although this magificent stylist must surely be high on most listings of great jazz trumpeters, he doesn't sound an apt accompanist for Billie. Both Red and Billie were strongly individualistic, and there seems little empathy when they worked together. Nobody on the session plays badly, but the only close link between band and singer is Teddy Wilson − impeccable as ever. Despite untidiness in the ensembles, and shortcomings in liaison between band and singer, Billie sings well throughout the session, particularly on 'My Last Affair', a good, but little-known tune by pianist Haven Johnson.

Soon after that February 1937 date, Billie joined Count Basie's Orchestra, and this meant that on every session from May 1937 to January 1938 she was accompanied in the recording studios by someone from within that band; the result is that almost every record from this period is exceptionally good. Billie's small-band recordings from this period have long been favourites with devotees, and in recent years, a few 'air-shots' (private recordings taken from radio broadcasts) of Billie with the full Basie Band have been issued on LP. and they reveal how favourably everyone in Basie's Band responded to Billie's inspiration (typified by Jo Jones' reaction 'Hasn't been one like Billie before, since, and never will be'). Lester Young surpasses himself on the full-band version of 'I Can't Get Started', his playing on the ballad is tender without being sentimental, and subtle without being obscure.

These were golden years for Lester too. His solo on take three of 'When You're Smiling' (recorded with Billie in January 1938) has been cited as one of the greatest tenor-saxophone solos ever recorded, but amazingly, his playing on the lesser-known take four, though substantially different, is almost as brilliant. There seemed no limit to the man's inventiveness, for on the next title recorded ('I Can't Believe That You're In Love With Me'), he plays two totally different solos on successive takes, and both creations are hauntingly beautiful. Billie was doubtless inspired; however, she retains her usual practice, and only makes small

213

variations here-and-there during the various takes.

Both 'When You're Smiling', and 'I Can't Believe ... ' were well-established standards by 1938; more and more evergreens were being included in Billie's sessions in place of current 'pop' songs. Inevitably some new material was recorded, and Billie sometimes has to prove that she could turn dross into silver. One notable exception is 'Born To Love'; Billie sound uninspired and most of the musicians present sound convincingly misanthropic. Billie once described how she and Lester Young often shared a bottle of top-and-bottom, (a 50-50 mixture of port and gin) at recording sessions. On this occasion the brew may well have temporarily taken its toll of inventive powers; however, heads must soon have cleared because both versions of 'Without Your Love' (the next tune recorded) are magnificent.

Billie left Basie's Band in the spring of 1938, and for two sessions following the break-up no Basie sidemen were present on Billie's recording dates. However, the pick-up band that accompanied her on the May 1938 session plays satisfactorily, and one of the tunes recorded, 'You Go To My Head', brought a glimmer of public acclaim to Billie. The magazine *Mademoiselle* picked it as their 'record of the month'. Billie made many better recordings, but the fact that there is very little instrumental improvising on the record may have been the factor that especially appealed to the magazine's selection panel.

A mention of Billie in the non-musical press was a rarity, but in the music magazines her name was appearing more frequently, and almost all of the reviews published were extremely favourable. In *Down Beat* (June 1937), George Frazier wrote, 'Billie Holiday's singing on "I Must Have That Man" is perfection itself, and stands her as one of the truly great vocalists of all time.'

But despite a regular stream of enthusiastic praise from music-critics Billie still lacked a large following. Possibly, her joining Artie Shaw could have provided this, but she was not contractually free to record with Shaw's Band, and therefore didn't get any of the promotional benefits that usually came to singers who recorded with big, white, swing bands. During Billie's year with Shaw they made one recording together, 'Any Old Time', and due to an argument over recording contracts the production of the disc was halted; few promotional copies reached disc-jockeys, and the air-time that the record received was minuscule.

Billie continued to record under her own name whilst she was with Shaw. Whenever possible she used her ex-colleagues from the Basie Band as accompanists, but often a pick-up band was assembled in the studio. By contrast, on a session in June 1938 she used the nucleus of the highly successful John Kirby Band, including the remarkable trumpet player Charlie Shavers. The date went well and produced two strong recordings, 'Says My Heart' and 'I'm Gonna Lock My Heart And Throw Away The Key'. Billie could work contentedly with backings that were no more than competent, but if sparks of real creativity came from the accompaniment she always responded with something extra.

She was well aware of the importance of supporting musicians, and stressed this when she was interviewed by Leonard Feather in 1938. Billie, commenting on the possibilities of a tour of Britain, said, 'I'd better bring a pianist with me. Those musicians over there, they can just about read and that's all, huh?' In January 1939, the *Amsterdam News* of New York reported, 'She once refused 250 dollars a week to go to England because she didn't believe that the Britishers had captured the feelings for swing well enough to inspire her.' The same feature mentioned that, 'Billie is quite definite about the choice of songs, and prefers to sing the way she feels, rather than the way audiences want her to.' By late 1938, this was certainly true of Billie's club dates; she chose her own programme, and though she often performed requests, she made it clear tht she didn't automatically sing a song in public simply because she had recorded it. But in the studios she still hadn't complete control over the choice of songs to be recorded, and on a session waxed soon after the feature in which she mentioned the necessity of careful selection she tackled four tunes that were very dubious contenders for lasting popularity. The backing band on this session (under Teddy Wilson's direction) was semi-arranged, and racially mixed, in that (like some previous Wilson dates) it included white musicians – in this instance Bobby Hackett, Bud Freeman and Toots Mondello. It was also the first time that trombonist Trummy Young had ever recorded with Billie; his reactions to the session are typical of the respect and admiration that most musicians felt for Lady Day, 'Billie thrilled us with her interpretation of these songs, she was a true stylist.'

But the adoration of the musicians didn't boost record sales, and by late 1938 Billie realised that she was getting nowhere fast with her recordings; sales figures rarely rose, and in some cases they dwindled. A change of format on the Teddy Wilson dates made little difference. By then Wilson was planning to start a big band, and the sides he made with Billie in the fall of 1938 reflect his ambitions, but despite magnificent singing and fine playing the general public remained uninterested.

Billie's next session with Wilson was to be the last that she did with him for over two years; she had begun her long residency at the Café Society and throughout her stay there she used the musicians who worked with her at the club on her record dates.

The bassist in the band, Johnny Williams, has fond memories of these sessions, 'I can see her now, coming in to record with a little taste for all the fellows, and we would be glad to go have a bite to eat with her after the date.'

On the first session with the Café Society musicians (recorded in March 1939) the band's leader, trumpeter Frankie Newton, was absent through illness and Hot Lips Page came in as a temporary replacement. The recordings prove that pianist Sonny White, though obviously an admirer of Teddy Wilson's playing, was not in the same class as his mentor. Sax-player Tab Smith is the dominating musician on the date, and his soprano-sax solo on 'Everything Happens For The Best' (a number he co-composed with Billie) is impressively dramatic. Trumpeter Hot Lips Page, whose

introduced 'Strange Fruit' into her club repertoire; on record the effect took a while to manifest itself. However, when Lady Day summarised the full impact of the 'Strange Fruit' recording in terms of record sales, publicity, prestige, and booking offers she realised that some of the general public were, at last, responding to her, and even if their numbers were not enormous, their reactions signified to Billie that she had been cast as a singer of slow ('messagy') songs. It was a role that some part of Billie's character found appealing. The days of hearing her sing an up-tempo song laced with buoyant humour were few and far between after 1941.

The success of 'Strange Fruit' meant that she now had the right to veto material that she felt to be unsuitable for recording, but this freedom didn't open up wider horizons for Billie; somehow it narrowed the scope of the material selected. Thenceforth, the preponderance of Billie's material was either slow, or medium-slow. Billie wanted every song to have the impact of 'Strange Fruit', but songs with such deep emotional content are rare; as substitutes, Billie chose to record several songs that were decidedly mawkish.

Throughout the rest of her career, Billie seldom sang new up-tempo songs; the few that she did include in her programmes were usually re-creations of tunes that she had sung in earlier years. Had she shown any rhythmic weaknesses when working at fast tempi one could more easily understand this embargo on speed.

Although 'Strange Fruit' brought a lot of publicity to Billie, the record itself got scant radio-time in the U.S.A. because of the stark clarity of its lyrics. Across the Atlantic, the British Broadcasting Corporation also practised a form of censorship by decreeing that the song was unsuitable for transmission. However, the recurring publicity connected with the song meant that by 1942 most disc-jockeys were aware of Billie's existence. It was ironical that by the time Billie had kindled the radio men's interest many of her bright performances were out-of-catalogue and unavailable. During the early 1940s, when the majority of American listeners heard Billie for the first time, she was invariably singing slow

songs. Small wonder that the general impression was that Billie only sang sombre ballads.

A chain reaction set in; most of the requests that Billie got were for her recent recordings, and the increased air-play and juke-box coverage meant that she got more requests than usual. This seemed to confirm to Billie that she had made the right decision in going along with those who had cast her image as a torch singer.

# CHAPTER THREE

        In June 1942, Billie recorded one song
('Travellin' Light') with Paul Whiteman's Orchestra —
because of the subsequent American Federation of
Musicians' ban on recordings, which affected all recording
artistes, the session was Billie's last studio-date until March
1944.

The melody of 'Travellin' Light' (a slow ballad) was
originally an instrumental feature for its composer,
trombonist Trummy Young. Johnny Mercer added the lyrics,
and Paul Whiteman (who is often criticised for inadequately
featuring the many jazzmen he employed) asked especially
that Billie record the number with his Orchestra. On the
record, Billie gives a telling performance but the benefits of
this one-off shot were minimal, since there was no likelihood
of Billie working regularly with Whiteman's Orchestra.

Billie's dramatic victory in the first Jazz Poll organised by
*Esquire* magazine meant that she was well featured at one of
the most star-studded jazz shows ever held — the January
1944 New York Metropolitan Opera House Concert. The
union ban on recordings was still in operation, but the
concert was recorded for issue on 'V' Discs — the war-time

recordings that were produced exclusively for service personnel. Billie is in great voice, and responds warmly to the inspired accompaniment; two of the three songs recorded are slow, the third being a medium-paced version of the war-time hit 'I'll Get By', a tune that Billie had originally recorded in the 1930s. Two months later, when commercial recordings were resumed, Billie waxed the same song for the Commodore label.

The accompaniment for all three 1944 Commodore sessions was directed by pianist Eddie Heywood, a fine musician, albeit a painstaking one. Although his band was strong in soloists, including trombonist Vic Dickenson, the emphasis is on arrangements rather than individual improvisation, the usual pattern being sustained band harmonies behind Billie's vocals, culminating in protracted endings. The band had rather a sedate style, despite the presence of the great drummer Sid Catlett.

As far as vocal technique, Billie is close to her best on these Commodore sessions; she swoops high and low inserting oblique notes that composers might well have kicked themselves for not including. During her heyday, Billie used a working range of a tenth – usually from low A to middle C sharp, occasionally she sang beyond these notes, but usually only for special effect. It was not an extensive range when compared to many other vocalists, (the exceptional Ella Fitzgerald is quite at ease over two octaves), but one never gets the feeling that Billie was technically restricted for she used countless inflections within her range.

One of the tunes recorded on Commodore was Johnny Green's composition 'I'm Yours'. Green gave his views on Billie's recording during one of Leonard Feather's famous blindfold tests. 'Vocally, it's wonderful, and the liberties taken are within the intent of the melody and the harmony. They're attractive, provocative, and infectious. The intonation is impeccable.'

But despite Billie's consummate musicianship, there is hint of pre-meditated vocal posing on many of the Commodore sides, a feeling that the languid vocal mannerisms are being

222

self-consciously grafted on to a style that was already perfectly formed. One of the best sides for the label is the trio version of 'On The Sunny Side Of The Street'; Billie seems to recapture the lilting humour that distinguished so many of her earlier records, probably due to the fact that the accompaniment is more relaxed and informal than usual. Heywood plays one of his most interesting solos, and Billie, weaving in and around the melody, gives a sparkling display of controlled casualness. Ironically, this was the last title that she made for Commodore; the label's owner, Milt Gabler, had by then begun his long association with Decca. Eventually, through Gabler's auspices Billie began to record for Decca.

Billie particularly favoured the idea of recording with a string section, accordingly, the orchestra assembled for her October 1944 debut session for Decca had violins to augment the trumpet and saxophone front-line – a much less common accompaniment procedure in those days than now. The whole of the backings are written out, save for a tenor-sax obbligato. On the two tunes recorded ('Lover Man' and 'No More') Billie sings throughout – both tunes are slow ballads. Sales figures were encouraging, and through the success of this recording, 'Lover Man' (which had been written in the early 1940s) became a standard song. The other tune from the session 'No More' (composed by Toots Camarata, who directed the session) is full of skilful musical devices, but seems to lack the assets of a really good song. Nevertheless, Billie (in 1952) cited 'No More' as one of her own three favourite recordings, together with 'Gloomy Sunday' and 'Fine and Mellow'.

There was no dramatic change in Billie's singing during the entire time she spent with Decca, but during her years with that company she became more and more subtle, and the subtlety eliminated a lot of the sparkle in her voice; but there is no monotony, for Billie's vocals were as bold and inventive as ever.

Bob Haggart, who was Billie's musical director on some of the Decca sessions, was always enthralled by her gift of reshaping melodies. Recently he said 'The release to the tune "There Is No Greater Love" (recorded in 1947) is an excellent example of how Billie could take a standard tune and add her Midas touch to the existing melody – giving the song a whole new value.'

The Decca recordings are less interesting to devotees of instrumental jazz, but many top-class vocalists find this period of Billie's work particularly satisfying. Peggy Lee once chose 'Good Morning Heartache' (from 1946) as her favourite Billie record, and Sarah Vaughan listed 'You Better Go Now' from the previous year as her top Billie record.

During 1945 and 1946, Billie's current boy-friend, trumpeter Joe Guy, played on most of her recordings; his presence adds a flavour of the be-bop sounds that were then filling most of the clubs on New York's 52nd Street. But Guy's contributions were usually restricted to short muted solos, or obbligati – usually the arrangements left few loopholes for inspired improvisation by the sidemen.

It was this change in the jazz proportion of the accompaniments that caused many of the fans who had regularly bought Billie's records since 1936 to prefer her earlier works. They had come to expect the accompanying musicians to sound as emotionally involved in the recording as Billie herself was; when the backings became smoother and more predictable, some fans found the change unwelcome. In effect, these people wanted a jazz-group which featured a great jazz singer, rather than a great jazz singer who was accompanied by session-musicians, some of whom might be jazz-orientated. There was a distinct change in the style of Billie's accompaniments from 1945 onwards, but this change in backings was more definite than any lessening of Billie's vocal prowess.

It would be all too easy to associate a decline in Billie's artistry with her dependence on hard drugs. We know that narcotics eventually contributed to her death, but during the mid-1940s, when she was heavily addicted, she still sang marvellously. This is apparent on a live recording made when Billie guested at a Louis Armstrong concert held at Carnegie

Hall in February 1947. Louis announces Billie as his co-star in the film *New Orleans,* she then sings 'Do You Know What It Means To Miss New Orleans' – a song from the film. The version is so moving and convincing that one could imagine Billie pining for old Louisiana; however Lady had no eyes for anywhere south of the Mason–Dixon line, and she had never got around even to visiting the Crescent City.

One becomes aware of the first signs of a change in Billie's voice on the records that she made in the year that she was released from Alderson Reformatory (1948). During the late 1930s when Billie was having great difficulty in finding happiness and security, she shielded her listeners from direct contact with her sadness. Adversity may have stimulated her genius, but it never overshadowed, or distorted, her singing. But from 1948 onwards, her despair is often given overt exposure; the humiliations and disappointments that scarred Billie's life so deeply became an inextricable part of the majority of her performances. By then, almost everyone throughout America knew her name, but she was known because of something that society judged an infamy rather than through the dozens of magnificent recordings that she had made. The popular press called Billie 'a talented songstress made tragic by drug addiction', and Billie's performances seem to emphasise this tragedy; an acrid discontent seeped into her vocals.

But despair wasn't completely immovable, and Billie could still achieve her earlier, happier approach, as she did on one of her last Decca recordings, in September 1949, when she shared a record-date with her childhood idol Louis Armstrong. Trumpeter Bernie Previn, who played on the session, recalls how excited Billie was at the prospect of working with Louis, but despite the array of talent, and the participants' enthusiasm, the records didn't sell well. A series of Billie recordings, featuring songs that Bessie Smith sang, were no more successful commercially, even though the vocal breaks on 'T'ain't Nobody's Business' are miraculous examples of jazz timing.

Despite Billie's artistry, or perhaps because of it, none of the recordings that Billie made for Decca were huge sellers at the time of their release. Various styles of accompaniment were tried, ranging from vocal choirs ('Weep No More'), through string sections ('Please Tell Me Now') to hard-hitting big band jazz ('Them There Eyes'); none brought an immediate jackpot to the recording company.

During the 1940s an unusual situation existed concerning issues of Billie's recordings – Columbia still had a number of Billie's recordings from the late 1930s that they had never issued; during the 1940s they began to release them periodically. In 1949, Michael Levin, then writing for *Down Beat* was emphatic in telling his readers that they would get a truer idea of Billie's immense talent by listening to her pre-1940 recordings. He was also emphatic in his denunciation of her first post-Alderson recordings. Apropos of 'Porgy', he wrote, 'There is a limit to the distortion to which you can subject a good song for purposes of your own interpretation, and this is it.' In the following year, Levin incurred the wrath of Billie's fans when he wrote of her October 1949 recording of 'You're My Thrill', 'it is rapidly becoming Lady Yesterday'.

Levin's words were more candid than those of many other writers who quietly hinted that they felt that Billie was over the hill, but in the midst of this critical hostility and indifference no one suggested that Billie had ceased to sing jazz. Lady would have found that impossible. However the general public, as a rule, do not usually buy huge numbers of any jazz recording: on the rare occasions that a jazz record does enter the hit parade it is usually because a tune, or the treatment of it, has some novelty value. Billie's work, devoid of gimmicks, stood little chance of achieving the sales figures that the post-war record industry demanded. Inevitably, Billie and Decca parted company.

Billie soon signed for the Aladdin label, a smaller, independent set-up. It was announced that Billie had a year's contract with the company, but only four titles were made for Aladdin, all recorded at the same session. The issues were given a lukewarm reception by the reviewers, though a brisk

226

'Blue Turning Gray Over You' received some praise. Unfortunately, the discs were practically ignored by America's disc-jockeys. For a long time after her imprisonment, Billie was shunned by the mass communications media. In 1951, *Metronome* magazine organised a poll that enabled disc-jockeys to pick their favourite female singers. Billie didn't gain a place in the entire listing.

Other than the four Aladdin sides, there would have been no other recordings of Billie from the year 1951 had not some of her radio performances and club appearances been taped 'live' and subsequently issued. Most notable of these recordings are the sides taken from broadcasts that originated from the Storyville Club in Boston. They were taken from a broadcast. It sounds possible that Billie may have had a taste or two before the show went on the air, here and there her pronunciation is slurred, but this doesn't detract, because the whole performance has a nonchalant air of merriness that is all too rare in Billie's later work. This flair graces the medium-paced 'You're Driving Me Crazy', on which tenorist Stan Getz, who was also working at the Storyville Club, can be heard playing a gentle, admiring accompaniment. Billie's pitching on these tracks isn't exemplary, but the zest with which she sings more than compensates. The high-spot of these Boston recordings is Gershwin's 'Porgy', infinitely superior to the acceptable version that Billie originally recorded in 1948.

# CHAPTER FOUR

1952 saw a big change in Billie's fortunes as far as income from recordings was concerned; that was the year she signed with Norman Granz's recording company. This development enabled her to resume recording with small groups jam-packed with top-class jazzmen. The Verve formula was similar to the early Teddy Wilson–Billie sessions, but one immediate difference was that a great percentage of tunes that Billie recorded for Granz's company were standards and evergreens – first-class tunes with memorable lyrics – the rest were re-makes of Billie's early successes. One sad aspect of this whole series is that by the time Billie was regularly recording songs that were commensurate with her vast talents her voice had begun to lose its elasticity and responsiveness. However, her gift for interpreting lyrics became even more astute, many of her Clef recordings show how often she was able to add a nuance to a song that had been sung by countless vocalists.

On every recording that Billie made for Norman Granz she was backed by top-class jazzmen, but despite their proficiency, invention and swing, it's easy to form the impression that the accompanists are not always in the same emotional compartment as Billie. In the 1950s, Billie told Jimmie Rowles of some of the problems she encountered in the recording studios. 'It's a pleasure working with you again. Jesus Christ! I've been with some pretty big shots and they don't dig me no kinda way ... they don't understand me, and I don't understand them. Like this last date, Norman (Granz) was in Japan, he called me ... he'd taken care of the date ... all the best musicians in the country – drunk. My date fucked up, the whole date, supposed to make at least eight sides, I made three good ones. Nearly broke my heart, and I needed the loot, at the time I was in kinda bad shape. I told Norman, please don't release nothing, but he did.'

Billie always had a particular need for sympathetic accompaniment, this is why the 1954 version of 'I Thought About You' is one of the most satisfying things that she did during the 1950s, for on this title Billie is accompanied only by pianist Bobby Tucker. His support is totally sympathetic and definitely enhances Billie's expressive interpretation of Johnny Mercer's poignant lyric. Those who heard Billie work at this time say that the track gives an accurate likeness of how she sounded on her night-club engagements.

Trumpeter Miles Davis was one who positively preferred hearing Billie with a minimum number of accompanists. In 1958 he told Nat Hentoff, 'I'd rather hear her with Bobby Tucker ... she doesn't need any horns. She sounds like one anyway.' The trumpeter also felt that Billie of the 1950s was 'much more mature than previously'. He added, 'You know, she's not thinking now what she was in 1937, and she's probably learned more about different things. And she still has control, probably more control now than then. No, I don't think she's in a decline. A lot of singers try to sing like Billie, but just the act of playing behind the beat doesn't make it sound soulful.'

A session recorded at a German concert, during Billie's long-awaited 1954 tour of Europe, shows how Billie could rise to the occasion. Leonard Feather who emceed the show, felt that if Billie had chosen to live in Europe permanently it might well have been her artistic and physical salvation; from the recorded evidence it seems that he has a valid point. Billie responds to the warm greeting of the eager audience and starts the show with a fine version of 'Blue Moon' – skilfully and flamboyantly backed by pianist Carl Drinkard, aided by a rhythm section. On this occasion, Billie sounds superb on the up-tempo songs, and 'Them There Eyes' shows that she hadn't lost the rhythmic freedom which allowed her to float over an emphatic four beats in a bar rhythm section and yet still swing. Lady sounds absolutely at ease when doubling up the tempo for the new version of 'I Cried For You'. Six of the titles recorded that evening were re-makes, amongst them a new version of 'My Man', which Billie recorded at least nine times during the 1950s, this song was always one of Billie's triumphs, and the fine vocalist Anita O'Day gave writer Don Gold her enthusiastic reaction to Billie's singing of this number, 'Only someone who has lived the way she does, who has lived such experiences could interpret "My Man" as she does – so beautifully, so grand, so sincere.'

Billie wasn't unduly worried that she was inviting comparisons with her earlier performances of the same songs. She felt that she had a new angle for each tune, and she was positive that the new accompaniments would be up-to-date enough to discourage people from airing the view that her finest work was done with pre-war bands.

During the early 1950s, writer Nat Hentoff was the undisputed champion of Billie's cause; he made a point of emphasising his devotion to her singing from all eras. In a *Down Beat* review dated 20 October 1954, he wrote of a new Clef LP, 'As for comparing it with earlier Teddy Wilson–Billie sessions, what's the point? Count your blessings in having both, and that's my general attitude on this business of separating Billie into time periods. Speaking of time, Billie's beat and variations thereon never cease to be among the seven wonders of jazz.'

Other critics were impressed by Billie's recordings for Norman Granz, and her new version of 'Yesterdays' (one of the first recordings that presented Oscar Peterson on organ) was compared to her earlier version, with honours even. Her re-make of 'What A Little Moonlight ...' (with the ingeniously different timing of the words, 'I Love You') also won widespread praise. None of Billie's re-makes were slavish copies of her earlier versions; many of the re-presentations were sung at tempos that varied from the originals. Lady also liked to introduce alternate lyrics on 'new' versions of her previous recordings; on 'He's Funny That Way' she adds the rarely-heard verse, whereas on 'Love Me Or Leave Me' she omits the verse that she had sung on her 1941 recording – this particular tune was one of several re-makes for which the key was lowered into an area more suited to Billie's deepened voice. Occasionally Billie was able to retain the original key, as on the 1955 version of 'I've Got My Love To Keep Me Warm', which is sung in the same key as the 1935 recording, but nothing could hide the fact that Billie's range was slowly becoming more restricted: yet unpredictable as ever, she could still amaze and delight her listeners by unexpectedly soaring to a high note. Billie never shirked songs that were impossible to coast on; her performance on Duke Ellington's challenging composition 'Do Nothing 'Til You Hear From Me' has some great moments, particularly on the concluding lines where she phrases the words 'hold a thrill' in a spine-tingling way. On the same session there's another great lyrical moment where Billie on the refreshingly fast 'Lover Come Back To Me' sings the word 'cold' in a way that throws snow into your face.

Both of these tunes were recorded with Tony Scott's Orchestra, an all-star studio group which featured trumpeter Charlie Shavers. Shavers' dazzling technique is well evident, as is his versatility – ranging from the cheekiness of his solo on 'I've Got My Love To Keep Me Warm', to the tenderness of his playing on 'Everything Happens To Me' (a number on which Billie makes the most of the expressive lyrics). On the same session, Billie did a re-make of 'I Wished On The Moon' – the first title that she ever recorded with Teddy Wilson (in 1935) – the latter version adds Dorothy Parker's subtle verse. Swinging versions of two standards, 'Always' and 'Ain't Misbehavin', were also recorded; on both of these

231

tunes Billie used an approach that was a stylistic habit in later years: when she felt that her listeners were totally familiar with the original melody, she boldy began improvising from the first note. Boldness is the keyword for Tony Scott's highly original (and technically formidable) clarinet work. Most of the arrangements from this session are neat and tidy affairs, the most effective being Irving Berlin's 'Say It Isn't So'. Billie sounds admirably relaxed during the changes in tempo, and the questioning tone that she adopts for the Berlin lyrics sounds convincingly realistic.

But from recordings made six months after that session it's easy to discern that ill health was plaguing Billie. On the August 1955 recordings (made in California), she is surrounded by old friends, including Benny Carter, Harry Edison, and Jimmie Rowles, and although these fine musicians gave her superb accompaniment they could not rejuvenate her. All too often Billie sounds so sad and tired that the listener feels that a sob, or a curse, are alarmingly close.

Most of the tunes are taken slowly, and although Carter's saxophone playing is the epitome of grace on the ballads, the medium-paced 'Please Don't Talk About Me' (with good solos by Carter, Edison and Barney Kessel) comes as something of a relief. Carter's alto-playing also distinguishes a new version of 'I Get A Kick Out Of You', but despite a crisply played latin-american rhythm, and appropriate trumpet work by Harry Edison, Billie's performance on this, like all the other titles from the August 1955 sessions, only lives from phrase to phrase — some of them are haphazard, others awe-inspiring.

There followed a ten-month gap in Billie's recordings which lasted until June 1956, when Billie did further recordings with Tony Scott's Orchestra. All of the songs recorded were re-makes, except for 'Lady Sings The Blues' (a new composition that tied-in with the promotion of Billie's auto-biography). This new work is, predictably, not a blues, but it is in slow tempo, as are all the other six songs recorded — the fastest being 'God Bless The Child'. Billie's selection of

songs that surveyed her career were all slow, sad themes that reeked of unrequited love — the exception being 'Strange Fruit'.

Billie is predictably intense on 'Strange Fruit'; on this re-make Charlie Shavers performs some brilliant, if entirely inappropriate, frahlich-styled trumpet work. There was apparently an air of friction in the studio between some of Billie's accompanists, but this doesn't seem to have caused a rush of blood to anybody's head, vocal chords, or finger tips. Billie usually worked well with Tony Scott, but on this occasion she sounds uninspired, and her constant repetition of the mannerism where she ends a song by singing the ninth note before the tonic makes for wearisome listening.

Anyone hearing this set could be forgiven for concluding that Billie Holiday's career as a great artiste was over, and that her only contribution to music was likely to be a series of pale, and at times distressing, re-runs of her old stand-bys. But Billie always retained her unpredictability, and on her next session (made during a return trip to California) she created a magnificent version of 'Do Nothing 'Til You Hear From Me'. She had made a satisfying version of the same tune during the previous year, but her August 1956 performance is an example of a great jazz singer giving a deep and passionate exhibition of her art. It is not Billie's swan song, but it is one of the last of her memorable performances.

The session marked a musical re-union between tenor-saxist Ben Webster and Billie. Ben (who had played on the first of the Teddy Wilson–Billie records in July 1935) hadn't recorded with Billie since 1936. In the intervening years he had become an even greater jazzman, his 16-bar solo on 'Do Nothing ...' is masterful, and the often enigmatic Harry Edison plays beautifully here, as does pianist Jimmie Rowles. Though there are several highspots on these sessions nothing eclipses 'Do Nothing ...', the nadir is 'All Or Nothing At All', where Billie's interpretation of the melody can only be called bizarre. Her gift of automatically enhancing a song deserted her during these last years. Sadly,

in this twilight time, she often gave renditions which seem to obscure composers' intentions.

During the last two years of her life, Billie proved that she could occasionally return to form, but from 1957 onwards, her work is usually a series of tantalising glimpses of genius mingled with self-parody. One gets the uneasy feeling that, by then, Billie felt that she was singing into a mirror. Her grimaces affect the delivery of her words, and some lyrics are hissed out – often haphazardly. Her pitching, once immaculate, drifted in and out of control, and the widened vibrato that she used in later days made her voice sound as though it belonged to a much older woman.

Billie once said, 'Anything I do sing, it's part of my life,' and during her last years she gives us clear indication of her anguished existence. But the strains that broke her heart, also crushed the rare ability whereby she could trigger-off a series of deep and varied emotions within her listeners. During the last years the response evoked was more often one of shocked pity. The deep melancholia that had lain just below the surface for so long was now rampant and in full command of Billie's every performance.

Billie's loyal friends and fans joined the sensation-seekers who flocked to Carnegie Hall in November 1956 to hear her sing at the concert that marked the publication of *Lady Sings The Blues*. Everyone there was moved by the occasion, the audience strained their eyes to catch a clearer glimpse of Billie waiting out of the spotlight as Gilbert Millstein read excerpts from the book, they admired the obvious loyalty and devotion that the accompanying musicians showed towards Billie, they called the star back for encore after encore. But the 'live' recordings taken from the concert show that although Billie was still capable of great moments nothing was halting the continued erosion of her vocal powers.

Early in 1957, Billie again returned to California and made yet another session with the Edison, Rowles, Webster alumni. Her spirit might have been willing, but her flesh seems to have been too desperately weak to respond. But whatever Lady's physical condition she commanded the undying

respect of her accompanists. Years later, Jimmie Rowles gave vent to this admiration, 'I think she had the most distinctive voice, interpretation, phrasing, and intrinsic musical feeling of anyone I ever heard. She didn't really sing, she transmitted feeling, she was Soul.'

Soon after Billie left California she began working regularly with Mal Waldron, a pianist who was to remain her accompanist for the rest of her life. Waldron also retains the staunchest admiration for Lady Day's talents; he said, 'Everything she sang meant something. She had a beautiful way with words.'

Mal Waldron's first recordings with Billie took place 'live' at the July 1957 Newport Jazz Festival. Despite fine accompaniment from Waldron on piano, Joe Benjamin on bass, and Jo Jones on drums, Billie sounds very unhappy and ill at ease. This was to be the last recording that Billie made for Norman Granz. It was the conclusion of a series of recordings that had begun by capturing Billie's last period of consistent greatness, and had gradually tracked her decline year by year. The records give us a clear, and extensive picture of Billie's work from 1952 through to 1957; one can only regret that the series didn't start a decade earlier.

Billie's new recording company was Columbia; her first recordings for them took place in December 1957, whilst she was rehearsing for a televised jazz spectacular sponsored by Timex. The backing band was crammed with jazz giants, including three patriarchs of the tenor saxophone, Coleman Hawkins, Ben Webster, and Lester Young. One of the songs that Billie sang on the show, 'Fine and Mellow', was recorded twice. The rehearsal version was issued on Columbia, but the 'live' version, issued later, has the edge — the adrenalin created by the big occasion seems to give added impetus to the performances. These dates were to give us the last examples of Billie working alongside Lester Young; the transformation that the years brought to both of these great artists is uncannily similar. The vigour and optimism that radiated through all their early work had gone, they were both world-weary and disconsolate, but on this occasion the

235

power of pride enabled both of them to give performances that were moving without being sorrowful.

Ten months later, Billie did another 'live' session for Columbia, taking part in a star-studded show held at the Plaza Hotel in New York. Duke Ellington's Orchestra and Jimmy Rushing were also on the session. Billie's two songs, 'When Your Lover Has Gone' and 'Don't Explain' were backed by a rhythm section and trumpeter Buck Clayton, whose tightly muted fill-ins are as elegant as ever. After an apprehensive start, Billie settles down to a medium version of 'When Your Lover ...' and follows it with her slow story-ballad 'Don't Explain'. Neither performance indicates that there had been a miraculous revival of all of Billie's talents during the last months of her life; nevertheless, they show that Lady Day could still turn in a performance that embarrassed no one.

In listening to these tracks it's difficult to believe that they were made in the middle of a long series of studio recordings that Billie had started in February 1958. The studio sessions were also for Columbia, with backings by Ray Ellis and his Orchestra. Billie had heard the scores that Ellis did for his 'Ellis in Wonderland' album, and had specifically asked that her next recordings be accompanied by him.

The emphasis of the arrangements is on the string section, woodwinds and vocal choir — there are brass-players present but the scoring for them is subdued. Two jazz trombonists Urbie Green and J. J. Johnson perform brilliantly in their short outings. The arrangements were not meant to be spectacular, they were to serve as a tasteful and unobtrusive background, one that would give Billie's harassed voice a mellow accompaniment.

Unfortunately, by the time of these recordings, Billie's voice is just not up to the scrutiny that the crystal-clear recordings provide. It's impossible to connect the sound of this crippled voice with the work of the young Billie Holiday. Billie said that she felt 'Lady In Satin' (the first of the LPs) was one of the best records that she ever made; that an artist of Lady's calibre should have thought this, indicates how

236

troubled she was during the last part of her life. Not that Billie was automatically satisfied with all of her latter-day recordings; during her final illness, MGM rushed test-pressings of her last LP to the Metropolitan Hospital, Billie was touched by the gesture, but disappointed with what she heard. Neither the sides with orchestral accompaniment, nor those with the small band backings brought her any joy. However, one of the small band sides, 'There'll Be Some Changes Made', did give her indirect satisfaction. She had particularly asked that this tune be included on the record, even though it had ended in an inconclusive fade-out – like several others on this series of recordings. Billie wanted the song issued as a token of her gratitude towards Herb Marks (the song's publisher), who had never stinted her whenever she had asked for advance payments of any composer royalties that were due to her.

Billie's skill with lyrics never deserted her, but in the end, her prowess as a singer had virtually disappeared, often reflexes alone seem to take her to the safety of a note within the song's harmony, and the listener is left with many anxious moments – both on 'Lady In Satin' and on the final LP.

Perhaps it is this anxiety that appeals to those who have made 'Lady In Satin' into one of Billie's bestselling albums. Allowing for the fact that two of the tracks, 'You've Changed' and 'I'm A Fool' give glimpses of Billie's former greatness, the other performances make for harrowing listening; the vocal sounds seem as private and distressing as photographs of a hopeless medical case.

The song from this session which really caught the public's imagination was 'For All We Know (we may never meet again)'. This is often described as Billie's last recorded performance; actually, it was thirty from the end. The song's love lyrics are given a sinister interpretation by those who actually want it to be Billie's last performance – thus making her ending as neat and clear-cut as the finish of a weepy movie.

It's convenient for the 'hear how she suffers' fans to listen to the sad recitatives on Billie's last recordings and convert them into an equation: born black in a white man's society plus terrifying childhood plus harrowing adolescence plus immense vocal talents plus narcotics plus unhappy love affairs equals Lady Day. Billie Holiday, like almost every black artist of her time, was exploited from the moment she earned her first dollar, her life *was* a terrifying sequence of tragedies, but, by the mysterious processes of artistic creation, her sufferings enabled her to communicate intense feelings to her listeners. It is not squeamishness to prefer hearing Billie when she was able to give an insight into the whole range of human emotions, rather than listen to those LPs which present the sounds of a sick woman in despair.

The anguish that tormented Billie for so long might not have been so disastrous if she had been able to cushion her feelings with the security and satisfaction that widespread success would have brought to her. But she could never bring herself to sing in a style that was commercial enough to achieve the acclaim that the insecure side of her character needed so desperately.

Billie tried to eliminate the miseries that this conflict brought to her by alcohol, narcotics and a succession of love affairs, but the aftermaths of these short-lived solutions only added to her sorrows. Yet, deep-down, she knew exactly what she wanted; long before her health began to fail she summarised her hopes, 'I want peace of mind. I want to sing.' She never achieved the first of those wishes, but for most of her life she offered the world the sound of a voice, the like of which it will never hear again.

# A selected bibliography of book references

| Author (or anthology title) | Title & publisher | Page references |
|---|---|---|
| Albertson, Chris. | BESSIE<br>Stein & Day, N.Y. 1972. | 188-9, et seq. |
| Allen, Walter C. | HENDERSONIA<br>Walter C. Allen, New Jersey 1973. | 129, 338, 357,<br>561, 564, 570. |
| Balliett, Whitney | THE SOUND OF SURPRISE<br>W. Kimber, London 1960. | 109, 135, 146. |
| Balliett, Whitney | DINOSAURS IN THE MORNING<br>J. Dent, London 1964. | 74-80 et seq. |
| Balliett, Whitney | SUCH SWEET THUNDER<br>Macdonald, London 1968. | 5, 51, 57 et seq. |
| Balliett, Whitney | ECSTASY AT THE ONION<br>Bobbs Merrill, N.Y. 1971. | 20, 30 et seq. |
| Berendt, Joachim | THE NEW JAZZ BOOK<br>Peter Owen, London 1964. | 57, 186, 224-7 |
| Black Music In Our Culture<br>(editor: Dominique-René de<br>Lerma) | Kent State Univ., Ohio 1970.<br>(contains John Hammond's 'An Experience in<br>Jazz History') | 51-2 |
| Blesh, Rudi | SHINING TRUMPETS<br>A. Knopf, N.Y. 1958. | 113, 143-4. |
| Blesh, Rudi | COMBO U.S.A.<br>Chilton Book Co, Philadelphia 1971. | 111-133 |
| Charters, Samuel<br>(and Leonard Kunstadt) | JAZZ – A HISTORY OF THE NEW YORK<br>JAZZ SCENE<br>Doubleday, N.Y. 1962. | 287-291. |
| Chilton, John | WHO'S WHO OF JAZZ<br>Bloomsbury Book Shop, London 1970.<br>Chilton Book Co., Phil. 1972. | 169-170. |
| Condon, Eddie<br>(and Richard Gehman) | EDDIE CONDON'S TREASURY OF JAZZ<br>(contains Gilbert Millstein's 'The Commodore<br>Shop')<br>Grove Press, N.Y. 1956. | 80-100. |
| Dance, Stanley | JAZZ ERA – THE FORTIES<br>Macgibbon & Kee, London 1961. | 142-4. |
| Dance, Stanley | THE WORLD OF SWING<br>Scribner's, N.Y. 1974. | 168-9 et seq. |
| Decca Book of Jazz<br>(editor: Peter Gammond) | Muller, London 1958.<br>(contains Vic Bellerby's 'Sing For Your Supper') | 204-216. |
| Dexter, Dave | JAZZ CAVALCADE<br>Criterion, N.Y. 1946. | 192-4 et seq. |
| Dexter, Dave | THE JAZZ STORY<br>Prentice-Hall, New Jersey 1964. | 97-9 et seq. |
| Esquire's Jazz Book 1944<br>(editor: Paul Eduard Miller) | Smith & Durrell, N.Y. 1944. | 192-4. |
| Esquire's Jazz Book 1945<br>(editor: Paul Eduard Miller) | A. S. Barnes, N.Y. 1945. | 97, 195. |
| Esquire's Jazz Book 1946<br>(editor: Paul Eduard Miller) | A. S. Barnes, N.Y. 1946. | 98, 112. |
| Esquire's Jazz Book 1947<br>(editor: Ernest Anderson) | Esquire Inc. N.Y. 1947. | 19. |
| Esquire's World of Jazz<br>(editor: Lewis W. Gillenson) | Arthur Barker, London 1962. | 126, 142-3<br>et seq. |

| | | |
|---|---|---|
| Evensmo, Jan | THE TENOR SAXOPHONISTS OF THE PERIOD 1930-42 N.C.C. Oslo, Norway 1969. | LY. 2-4 et seq. |
| Feather, Leonard | THE BOOK OF JAZZ Arthur Barker, London 1957. | 43, 75, et seq. |
| Feather, Leonard | THE ENCYCLOPEDIA OF JAZZ (New Edition) Arthur Barker, London 1960. | 257-8. |
| Feather, Leonard | FROM SATCHMO TO MILES Quartet Books, London 1974. Stein & Day, N.Y. 1972. | 67-86. |
| Fox, Charles | THE JAZZ SCENE Hamlyn, London 1972. | 40, 53, 73-4. |
| Finkelstein, Sidney | JAZZ – A PEOPLE'S MUSIC Citadel Press, N.Y. 1948. | 40, 58, 170. |
| Goffin, Robert | JAZZ – From Congo to the Metropolitan Doubleday, Doran. N.Y. 1944. | 218-9. |
| Gonzales, Babs | I PAID MY DUES Expubidence Publishing, U.S.A. 1967. | 32-3, 56-7. |
| Green, Benny | THE RELUCTANT ART Macgibbon & Kee. London 1962. | 119-158. |
| Green, Benny | DRUMS IN MY EARS Davis-Poynter, London 1973. | 132-140. |
| Harlem On My Mind (editor: Allon Schoener) | Random House, N.Y. 1968. | 145. |
| Hawes, Hampton (and Don Asher) | RAISE UP OFF ME Coward, McCann & Geoghegan, N.Y. 1974. | 25-7. |
| Hear Me Talkin' To Ya (editors: Nat Shapiro and Nat Nentoff) | Peter Davies, London 1955 | 44, 154, 181-3. |
| Hentoff, Nat | THE JAZZ LIFE Dial Press, N.Y. 1961. | 49 |
| Hodeir, Andre | TOWARD JAZZ Grove Press, N.Y. 1962. | 62, 191-5. |
| Holiday, Billie (with William Dufty) | LADY SINGS T°BLUES Doubleday, N.Y. 1956. (republished by Barrie & Rockliffe, London with additional discography by Albert J. McCarthy.) | 1-250. |
| Horne, Lena | LENA HORNE IN PERSON (as told to Helen Arstein & Carlton Moss) Greenberg, N.Y. 1950. | 192 |
| Horne, Lena (and Richard Schickel) | LENA A. Deutsch, London 1966. | 114-6. |
| Horricks, Raymond | COUNT BASIE & HIS ORCHESTRA V. Gollancz, London 1957. | 113-4. |
| Hughes, Langston (and Milton Meltzer) | BLACK MAGIC Prentice Hall, New Jersey 1967. | 79, 282-5 et seq. |
| Hughes, Spike | SECOND MOVEMENT Museum Press, London. 1951. | 259-261. |
| Jam Session (editor: Ralph J. Gleason) | Putnam's, N.Y. 1958. | 243-264. |
| James, Burnett | ESSAYS ON JAZZ Sidgwick & Jackson, London 1961. | 45-60. |
| Jazzbook 1947 (editor: Albert McCarthy) | P. L. Editions, London 1947. (contains poem 'For Billie Holiday' by Nicholas Moore) | 161. |
| Jazz On Record | Hanover Books, London 1968. | 136-8. |

| (editors: McCarthy, Morgan, Oliver, Harrison) | (Billie Holiday entry by Pat Burke) | |
|---|---|---|
| Jazz Panorama (editor: Martin Williams) | Crowell-Collier, USA. 1962. (contains 'Billie Holiday' by Glenn Coulter and 'Lester Young' by Francois Postif). | 139-153. |
| Jazz Record Book (editors: Smith, Ramsey, Rogers, Russell) | Smith & Durrell, USA. 1942. | 431-3, 497-9. |
| Jazz Street (photos: Dennis Stock, text: Nat Hentoff) | A. Deutsch, London 1960. | 47-8, 53. |
| Jepsen, Jorgen Grunnet | A Discography of Billie Holiday Knudsen, Denmark 1969. | 1-37. |
| Jones, Max (and John Chilton) | LOUIS – THE LOUIS ARMSTRONG STORY Studio Vista, London 1971. | 36, 138, 167, 180. |
| Just Jazz (editors: Sinclair Traill and the Hon. Gerald Lascelles) | Peter Davies, London 1957. (contains Jerome Shipman's 'New York Today') | 130-2. |
| Just Jazz 2 (editors: Traill and Lascelles) | Peter Davies, London 1958. (contains 'Jazz at the Philharmonic' by Sinclair Traill) | 15-21. |
| Just Jazz 3 (editors: Traill and Lascelles) | Four Square, London 1959. (contains 'Man With A Hat' by Benny Green) | 47-54. |
| Just Jazz 4 (editors: Traill and Lascelles) | Souvenir Press, London 1960. (contains 'Stop, Look and Listen' by Dan Morgenstern) | 69-72. |
| Kaminsky, Max (and V. E. Hughes) | MY LIFE IN JAZZ Harper & Row, N.Y. 1963. | 87-9 et seq. |
| Larkin, Philip | ALL WHAT JAZZ Faber, London 1970. | 67-8 et seq. |
| Lee, Edward | JAZZ, AN INTRODUCTION Kahn & Averill, London 1972. | 137-9. |
| Leonard, Neil | JAZZ AND THE WHITE AMERICANS University of Chicago 1962. | 111-3 et seq. |
| McCarthy, Albert | THE TRUMPET IN JAZZ Citizen Press, London 1945. | 38, 55 et seq. |
| McCarthy, Albert | BIG BAND JAZZ Barrie & Jenkins, London 1974. | 60, 203, 263. |
| Mellers, Wilfrid | MUSIC IN A NEW FOUND LAND Barrie & Rockliffe, London 1964. | 379-382, 384. |
| Miller, Paul Eduard | MILLER'S YEARBOOK OF POPULAR MUSIC PEM Publications, U.S.A. 1942. | 53-4. |
| Newton, Francis | THE JAZZ SCENE Penguin Special, London 1961. | 24, 69 et seq. |
| New York Jazz Museum | BILLIE HOLIDAY REMEMBERED (compiled by Kuehl, Morgenstern, Schocket) New York Jazz Museum 1973. | 1-20. |
| Noble, Peter | THE NEGRO IN FILMS Skelton Robinson, London n/d c. 1950. | 80, 97. |
| Panassié, Hugues | DICTIONARY OF JAZZ Cassell, London 1956. | 115. |
| Panassié, Hugues | DISCOGRAPHIE CRITIQUE DE JAZZ Laffont, Paris 1958. | 330-1. |
| Pleasants, Henry | SERIUS MUSIC – AND ALL THAT JAZZ Gollancz, London 1969. | 56, 130, 164, 168. |

| | | |
|---|---|---|
| Pleasants, Henry | THE GREAT AMERICAN POPULAR SINGERS<br>Simon & Schuster, N.Y. 1974. | 157-167. |
| Postgate, John | A PLAIN MAN'S GUIDE TO JAZZ<br>Hanover, London 1973. | 55, 72 et seq. |
| Rosenkrantz, Timme | SWING PHOTO ALBUM 1939<br>Scorpion Press, London 1964. | 41. |
| Russell, Ross | BIRD LIVES!<br>Quartet Books, London 1973 | 194, 261, 272,<br>304, 334, 362. |
| Schiffman, Jack | UPTOWN – THE STORY OF HARLEM'S APOLLO THEATRE<br>Cowles, N.Y. 1971. | 38, 43, et seq. |
| Shaw, Arnold | THE STREET THAT NEVER SLEPT<br>Coward, McCann & Geoghegan, 1971. | 21-2 et seq. |
| Shaw, Arnold | SINATRA – A BIOGRAPHY<br>W. H. Allen, London 1968. | 13, 27-8 et seq. |
| Shaw, Artie | THE TROUBLE WITH CINDERELLA<br>Jarrolds, London 1955 | 168. |
| Simon, George T. | THE BIG BANDS<br>Macmillan, N.Y. 1971. | 39, 82 et seq. |
| Simon, George T. | SIMON SAYS<br>Arlington House, N.Y. 1971. | 97, 266 et seq. |
| Sinatra and the Great Song Stylists<br>(editor: Ken Barnes) | Ian Allan, London 1972.<br>(contains: 'Bessie and Billie' by Stan Britt) | 145-9. |
| Smith, Willie 'The Lion'<br>(with George Hoeffer) | MUSIC ON MY MIND<br>Doubleday, U.S.A. 1964. | 167 et seq. |
| Southern, Eileen | THE MUSIC OF BLACK AMERICANS<br>Norton, N.Y. 1971 | 394-7-9,<br>497 |
| Stearns, Marshall | THE STORY OF JAZZ<br>Oxford Univ. Press, N.Y. 1970. | 208, 220. |
| Terkel, Studs | GIANTS OF JAZZ<br>Crowell, N.Y. 1957. | 134-146. |
| The Art of Jazz<br>(editor: Martin Williams) | Oxford Univ. Press, N.Y. 1959.<br>(contains 'Billie Holiday' by Glenn Coulter) | 161-172. |
| The Jazz Makers<br>(editors: Nat Shapiro,<br>Nat Hentoff) | Rinehart, N.Y. 1957.<br>(contains 'Billie Holiday' by C. E. Smith) | 276-295. |
| The Jazz Word<br>(editors: Cerulli, Korall,<br>Nasatir) | Denis Dobson, London 1962 1962.<br>(contains 'Billie's Blues' by Burt Korall) | 85-87. |
| This is Jazz<br>(editor: Ken Williamson) | Newnes, London 1960.<br>(contains 'The Three Graces of Jazz' by Leonard Feather) | 146-158. |
| Ulanov, Barry | A HISTORY OF JAZZ IN AMERICA<br>Viking Press, N.Y. 1952. | 323, 189<br>et seq. |
| Ulanov, Barry | A HANDBOOK OF JAZZ<br>Hutchinson's, London 1958. | 26, 30 et seq. |
| Warren, Guy | I HAVE A STORY TO TELL<br>Guinea Press, Accra 1963. | 191-5. |
| Williams, Martin | WHERE'S THE MELODY?<br>Pantheon Books, N.Y. 1966. | 19-20, 159-66. |
| Williams, Martin | THE JAZZ TRADITION<br>Oxford Univ. Press, N.Y. 1970. | 78-86. |
| Wilson, John S. | THE COLLECTOR'S JAZZ<br>(TRADITIONAL & SWING)<br>Lippincott, N.Y. 1958. | 87, 128, 164-7 |

# A selected bibliography of magazine and newspaper references

Abbreviations:
Melody Maker = M.M.
Jazz Journal = J.J.
Down Beat = d.b.

Leonard Feather's Blindfold Test
= L.F.B.T.
Billie Holiday = B.H.
Record review = r.r.

**1933**

| April | M.M. | p. 271 | 'More Places with Spike', John Hammond. |
|---|---|---|---|

**1934**

| Dec 1 | New York Age | | Bobby Henderson-B.H. no longer engaged. |
|---|---|---|---|

**1935**

| Aug | Hot News | p. 21 | Teddy Wilson – B.H. to record for Brunswick |
|---|---|---|---|
| Aug 10 | M.M. | p. 12 | Praise for B.H., R. Edwin Hinchliffe |
| Sept | Swing Music | p. 185 | John Hammond on Teddy Wilson |
| Sept 21 | M.M. | p. 5 | First Teddy Wilson-B.H. records, John Hammond |
| Oct | Swing Music | p. 223 | 'Miss Brown To You' r.r. Leonard Hibbs |
| Dec | Rhythm | p. 21 | 'What A Night' r.r. John Hammond |

**1936**

| Jan-Feb | Swing Music | p. 288 | 'These'n'That ...' r.r. Leonard Hibbs |
|---|---|---|---|
| Feb 8 | M.M. | p. 13 | B.H. has ptomaine poisoning |
| Mar | Swing Music | p. 27 | 'Spreading Rhythm Around' r.r. Eric Ballard |
| Mar 21 | M.M. | p. 12 | B.H. – Teddy Wilson audition for Europe |
| Apr | Rhythm | p. 28 | 'Eeny Meeny ...' r.r. John Hammond |
| Apr | Jazz Hot | | B.H. at Connie's; to do theatre work. |
| Apr 11 | M.M. | p. 9 | B.H. does theatre work |
| May | Rhythm | p. 9 | B.H. 'Idol Of The Month' |
| May | Rhythm | p. 41 | 'If You Were Mine' r.r. John Hammond |
| Aug 1 | M.M. | p. 7 | News From New York: Leonard Feather |
| Sept 19 | M.M. | p. 11 | B.H. to open at Onyx Club |
| Sept | d.b. | | Stuff Smith and B.H. disagree |
| Oct 3 | M.M. | p. 5 | 'No Regrets' r.r. 'Rophone'. |
| Oct 10 | M.M. | p. 11 | B.H. no longer at The Onyx. |
| Oct 31 | M.M. | p. 12 | B.H. – anon. tribute in rhyme. |
| Dec 5 | M.M. | p. 6 | B.H. to return to The Onyx.. |
| Dec 19 | M.M. | p. 7 | 'Billie's Blues' r.r. 'Rophone' |

**1937**

| Jan 23 | M.M. | p. 2 | Artie Shaw comments on B.H. |
|---|---|---|---|
| Feb 6 | M.M. | p. 15 | 'I Can't Give You ...' r.r. 'Rophone' |
| Feb 13 | M.M. | p. 6 | B.H. at Uptown House |
| Feb | Rhythm | p. 12 | 'Billie's Blues' r.r. John Hammond |
| Mar | d.b. | p. 3 | John Hammond visits Uptown House |
| Mar | d.b. | p. 18 | 'One Never Knows ...' r.r. 'E. Greentree'. |
| Mar | Jazz Hot | | Stanley Dance reviews Basie at Scranton |
| Apr 3 | M.M. | p. 9 | B.H. to join Count Basie |
| May | Rhythm | p. 9 | 'I Must Have That Man', r.r. John Hammond |

| | | | |
|---|---|---|---|
| May | d.b. | pp. 3, 5 | B.H. with Basie at Apollo and Savoy. |
| May 22 | M.M. | p. 9 | More recordings for B.H. |
| Jun 12 | M.M. | p. 16 | Dick Lander on B.H. with Basie |
| Jun | d.b. | p. 2 | George Frazier comments on B.H.'s skills. |
| Jul 24 | M.M. | p. 11 | 'Where Is The Sun?' r.r. 'Rophone' |
| Aug 21 | M.M. | p. 15 | 'Let's Call The Whole Thing Off' r.r. |
| Sept | Rhythm | p. 9 | 'Moanin' Low' r.r. John Hammond |
| Sept 4 | M.M. | p. 5 | 'This Year's Kisses' r.r. Edgar Jackson. |
| Oct | Rhythm | p. 33 | 'He Ain't Got Rhythm' r.r. John Hammond |
| Oct | d.b. | p. 10 | Letter commenting on B.H.'s singing |
| Oct | d.b. | p. 32 | B.H. and Basie Band in Boston |
| Oct 9 | M.M. | p. 9 | 'Me, Myself & I' r.r. 'Rophone' |
| Nov 27 | M.M. | p. 2 | First ever M.M. poll, results: |
| | | | 1st. Ella Fitzgerald |
| | | | 2nd. Mildred Bailey |
| | | | 3rd. B.H. |

## 1938

| | | | |
|---|---|---|---|
| Feb 12 | M.M. | p. 8 | 'Summertime' r.r. 'Rophone' |
| Mar 5 | M.M. | p. 11 | N.Y. News (L. Feather): Billie leaves Basie |
| Apr | Rhythm | p. 7 | 'How Could You?' r.r. 'Mike' |
| Apr 2 | M.M. | p. 11 | B.H. now with Artie Shaw |
| Apr 16 | M.M. | p. 2 | Leonard Feather interviews B.H. |
| Apr 23 | M.M. | p. 4 | 'When You're Smiling' r.r. 'Rophone' |
| May | d.b. | p. 4 | George Frazier on B.H. with Artie Shaw |
| May 14 | M.M. | p. 14 | L. Feather on Shaw-B.H. broadcasts |
| May 21 | M.M. | p. 7 | 'I Can't Believe ...' r.r. 'Rophone' |
| June | Metronome | p. 9 | B.H. remains with Shaw |
| June | d.b. | p. 6 | John Munro reviews Artie Shaw's Band |
| June 4 | M.M. | p. 7 | 'He's Funny That Way' r.r. 'Rophone' |
| June 4 | M.M. | p. 14 | Artie Shaw signs second girl singer |
| June 18 | M.M. | p. 14 | L. Feather on Shaw – B.H. broadcasts |
| June-July | Jazz Hot | pp. 8, 9 | B.H. by Jack Armitage |
| July | Rhythm | p. 49 | 'He's Funny That Way' r.r. 'Mike' |
| July | Metronome | p. 32 | 'You Go To My Head' r.r. |
| Aug | d.b. | p. 5 | Ted Locke interviews B.H. |
| Aug | Metronome | p. 11 | B.H. with Artie Shaw in Atlantic City |
| Sept | d.b. | p. 6 | Willard Alexander's statement on B.H. |
| Sept | Metronome | p. 17 | Artie Shaw's Band Background |
| Sept 24 | M.M. | p. 17 | 'My Man' r.r. 'Rophone' |
| Oct | Metronome | p. 15 | Photo: B.H. with Les Burness |
| Oct 15 | M.M. | p. 4 | 'You Go To My Head' r.r. 'Rophone' |
| Oct 15 | M.M. | p. 9 | U.S. News: B.H. still with Artie Shaw |
| Oct 22 | M.M. | p. 9 | 'Getting Some Fun ...' r.r. 'Rophone' |
| Nov | Rhythm | p. 17 | 'Easy To Love' r.r. L. Hibbs |
| Nov | d.b. | p. 33 | B.H. with Artie Shaw at Savoy |
| Nov 12 | M.M. | p. 9 | 'Easy To Love' r.r. 'Rophone' |
| Dec 10 | M.M. | p. 2 | Leonard Feather on Count Basie |
| Dec 10 | M.M. | p. 6 | B.H. leaves Artie Shaw |
| Dec 17 | M.M. | p. 5 | L. Feather on Shaw – B.H. break up |

## 1939

| | | | |
|---|---|---|---|
| Jan | Rhythm | p. 26 | 'I Can't Get Started' r.r. L. Hibbs |
| Jan | Metronome | p. 57 | Poll Results: 1st. Ella Fitzgerald |
| | | | 5th. B.H. |

| | | | |
|---|---|---|---|
| Jan | d.b. | p. 16 | Poll Results: 1st. Ella Fitzgerald |
| | | | 4th. B.H. |
| Jan | d.b. | p. 3 | Onah Spencer on B.H.-Shaw controversy |
| Jan | N.Y. Amsterdam | | Bill Chase interviews B.H. |
| | News | | |
| Jan | d.b. | p. 17 | B.H. rounding up own band |
| Feb | Rhythm | p. 40 | 'The Very Thought Of You' r.r. L. Hibbs |
| Feb | d.b. | p. 3 | Cafe Society opens |
| May 6 | M.M. | p. 14 | L. Feather visits Cafe Society |
| May | Rhythm | p. 42 | 'Sugar' r.r. L. Hibbs |
| May 20 | M.M. | p. 9 | B.H. to marry |
| June | d.b. | p. 5 | B.H.'s latest is 'Strange Fruit' |
| July | Rhythm | pp. 19-23 | Models for Croonettes (B.H. etc) by |
| | | | Phyllis Frost |
| July | Metronome | p. 14 | 'Strange Fruit' r.r. George T. Simon |
| July | d.b. | p. 24 | 'Strange Fruit' r.r. and photo. of |
| | | | session |
| July 15 | M.M. | p. 15 | Cartoon drawing of B.H. |
| Sept | d.b. | p. 33 | B.H. to open in Chicago |
| Oct 1 | d.b. | p. 1 | B.H., McPartland are Off-Beat stars |
| Oct 15 | d.b. | p. 2 | B.H. in Chicago |
| Oct 15 | d.b. | p. 4 | B.H. says 'Les Young wasn't carved' |
| Nov 1 | d.b. | p. 4 | Dave Dexter interviews B.H. |
| Nov 15 | d.b. | p. 1 | Jam sessions at the Green Haven |
| Nov 15 | d.b. | p. 10 | Les Zimmerman letter on B.H.-Shaw row |
| Dec 1 | d.b. | p. 17 | Brother Jackson's Holiday Carbons |
| Dec 15 | d.b. | p. 17 | B.H. opened at Kelly's Stables |

**1940**

| | | | |
|---|---|---|---|
| Jan 1 | d.b. | p. 13 | Poll Results: 1st. Ella Fitzgerald |
| | | | 2nd. Mildred Bailey |
| | | | 3rd. B.H. |
| Apr 1 | d.b. | p. 22 | B.H. at Ernie's, N.Y. |
| May 1 | d.b. | p. 22 | B.H.-Roy Eldridge at Kelly's |
| May 11 | M.M. | p. 6 | B.H. biog. by Leonard Feather |
| July 15 | d.b. | p. 15 | B.H.-Roy Eldridge 18th week at Kelly's |
| Sept 15 | d.b. | p. 23 | New Cafe Society will open Sept. 27th |
| Oct 15 | d.b. | p. 1 | B.H. fails to show up |
| Nov | Swing | p. 9 | B.H. into Cafe Society |
| Dec 15 | d.b. | p. 16 | 'I Hear Music' r.r. |

**1941**

| | | | |
|---|---|---|---|
| Jan 1 | d.b. | p. 1 | Poll Results: 1st. Helen O'Connell |
| | | | 2nd. Billie Holiday |
| | | | (Ella Fitzgerald then leading her own |
| | | | band was ineligible). |
| Feb 22 | M.M. | p. 3 | B.H. at Milt Gabler's jam sessions |
| Mar 15 | d.b. | p. 21 | Una Mae Carlisle replaces B.H. at Kelly's |
| May 15 | d.b. | p. 2 | B.H. considered for Basie Band |
| May 15 | d.b. | p. 14 | 'Let's Do It' r.r. Dave Dexter |
| Aug 1 | d.b. | p. 14 | B.H. opens at Famous Door |
| Aug 15 | d.b. | p. 14 | 'Solitude' r.r. Dave Dexter |
| Sept 15 | d.b. | pp. 1, 20 | B.H. weds Jimmy Monroe |
| Oct 15 | d.b. | p. 4 | B.H. at Californian Cafe Society |
| Dec 15 | d.b. | p. 16 | 'Gloomy Sunday' r.r. Dave Dexter. |

**1942**

| | | | |
|---|---|---|---|
| Jan 3 | M.M. | p. 5 | B.H. marries |
| April | Music & Rhythm | p. 11 | Dinah Shore's 'Top Ten Vocalistes' |
| May 15 | d.b. | p. 8 | B.H. Theatre dates, and Cleveland booking |
| June 1 | d.b. | p. 12 | Trouville adds B.H. |
| June 15 | d.b. | p. 6 | Ted Le Berthon's 'Strange Fruit' story |
| July 15 | d.b. | p. 12 | Marie Bryant replaces B.H. at Trouville |
| Sept 1 | d.b. | p. 4 | B.H. opens in Chicago |
| Oct 1 | d.b. | p. 5 | B.H. to stay at Garrick Show Bar |
| Oct 15 | d.b. | p. 4 | B.H. jailed in comedy of errors |
| Nov 1 | d.b. | p. 5 | B.H. threatens walk-out |
| Dec 1 | d.b. | p. 18 | Dixon Gayer reviews B.H. in Chicago |

**1943**

| | | | |
|---|---|---|---|
| Jan 1 | d.b. | p. 14 | Poll Results: 1st. Helen Forrest |
| | | | 4th. B.H. |
| Jan 16 | M.M. | p. 4 | B.H. arrested in Chicago |
| Jan 15 | d.b. | p. 4 | B.H. in Chicago for New Year's Eve |
| Mar 1 | d.b. | p. 9 | B.H. at Kelly's Stables |
| Apr 1 | d.b. | p. 7 | B.H. and L. Feather journey to L.A. |
| July 1 | d.b. | p. 2 | Cozy Cole Trio back B.H. at Onyx |
| Aug 15 | d.b. | p. 15 | B.H. still at Onyx |
| Sept 1 | Jazz Record | p. 2 | B.H. at Gjon Mili's party |
| Oct 1 | Jazz Record | p. 13 | Al Casey Trio back B.H. at Onyx |
| Nov | Jazz Music | p. 50 | Poem for B.H. by Nicholas Moore |
| Nov | Metronome | p. 6 | B.H.'s brother-in-law fronts band |
| Dec | Music Dial | p. 24 | B.H. to tour with Ted McRae's Band |
| Dec 25 | M.M. | p. 5 | B.H., Pete Brown at Onyx |

**1944**

| | | | |
|---|---|---|---|
| Jan 1 | d.b. | p. 1 | Poll Results: 1st. Jo Stafford |
| | | | 5th. B.H. |
| Mar 15 | d.b. | p. 3 | B.H. at Onyx with Dizzy Gillespie |
| Apr 1 | d.b. | p. 3 | Pianist Joe Springer at Onyx |
| Apr | Music Dial | p. 5 | B.H. at Onyx |
| Apr | Metronome | p. 10 | B.H. to record again |
| May | Music Dial | p. 3 | B.H. at Action Rally |
| May | Jazz Record | p. 2 | Another Gjon Mili party: B.H. leaves |
| | | | Onyx |
| June 1 | d.b. | p. 1 | B.H. at Ruban Bleu |
| June | Jazz Record | p. 13 | B.H. at Breakfast Dance |
| July 1 | d.b. | p. 2 | Film studios 'find' B.H. |
| July 15 | d.b. | p. 4 | B.H. returns to Chicago |
| Aug 15 | d.b. | p. 4 | B.H. at Regal, Chicago with Tiny Hill. |
| Sept | Record Changer | p. 53 | B.H. opens at Downbeat Club |
| Sept | Metronome | p. 30 | 'My Man' r.r. Barry Ulanov |
| Oct | Metronome | p. 10 | Norvo men back B.H. at Downbeat |
| Oct | Record Changer | p. 71 | B.H. & Mamie Smith at Actor's Guild Jamboree |
| Oct 15 | d.b. | p. 5 | B.H. to record for Decca |
| Nov 15 | d.b. | p. 2 | Streamlined B.H. now at Downbeat |
| Nov | Bandleaders | p. 61 | Warner Brothers discover B.H. |
| Dec 16 | M.M. | p. 2 | B.H.'s husband jailed |
| Dec 22 | France-Belgique | pp. 1, 8 | Fruit Etrange |

**1945**

| | | | |
|---|---|---|---|
| Jan | Jazz Record | p. 2 | B.H. at Spotlight |

| | | | |
|---|---|---|---|
| Jan | Record Changer | p. 61 | B.H. opened at Spotlight Dec 8th |
| Jan 15 | d.b. | p. 2 | B.H. at Esquire's L.A. concert |
| Jan 27 | M.M. | p. 5 | Esquire's 2nd Annual Concert |
| Feb 1 | d.b. | p. 6 | B.H. at Philharmonic Hall |
| Feb 15 | d.b. | p. 6 | B.H. at New Plantation in L.A. |
| Mar | Record Changer | p. 29 | B.H. on Coast |
| Mar 3 | M.M. | p. 5 | B.H. closes at Spotlight |
| Mar 15 | d.b. | p. 6 | B.H. at Granz concert March 5th |
| Apr | Metronome | p. 13 | 'Lover Man' r.r. |
| Apr | Jazz Record | p. 16 | B.H. at Philharmonic, L.A. |
| Apr 1 | d.b. | p. 9 | "Lover Man" r.r. |
| May 1 | Jazz (Brussels) | p. 3, 4 | Une Grande Chanteuse Noire by A. Bettonville |
| May | Metronome | p. 34 | Jo Stafford comments on B.H. |
| May 5 | M.M. | p. 7 | B.H. in Los Angeles |
| June 1 | d.b. | p. 5 | B.H. gets 'divorce' |
| June 2 | M.M. | p. 5 | B.H. in St. Louis Plantation incident |
| June | Metronome | p. 16 | 'I Cover The Waterfront' r.r. |
| June | Jazz Notes (Australia) | p. 1 | 52nd Street by George Avakian |
| June 15 | d.b. | p. 1 | B.H. opens at Downbeat |
| July 15 | d.b. | p. 1 | B.H. is worrying her associates |
| Aug | Record Changer | p. 33 | B.H. at Savoy in San Francisco |
| Aug 1 | d.b. | p. 3 | B.H. irregularly at Downbeat |
| Aug 15 | d.b. | p. 3 | B.H. – Joe Guy to tour after Redman dates |
| Sept | Metronome | p. 35 | B.H. one-nighters with own band |
| Sept 1 | d.b. | p. 13 | B.H. tours with Joe Guy |
| Sept 22 | M.M. | p. 5 | B.H. – Don Redman open new theatre |
| Oct 1 | d.b. | p. 13 | B.H. band itinerary |
| Oct 20 | M.M. | p. 3 | B.H. to go on road with 15 piece band |
| Nov 1 | d.b. | p. 3 | B.H. returns to Downbeat |
| Nov | Metronome | p. 14 | B.H. – Joe Guy in Chicago |
| Nov | Metronome | p. 15 | Glaser's stars at Downbeat |
| Dec 8 | M.M. | p. 5 | B.H. & Louis Armstrong may tour Britain |

**1946**

| | | | |
|---|---|---|---|
| Jan 1 | d.b. | p. 1 | Poll Results: 1st. Jo Stafford 2nd. B.H. |
| Jan | Metronome | p. 31 | Records of the Year – B.H.'s 'That Ole Devil Called Love' cited. |
| Jan | Metronome | p. 64 | Poll Results: 1st. B.H. 2nd. Anita O'Day |
| Feb | Metronome | p. 13 | B.H. at Philadelphia Academy of Music |
| Mar 11 | d.b. | p. 1 | B.H. Concert makes jazz history |
| Mar 16 | M.M. | p. 7 | L. Feather on B.H. New York Town Hall concert |
| Mar | Metronome | p. 32 | Dave Bittan reviews B.H. in Philadelphia |
| Mar | Metronome | p. 40 | B.H. at N.Y. Town Hall, and Downbeat club |
| Apr | Jazz Hot | | B.H. now with Springer, Catlett and Casey. |
| May | Record Changer | p. 30 | Bill Gottlieb reports B.H. earns $1,250 a week |
| May | Metronome | p. 27 | 'You Better Go Now' r.r. |
| May | Hollywood Notes | p. 6 | John Hammond reviews B.H. Town Hall Concert |
| June 17 | d.b. | p. 1 | B.H. back after tour |
| June 22 | M.M. | p. 3 | B.H. at Carnegie Hall – L. Feather review |
| July | Jazz Record | p. 7 | Lester Young interviewed by Allan Morrison |

247

| | | | |
|---|---|---|---|
| Aug | Metronome | p. 28 | Four sides by B.H. r.r. |
| Aug | Australian Jazz Quarterly | pp. 3-10 | 'Billie' by William H. Miller |
| Aug 17 | M.M. | p. 3 | Louis and B.H. signed for film |
| Sept 3 | Look | p. 59 | B.H. report |
| Sept 21 | M.M. | p. 5 | B.H. Californian booking . |
| Sept 28 | M.M. | p.5 | B.H. may work with John Kirby on Coast |
| Dec 16 | d.b. | p. 4 | B.H. – Eddie Heywood dispute |
| Dec 21 | M.M. | p. 9 | Teddy Wilson looks back |
| Dec | Metronome | p. 31 | 'Big Stuff' r.r. |
| Dec | Jazzology | pp. 7-9 | 'On Holiday' by Charles Saunders |

**1947**

| | | | |
|---|---|---|---|
| Jan | Metronome | p. 49 | Poll Results: 1st. June Christy<br>2nd. B.H. |
| Jan | Metronome | p. 34 | 'Good Morning Heartache' r.r. |
| Jan 1 | d.b. | p. 7 | Premiere of 'New Orleans' film. |
| Jan 15 | d.b. | p. 3 | B.H. contract problems |
| Jan | Jazz Hot 14 | p. 2 | New York '47, by Charles Delaunay |
| Feb | Metronome | p. 31 | L.F.B.T. Peggy Lee on B.H.'s 'Any Old Time' |
| Feb 12 | d.b. | p. 1 | B.H. – 20% salary reduction |
| Feb 12 | d.b. | p.20 | 'Good Morning Heartache' r.r. |
| Feb 26 | d.b. | p. 14 | B.H. on WNEW music show |
| Mar | Metronome | p. 8 | B.H. sings at Louis Armstrong concert. |
| Mar 8 | M.M. | p. 3 | George Shearing hears B.H. in New York |
| Apr | Metronome | p. 43 | L. Feather reviews New Orleans |
| Apr 9 | d.b. | p. 1 | B.H. gets check-up |
| May | Metronome | p. 7 | B.H. recuperates in hospital |
| May | Metronome | p. 40 | Judy Garland picks Ella, Kate Smith & B.H. |
| May 21 | d.b. | p.18 | 'Solitude' r.r. |
| June | Jazz Hot 16 | p. 16 | Review of film New Orleans |
| June | Metronome | p. 27 | 'Solitude' r.r. |
| June 4 | d.b. | p. 16 | 'Don't Blame Show Biz' says B.H. |
| June 4 | d.b. | p. 7 | Radio station bans B.H. records |
| June 14 | M.M. | p. 5 | Star U.S. singer jailed |
| June 18 | d.b. | p. 1 | B.H. pleads guilty |
| July 2 | d.b. | p. 2 | B.H. no longer at '18 Club'. |
| July | Metronome | p. 7 | B.H. sentenced |
| Aug | Metronome | p. 7 | 'Musicians not dope fiends' by Barry Ulanov |
| Aug | Metronome | p. 31 | 'I'm Yours' r.r. |
| Sept 24 | d.b. | p. 24 | 'Long Gone Blues' r.r. |
| Oct 8 | d.b. | p. 1 | B.H. testimony saves Joe Guy |
| Oct | Metronome | p. 23 | 'Long Gone Blues' r.r. |
| Nov | Pickup | pp. 6-7 | B.H. – Blues Singer or Crooner? |
| Nov | Metronome | p. 46 | 'Body and Soul' r.r. |
| Dec 3 | d.b. | p. 2 | B.H. Testimonial Concert |
| Dec | Metronome | p. 45 | 'Easy Living' r.r. |
| Dec 17 | d.b. | p. 6 | B.H. wants no part of charity show |
| Dec 17 | d.b. | p. 12 | Poll Results: 1st. Sarah Vaughan<br>5th. B.H. |
| Dec 17 | d.b. | p. 16 | 'Night and Day' r.r. |
| Dec | Jazz Music (Vol.3. No.5.) | pp. 3-5 | Harald Grut on B.H. |

**1948**

| | | | |
|---|---|---|---|
| Jan | Metronome | p. 40 | Poll Result: 1st. Sarah Vaughan<br>4th. B.H. |
| Jan 14 | d.b. | p. 16 | 'Body and Soul' r.r. |
| Jan | Metronome | p. 7 | Granz-Glaser row |
| Mar 10 | d.b. | p. 1 | B.H. to appear at Carnegie Hall |
| Mar 13 | M.M. | p. 4 | 52nd Street Obituary by L. Feather |
| Apr 21 | d.b. | p. 1 | Billie at Carnegie — Jack Egan |
| May | Metronome | p. 22 | B.H. in 'Hall of Fame' |
| May 5 | d.b. | p. 1 | B.H. agency dispute |
| May | Record Changer | p. 8 | B.H. at Carnegie |
| June | Record Changer | pp. 8-9 | Lady Day Returns |
| June | Metronome | p. 6 | B.H. on Broadway |
| June 2 | d.b. | p. 1 | B.H. opens at Ebony Club |
| June 30 | d.b. | p. 1 | B.H. to play Strand |
| July 14 | d.b. | p. 5 | B.H. at Blue Note |
| Aug | J.J. | p. 7 | Charles Snape on B.H. |
| Aug-Sept | Jazz Hot | p. 25 | B.H. at Strand with Basie |
| Sept | J.J. | p. 3 | B.H. at Strand, N.Y. |
| Oct | Metronome | p. 1 | B.H. cover photo |
| Oct | Metronome | p. 3,<br>13-14<br>31, 33 | 'A Great Lady' by Barry Ulanov |
| Oct 6 | d.b. | p. 1 | B.H. to again play Ebony Club |
| Oct 6 | d.b. | p. 2 | B.H. planning concerts |
| Nov 3 | d.b. | p. 4 | B.H. in Chicago |
| Nov 17 | d.b. | p. 4 | B.H. at Silhouette |
| Dec 1 | d.b. | p. 4 | B.H. commotion at Silhouette |
| Dec 15 | d.b. | p. 6 | B.H. to play Billy Berg's |
| Dec 29 | d.b. | p. 1 | Norvo Septet to back B.H. |
| Dec 29 | d.b. | p. 6 | B.H. to appear on Coast |
| Dec 29 | d.b. | p. 6 | Poll Results: 1st. Sarah Vaughan<br>10th. B.H. |

**1949**

| | | | |
|---|---|---|---|
| Jan | Metronome | p. 32 | Poll Results: 1st. Sarah Vaughan<br>4th. B.H. |
| Jan 5 | San Francisco<br>Chronicle | p. 3 | B.H. out on bail after melee |
| Jan 14 | d.b. | p. 5 | B.H. and press agent Jerome Lee fall out |
| Jan 22 | San Francisco<br>Chronicle | p. 1 | B.H. is held on opium charge |
| Jan 28 | d.b. | p. 1 | B.H. and manager face 3 assault counts |
| Jan | Jazz Hot<br>(issue 40) | p. 13 | B.H. by Robert Aubert |
| Feb 25 | d.b. | p. 5 | B.H. and John Levy on opium count |
| March | Metronome | p. 42 | B.H. stands accused |
| Mar 26 | M.M. | p. 6 | B.H. trial deferred |
| Apr 8 | d.b. | p. 1 | B.H. trial delayed a month |
| Apr 9 | M.M. | p. 2 | 'Am I Blue' r.r. Edgar Jackson |
| Apr 22 | d.b. | p. 13 | B.H. skips tour |
| May 6 | d.b. | p. 1 | B.H. in Detroit |
| May 6 | d.b. | p. 3 | B.H. Cabaret Card appeal dismissed |
| May 6 | d.b. | p. 15 | Article on Lester Young |
| June | Metronome | p. 28 | 'Weep No More' r.r. |

| July | Ebony | pp. 26-32 | 'I'm Cured For Good' says B.H. |
|------|-------|-----------|-------------------------------|
| July 1 | d.b. | p. 15 | 'Porgy' r.r. Mike Levin |
| July 15 | d.b. | p. 3 | B.H. 'Broke and alone'. |
| July 29 | d.b. | p. 1 | B.H. sued for missing dates |
| Aug | Metronome | p. 28 | 'Porgy' r.r. |
| Aug | J.J. | p. 11 | 'Easy Living' r.r. |
| Sept | Metronome | p. 27 | First 'all time all star' poll. 1st. B.H. 2nd. Ella Fitzgerald |
| Oct | J.J. | p. 13 | B.H. at Apollo |
| Oct 21 | d.b. | p. 18 | 'Baby Get Lost' r.r. |
| Nov | Metronome | p. 14 | Whole page ad. for B.H. |
| Nov | Metronome | p. 47 | 'Wherever You Are' r.r. |
| Nov 4 | d.b. | pp. 5-18 | B.H. has gigs in New York and Detroit |
| Nov 12 | M.M. | p. 6 | B.H. & Chuck Peterson in Detroit incident |
| Nov 18 | d.b. | p. 1 | Tour planned for B.H. |
| Nov 18 | d.b. | p. 15 | 'Wherever You Are' r.r. |
| Dec | Metronome | p. 33 | 'My Sweet Hunk Of Trash' r.r. |
| Dec 30 | d.b. | p. 30 | Norvo to back B.H. in Hollywood |
| Dec 30 | d.b. | p. 15 | 'My Sweet Hunk Of Trash' r.r. |

**1950**

| Jan | Metronome | | Poll Result. 1st. Sarah Vaughan. 5th. B.H. |
|-----|-----------|--|--------------------------------------------|
| Jan | J.J. | p. 11 | 'Baby Get Lost' r.r. |
| Jan 13 | d.b. | pp. 7-8 | B.H. in Chicago, to tour Mid-West |
| Jan 27 | d.b. | p. 14 | 'You're My Thrill' r.r. |
| Feb | Metronome | pp. 16, 30 | L.F.B.T. 'Lady Day Has Her Say' B.H. interview |
| March | Metronome | pp. 18, 25 | L.F.B.T. Roy Kral and Jackie Cain. |
| March | J.J. | p. 12 | B.H. mentioned in 'Lightly & Politely' column |
| Mar 24 | d.b. | p. 4 | B.H. in San Francisco |
| May | Metronome | p. 22 | Mel Torme comments on B.H. |
| May | Metronome | p. 27 | B.H. with Basie. Barbara Hodgkins review |
| May 5 | d.b. | p. 1 | Two judgments against B.H. |
| May 5 | d.b. | p. 14 | 'Please Tell Me Now' r.r. |
| June 16 | d.b. | p. 15 | 'God Bless The Child' r.r. |
| Sept 8 | d.b. | p. 13 | B.H. and John Levy part |
| Sept 22 | d.b. | p. 13 | B.H. in Los Angeles |
| Oct 6 | d.b. | p. 14 | 'Keeps On Raining' r.r. |
| Nov | Metronome | p. 35 | B.H. sides to be re-issued on LP |
| Nov 3 | d.b. | p. 1 | B.H. set for Long Bar, San Francisco |
| Nov 17 | d.b. | p. 1 | B.H.'s car impounded |
| Dec | Metronome | p. 31 | 'Keeps On Raining' r.r. |
| Dec 15 | d.b. | p. 16 | B.H. leaves Long Bar |
| Dec 29 | d.b. | p. 5 | Jack Russin accompanying B.H. |
| Dec 29 | d.b. | p. 14 | Poll Results: 1st. Sarah Vaughan 7th. B.H. |

**1951**

| Metronome | Yearbook 1951 | p. 25 | B.H.'s Ten Favorite Records |
|-----------|---------------|-------|-----------------------------|
| Jazz Music | Vol. 4. no's 7/8 | | Jack Millar listing of B.H. on Vocalion |
| Jan 26 | d.b. | p. 6 | B.H. at Hi-Note, Chicago |
| Feb 23 | d.b. | p. 12 | Bobby Tucker biog. by Sharon Pease |
| Apr 23 | d.b. | p. 1 | B.H. signs for Aladdin Records |

| | | | |
|---|---|---|---|
| June 1 | d.b. | p. 13 | B.H. first dates for Aladdin |
| June | Metronome | p. 7 | B.H. leaves Decca |
| June 29 | d.b. | p. 14 | 'Detour Ahead' r.r. Jack Tracy |
| June 29 | d.b. | p. 13 | L. Feather covers Artie Shaw's career |
| Aug | Metronome | p. 15 | B.H. liked Nat Jaffe's playing |
| Aug 24 | d.b. | p. 6 | B.H. to work with Herbie Fields |
| Aug 24 | d.b. | p. 14 | 'Rocky Mountain Blues' r.r. |
| Nov 2 | d.b. | p. 11 | Letter re. B.H./Basie film |
| Nov 16 | d.b. | p. 3 | B.H. in Boston |
| Nov 30 | d.b. | p. 1 | B.H. to be in 'Carnival of Jazz' |
| Dec | Metronome | p. 27 | 'Rocky Mountain Blues' r.r. |
| Dec 28 | d.b. | p. 12 | Poll Results: 1st. Sarah Vaughan |
| | | | 9th. B.H. |

**1952**

| | | | |
|---|---|---|---|
| Jan 11 | d.b. | p. 2 | 'B.H. finds happiness' – Nat Hentoff |
| Jan 12 | M.M. | p. 7 | Death of club owner Dickie Wells |
| Jan | Metronome | p. 8 | B.H. returns to Detroit |
| Feb | Metronome | p. 16 | Poll Results: 1st. Sarah Vaughan |
| | | | 4th. B.H. |
| Feb 8 | d.b. | p. 17 | B.H. to work on Coast |
| Feb 22 | d.b. | p. 13 | B.H. back to San Francisco |
| Mar 7 | d.b. | p. 4 | Maxine Sullivan mentions B.H. |
| Mar 8 | M.M. | p. 4 | B.H. in short film with Basie |
| Mar | Metronome | p. 25 | 'Do Your Duty' r.r. |
| Apr 4 | d.b. | p. 7 | B.H. draws capacity crowds |
| Apr 26 | M.M. | p. 4 | No Bop For Lady Day |
| May 21 | d.b. | p. 12 | L.F.B.T. Gordon Jenkins on B.H. |
| June | Metronome | p. 8 | Letter re. B.H. |
| June 4 | d.b. | p. 12 | L.F.B.T. Johnnie Ray on B.H. |
| July 2 | d.b. | p. 1 | B.H. recording for Norman Granz |
| July 19 | M.M. | p. 1 | B.H. booked for tour of Britain |
| Aug 2 | M.M. | p. 12 | B.H. records for Norman Granz |
| Aug 13 | d.b. | p. 6 | Ralph Cooper reminisces |
| Sept 6 | M.M. | p. 3 | Jose Ferrer mentions B.H. |
| Sept 10 | d.b. | p. 18 | David Rose is m.d. for B.H. t.v. show |
| Oct 8 | d.b. | p. 17 | No Europe Tour yet for Lady Day |
| Oct 22 | d.b. | pp. 3, 7, 18 | B.H. in Boston – Nat Hentoff |
| Oct 22 | d.b. | p. 15 | B.H. to headline at Chicago Civic |
| Dec 3 | d.b. | p. 3 | Frank Holzfeind reminisces |
| Dec 31 | d.b. | p. 17 | Lady Day to wax 8 sides |
| Dec 31 | d.b. | p. 1 | Poll Results: 1st. Sarah Vaughan |
| | | | 7th. B.H. |

**1953**

| | | | |
|---|---|---|---|
| Metronome | Year Book 1953 | p. 30 | B.H. photo and caption. |
| Jan | Metronome | p. 32 | B.H. at Duke's 25th Anniv. concert |
| Jan 14 | d.b. | p. 1 | B.H./Basie/Eckstine discuss tour |
| Feb | Tan | | Feature on B.H. |
| Feb | Metronome | p. 3 | Poll Results: 1st. Sarah Vaughan |
| | | | 4th. B.H. |
| Feb 11 | d.b. | p. 21 | B.H. in San Francisco |
| Mar 21 | M.M. | p. 4 | Lester Young interview |

| Apr 22 | d.b. | p. 20 | 'Yesterdays' r.r. |
|---|---|---|---|
| June | Metronome | p. 25 | 'Yesterdays' r.r. |
| July 1 | d.b. | p. 3 | B.H. at Hi-Hat, Boston |
| July 29 | d.b. | p. 3 | B.H. to play Chicago d.j. benefit |
| Aug 26 | d.b. | p. 1 | First Annual Critics' Poll: |
| | | | 1st. Ella Fitzgerald |
| | | | 2nd. Tie between B.H. and Sarah Vaughan |
| Sept 23 | d.b. | p. 3 | B.H. has abscessed jaw |
| Oct 31 | M.M. | p. 3 | B.H. on 'Comeback' t.v. show |
| Nov 4 | d.b. | p. 3 | B.H. sings on Stan Kenton concert |
| Nov 18 | d.b. | p. 3 | B.H. in California |
| Dec 5 | M.M. | p. 2 | B.H. & Louis McKay prepare for Europe |
| Dec 19 | M.M. | p. 2 | B.H. & Louis McKay drive to Coast |
| Dec 30 | d.b. | p. 1 | B.H. to make European Tour |
| Dec 30 | d.b. | p. 6 | Poll Results: 1st. Ella Fitzgerald |
| | | | 7th. B.H. |
| Dec 30 | d.b. | p. 14 | 'My Man' r.r. Nat Hentoff |

## 1954

| Jan 9 | M.M. | p. 7 | Death of 'Pods' Hollingsworth |
|---|---|---|---|
| Jan 13 | d.b. | p. 3 | B.H. at Tiffany Club |
| Jan 23 | M.M. | p. 1 | B.H. to appear at Albert Hall, London |
| Jan 23 | M.M. | p. 6 | 'Jazz Club U.S.A.' in Scandinavia |
| Jan 30 | M.M. | p. 3 | Max Jones int. Joe Shribman re. Artie Shaw |
| Jan 30 | M.M. | pp. 3, 9 | B.H. in Berlin |
| Feb | Metronome | p. 21 | Poll Results: 1st. Ella Fitzgerald |
| | | | 3rd. B.H. |
| Feb 10 | d.b. | p. 2 | B.H. birth certificate untraceable |
| Feb 13 | M.M. | p. 1 | B.H. in Britain |
| Feb 20 | M.M. | pp. 7-10 | 'Holiday with Billie' by Max Jones |
| Feb 24 | d.b. | p. 14 | L. Feather reports on 'Jazz Club U.S.A.' |
| | | | tour |
| Feb 27 | M.M. | p. 12 | 'The Art of Holiday' by Vic Bellerby |
| March | Metronome | p. 24 | 'Yesterdays' r.r. |
| Apr 3 | M.M. | p. 2 | Lee Young interviewed |
| May 5 | d.b. | pp. 3, 17 | B.H. at Carnegie, then to Washington. |
| May 5 | d.b. | p. 13 | L.F.B.T. Dinah Washington on B.H. |
| June 2 | d.b. | p. 13 | L.F.B.T. Jane Russell on B.H. |
| July | Metronome | p. 24 | 'Autumn in New York' r.r. |
| July 28 | d.b. | p. 3 | B.H. again scheduled for Carnegie Hall |
| Aug 25 | d.b. | p. 1 | B.H. – Lester Young 'feud' is over |
| Aug 25 | d.b. | p. 2 | B.H. at First Newport Jazz Festival |
| Sept | Metronome | p. 17 | Bill Coss on B.H. at Newport |
| Sept 18 | M.M. | p. 17 | Max Jones reviews new B.H. LP |
| Oct 20 | d.b. | p. 5 | B.H. receives special Down Beat award |
| Oct 20 | d.b. | p. 16 | Nat Hentoff r.r. B.H. Clef LP |
| Nov | Jazz Hot. No 93 | | B.H. may go to Alaska |
| Nov | J.J. | p. 9 | B.H. Golden Age by Jim Sylvester |
| Nov 3 | d.b. | pp. 18, 20 | B.H. in Boston, then to Carnegie Hall |
| Dec | Metronome | p. 21 | Ralph Watkins reminisces about B.H. |
| Dec | J.J. | p. 6 | Stanley Dance mentions B.H. |
| Dec 29 | d.b. | p. 6 | Poll Results: 1st. Ella Fitzgerald |
| | | | 5th. B.H. |
| Vol.5. No.5. Jazz Music | | pp. 22-24 | Lady Day by Bert Rehneberg |

**1955**

| | | | |
|---|---|---|---|
| | Metronome Year Book 1955 | pp. 34, 44 | Photo and poem by Donald Smith |
| Feb 19 | M.M. | p. 9 | Max Jones r.r. B.H. LP./Comments from Camarata |
| Mar 23 | d.b. | p. 4 | B.H. waxes in New York |
| May | Jazz Monthly | p. 9 | Charles Fox on B.H. |
| May 4 | d.b. | p. 14 | B.H.'s 'J.A.T.P.' r.r. |
| May 4 | d.b. | p. 19 | L.F.B.T. Hazel Scott on B.H. |
| May 7 | M.M. | p. 3 | B.H. sings at Charlie Parker memorial concert |
| June 29 | d.b. | p. 13 | 'Willow Weep For Me' r.r. Nat Hentoff |
| July | Metronome | p. 26 | 'Stormy Blues' r.r. George T. Simon |
| July 16 | M.M. | p. 2 | Jeff Kruger says B.H. 'definitely booked'. |
| July 27 | d.b. | p. 42 | B.H. at Hi-Hat, Boston. |
| July 30 | M.M. | p. 7 | Teddy Wilson/B.H. re-issues on LP. r.r. Max Jones |
| Aug 10 | d.b. | p. 23 | 'Lady Day' LP r.r. Nat Hentoff |
| Aug 22 | M.M. | p. 6 | B.H. to write *Bitter Crop* book |
| Aug 24 | d.b. | p. 1 | Annual Critics' Poll. 1st. Ella Fitzgerald 2nd. B.H. |
| Sept 7 | d.b. | p. ˙18 | 'Love Me Or Leave Me' r.r. Nat Hentoff |
| Sept 21 | d.b. | p. 9 | B.H. writing life story |
| Oct | Jazz Journal | p. 11 | 'B.H. Sings' by Derrick Stewart-Baxter |
| Oct 5 | d.b. | p. 51 | L.F.B.T. Ella Fitzgerald on B.H. |
| Nov | Metronome | p. 20 | Lady Day at Hollywood Bowl |
| Nov 30 | d.b. | p. 6 | Dom Cerulli reports on B.H. in Boston |
| Dec | Metronome | p. 29 | Commodore re-issues reviewed |
| Dec 14 | d.b. | p. 14 | 'Music For Torching' r.r. Nat Hentoff |
| Dec 28 | d.b. | p. 1 | Poll Results: 1st. Ella Fitzgerald 6th. B.H. |

**1956**

| | | | |
|---|---|---|---|
| Mar | Jazz Monthly | pp. 2-5, 32 | Edward Towler on B.H. |
| Mar 7 | d.b. | p. 10 | Lester Young int. by Nat Hentoff |
| Apr | J.J. | p. 10 | 'B.H. Today' by Derrick Stewart-Baxter |
| Apr 4 | d.b. | p. 7 | B.H. out on bail |
| May 19 | M.M. | p. 6 | Trummy Young int. by Max Jones |
| May 30 | d.b. | p. 27 | L.F.B.T. Jeri Southern on B.H. |
| June 13 | d.b. | p. 33 | B.H. in Detroit |
| June 27 | d.b. | p. 29 | L.F.B.T. Maxine Sullivan on B.H. |
| Aug 8 | d.b. | p. 9 | Nat Hentoff reviews *Lady Sings The Blues* book. |
| Aug 8 | d.b. | pp. 34-35 | Chicago booking and Hollywood dates for B.H. |
| Aug 22 | d.b. | p. 23 | Nat Hentoff r.r. 1955 recordings |
| Aug 25 | M.M. | p. 9 | B.H. draws crowds to Jazz City, L.A. |
| Sept | Metronome | p. 6 | B.H. at Randall's Island Festival |
| Sept 5 | d.b. | p. 35 | Louis McKay's Chicago club features B.H. |
| Sept 19 | d.b. | pp. 32-33 | B.H. Honolulu and Hollywood dates |
| Oct 17 | d.b. | p. 24 | Nat Hentoff r.r. Clef LP. |
| Oct 27 | M.M. | p. 10 | B.H. Carnegie Hall plans |
| Nov 3 | M.M. | p. 13 | B.H. with J.A.T.P. r.r. Max Jones |
| Nov 14 | d.b. | p. 8 | B.H. at Carnegie Hall, Nov 10th. |
| Nov | J.J. | p. 11 | Berta Wood on B.H. at Jazz City |
| Nov | Metronome | p. 47 | Bill Coss reviews B.H. book |
| Nov | Jazz Today | p. 6 | B.H. to sing at Carnegie Hall |
| Nov | Jazz Today | p. 34 | Bill Coss r.r. 'Velvet Mood' LP |
| Nov 28 | d.b. | p. 37 | Triple encores for B.H. in Washington |

| Dec | Jazz Monthly | pp. 7, 31 | Svein Haagensen on 'Lester with B.H.' |
| Dec | Jazz Today | p. 44 | Lady Day at Carnegie by Jack Maher |
| Dec | Jazz Today | p. 6 | Carnegie Hall summary |
| Dec 12 | d.b. | p. 10 | Nat Hentoff reviews Carnegie Hall concert |
| Dec 12 | d.b. | p. 45 | B.H. to return to Jazz City |
| Dec 15 | M.M. | p. 8 | B.H. again at Jazz City |
| Dec 26 | d.b. | p. 1 | Poll Results: 1st. Ella Fitzgerald 3rd. B.H. |
| Dec 29 | M.M. | p. 2 | B.H.'s ex-manager John Levy dies. |

**1957**

| | Metronome Year Book 1957 | p. 26 | Photo and caption |
| Jan | Metronome | p. 20 | Review of B.H. at Carnegie Hall |
| Jan 9 | d.b. | p. 8 | Plan to film B.H.'s life story |
| Jan 9 | d.b. | pp. 44-45 | Chicago and Hollywood bookings. |
| Jan 23 | d.b. | p. 3 | Death of John Levy |
| Jan 23 | d.b. | p. 25 | 'Lady Sings The Blues' r.r. |
| Jan 23 | d.b. | pp. 36, 37 | Chicago, Miami bookings |
| Feb | Metronome | pp. 24, 25 | Willis Conover's interview with B.H. |
| Feb | Jazz Monthly | p. 11 | Langston Hughes poem for B.H. |
| Feb 16 | M.M. | p. 11 | B.H. in Santa Monica |
| Feb 20 | d.b. | p. 37 | B.H. in California |
| Feb 23 | M.M. | p. 17 | B.H. on Clef r.r. Sinclair Traill |
| Mar 6 | d.b. | pp. 13, 60 | B.H. in L.A. and S.F. |
| Mar 21 | d.b. | p. 8 | B.H. film project |
| Apr 4 | d.b. | p. 8 | Narcotics trial postponed |
| Apr 4 | d.b. | p. 32 | B.H. at Mister Kelly's |
| May 2 | d.b. | p. 8 | Dorothy Dandridge may star in B.H. film |
| May 11 | M.M. | p. 2 | B.H. may sue City of New York |
| June 27 | d.b. | p. 40 | Detroit, Baltimore bookings |
| July 11 | d.b. | p. 38 | Philadelphia dates |
| July 25 | d.b. | p. 3 | Mal Waldron's new LP |
| July 25 | d.b. | p. 44 | B.H. nearly blows her top |
| July 27 | M.M. | p. 2 | Who plays B.H. in film? |
| Aug 8 | d.b. | p. 16 | Don Gold reports on B.H. at Newport |
| Aug 17 | M.M. | p. 17 | B.H. in Toronto |
| Aug 22 | d.b. | p. 1 | Jazz Critics' Poll: 1st. Ella Fitzgerald 2nd. B.H. |
| Aug 24 | M.M. | p. 5 | Jazz in Central Park |
| Sept | Metronome | pp. 6, 19 | Details of jazz festivals |
| Sept 5 | d.b. | p. 8 | B.H. and Mal Waldron sit-in |
| Sept 5 | d.b. | p. 41 | B.H. at Stratford, Ontario. |
| Sept 7 | M.M. | p. 3 | Jimmy Rushing on B.H. and Lester Young |
| Sept 7 | M.M. | p. 8 | B.H. success in Toronto |
| Sept 19 | d.b. | p. 37 | L.F.B.T. Johnny Green on B.H. |
| Oct | Jazz Today | p. 10 | Lester Cowan to film B.H. story |
| Oct | Jazz Today | p. 33 | B.H. at Randall's Island Concert |
| Oct 3 | d.b. | p. 14 | B.H. has split from Verve |
| Oct 5 | M.M. | p. 2 | B.H. has left Verve |
| Oct 17 | d.b. | p. 40 | B.H. in Toronto |
| Oct 12 | M.M. | p. 14 | 'Lady Sings The Blues' r.r. Max Jones |
| Nov | Metronome | p. 29 | Newport Festival LP. r.r. |
| Nov 9 | M.M. | p. 9 | Lucy Ann Polk replaces B.H. |
| Dec 12 | d.b. | p. 52 | B.H. ill on Coast |
| Dec 26 | d.b. | p. 4 | Letter on B.H. |
| Dec 26 | d.b. | p. 6 | B.H. at Carnegie Hall, late November. |

| | | | |
|---|---|---|---|
| Dec 26 | d.b. | p. 1 | Poll Results: 1st. Ella Fitzgerald<br>7th. B.H. |
| Dec 26 | d.b. | p. 42 | Mal Waldron with B.H. in Hollywood |

**1958**

| | | | |
|---|---|---|---|
| Jan | Metronome | p. 34 | B.H. on 'Seven Lively Arts' TV show |
| Jan 23 | d.b. | p. 31 | L.F.B.T. Jimmy Rushing on B.H. |
| Feb 6 | d.b. | p. 24 | B.H. at Newport r.r. Don Gold |
| Feb 20 | d.b. | p. 8 | B.H. planning European tour |
| Feb 22 | M.M. | p. 20 | B.H. to sing in London |
| Mar 20 | d.b. | p. 14 | Teddy Wilson mentions B.H. |
| Apr 19 | M.M. | p. 11 | B.H. film soundtrack plans |
| Apr 26 | M.M. | p. 2 | B.H. to record film music |
| May 17 | M.M. | p. 20 | B.H. to appear at Festival Hall, London |
| May 31 | M.M. | p. 13 | B.H.'s book to be published in Britain |
| June 7 | M.M. | p. 10 | B.H. concert is off |
| June 12 | d.b. | p. 15 | Anita O'Day mentions B.H. |
| June 14 | M.M. | p. 5 | Cleo Laine praises B.H. |
| July | Metronome | pp. 14, 15 | Abbey Lincoln and Marilyn Moore speak of<br>B.H. |
| July | J.J. | p. 32 | Dan Morgenstern's American News Letter |
| July 5 | M.M. | p. 5 | Bob Dawbarn reviews *Lady Sings The Blues*<br>book |
| July 10 | d.b. | p. 13 | Shorty Rogers lists favorite singers |
| July 24 | d.b. | p. 14 | Tony Scott on B.H. |
| Aug | Metronome | p. 36 | B.H.'s favorite records |
| Aug 7 | d.b. | p. 24 | 'Lady In Satin' r.r. Martin Williams |
| Aug 21 | d.b. | p. 1 | Jazz Critics' Poll: 1st. Ella Fitzgerald<br>2nd. B.H. |
| Sept | J.J. | p. 31 | Sinclair Traill reviews B.H. book |
| Sept 4 | d.b. | p. 8 | B.H. at Wallingford jazz festival |
| Sept 18 | d.b. | pp. 55-57 | N.Y. Town Hall and California bookings<br>for B.H. |
| Oct | Metronome | p. 26 | 'Lady In Satin' r.r. Bill Coss |
| Oct | Jazz Hot | p. 33 | B.H. will play at Olympia, Paris |
| Oct 2 | d.b. | p. 57 | B.H. in San Francisco |
| Oct 18 | M.M. | p. 4 | B.H. files for final decree from Louis<br>McKay |
| Oct 30 | d.b. | p. 8 | B.H.–Basie reunion; B.H. records at Hotel Plaza |
| Nov | Jazz Monthly | p. 12 | Albert McCarthy reports on Monterey |
| Nov | Jazz Hot | p. 12 | B.H. in Paris |
| Nov 1 | M.M. | p. 30 | B.H. may move to London |
| Nov 15 | M.M. | p. 2 | Milan theatre manager asks B.H. to quit |
| Nov 22 | M.M. | p. 15 | B.H. interviewed |
| Dec | Jazz Review | p. 3 | Miles Davis on B.H. Nat Hentoff interview |
| Dec | Jazz Monthly | pp. 9-12 | Berta Wood reviews B.H.'s TV show |
| Dec | Metronome | p. 20 | Howard Lucraft reviews Monterey |
| Dec | Jazz Hot | p. 29 | Mal Waldron by Francois Postif |
| Dec | Jazz Hot | p. 33 | Kurt Mohr reports on Olympia concerts |
| Dec | Jazz Hot | p. 37 | B.H. to sing at Blue Note |
| Dec 11 | d.b. | p. 39 | B.H.'s new manager is George Treadwell |
| Dec 11 | d.b. | p. 8 | The Voices of Jazz by Charles E. Smith |
| Dec 25 | d.b. | p. 17 | Poll Results: 1st. Ella Fitzgerald<br>7th. B.H. |

**1959**

| | | | |
|---|---|---|---|
| Jan | J.J. | p. 30 | Berta Wood reviews Monterey |

255

| | | | |
|---|---|---|---|
| Jan | Jazz Hot | p. 36 | B.H. at Mars Club, Paris |
| Jan | Jazz Monthly | p. 12 | Hal Singer mentions B.H. |
| Jan 8 | d.b. | p. 36 | 'Lover Man' LP r.r. Dom Cerulli |
| Jan 17 | M.M. | p. 8 | Raymond Scott praises B.H. |
| Feb | Metronome | pp. 5, 19 | 'The Jazz Singer' B.H. cover photo |
| Feb 21 | M.M. | p. 5 | Steve Race's Great Records: 'Porgy' by B.H. |
| Feb 28 | M.M. | pp. 5, 30 | 'I'm settling in Britain' B.H. tells Max Jones |
| Mar | Metronome | p. 12 | Mal Waldron back from Europe |
| Mar | Metronome | pp. 32, 43 | B.H. recordings, and Timex TV show |
| Mar 19 | d.b. | p. 38 | 'Songs For Distingue Lovers' r.r. |
| Mar 19 | d.b. | p. 48 | Sam Cooke records 'Tribute to the Lady' |
| Mar 21 | M.M. | p. 16 | B.H. 'nervous' |
| Mar 28 | M.M. | p. 2 | Goodbye to Lester Young |
| Apr 11 | M.M. | p. 11 | B.H. waxes LP for M.G.M. |
| Apr 18 | M.M. | p. 8 | B.H.'s birthday party |
| Apr 30 | d.b. | p. 10 | Lester Young's funeral |
| May 14 | d.b. | p. 9 | B.H. still unable to get cabaret card |
| May 14 | d.b. | p. 40 | B.H. in Philadelphia |
| May 30 | M.M. | p. 2 | B.H. too ill to work |
| June 6 | M.M. | p. 1 | B.H. critically ill |
| June 11 | d.b. | p. 8 | Doctors warn B.H. |
| June 13 | M.M. | p. 1 | B.H. recovering |
| June 20 | M.M. | p. 1 | Lady Day arrested |
| June 20 | M.M. | pp. 2, 9 | Dinah Washington, Abbey Lincoln on B.H. |
| June 25 | d.b. | p. 49 | B.H. not moving to England |
| Summer | Jazz (a quarterly in American Music) | pp. 183-4 | John Hammond on Lester Young |
| July | Coda | p. 13 | B.H. ill with hepatitis |
| July 9 | d.b. | pp. 10-11 | B.H. in hospital, report by George Hoeffer |
| July 18 | New York Times | | B.H. dies here at 44. |
| Aug | Coda | pp. 23-25 | B.H. obituary by William Dufty (reprinted from the *New York Post*) |
| Aug | Jazz Review | pp. 7-8 | 'What Is a Jazz Singer?' by Nesuhi Ertegun |
| Aug | Jazz Monthly | pp. 9-11, 31 | The Art of Communication by Burnett James |
| Aug 8 | M.M. | p. 5 | Josh White and others pay tribute to B.H. |
| Aug 6 | d.b. | p. 1 | Jazz Critics' Poll: 1st. Ella Fitzgerald 2nd. B.H. |
| Aug 20 | d.b. | pp. 17, 20, 21 | Requiescat In Peace. L. Feather on B.H. |
| Sept | Coda | pp. 13-14 | Gerry Bahl reports on B.H. funeral |
| Sept | Jazz Review | pp. 8-9 | F. Postif 'Lester's Last Interview' (Jazz Hot) |
| Sept | Playboy | | Lester Young by L. Feather |
| Sept 3 | d.b. | pp. 6, 9, 31 | Coda for B.H., also letter from Dexter Gordon |
| Sept 17 | d.b. | p. 30 | 'Stay With Me' r.r. |
| Oct | J.J. | p. 3 | Dan Morgenstern on B.H.'s funeral |
| Nov | Jazz Review | pp. 36-37 | 'Distingue Lovers' r.r. Maitland Carey |
| Dec 10 | d.b. | p. 10 | B.H.'s estate amounts to $100,000. |
| Dec 24 | d.b. | p. 46 | 'All Or Nothing At All' r.r. |

**1960**

| | | | |
|---|---|---|---|
| May | Jazz Review | p. 25 | The B.H. Story r.r. Bill Crow |

| | | | |
|---|---|---|---|
| May 26 | d.b. | pp. 6, 10 | B.H. grave still not marked |
| June 23 | d.b. | p. 14 | A stone for Lady Day. |
| July | J.J. | p. 3 | Herbert Corby poem for B.H. |
| July | J.J. | p. 4 | A Reflection on B.H. by Benny Green |
| July 21 | d.b. | p. 16 | B.H. Memorial Foundation |
| Aug | J.J. | p. 12 | Valerie Wilmer interviews Earle Warren |
| Oct 13 | d.b. | p. 14 | Premiere of John Butler's ballet *Portrait of Billie.* |
| Dec 31 | Jazz News | p. 6 | Lady Day by Mike Butcher |

**1961**

| | | | |
|---|---|---|---|
| Jan | J.J. | p. 5 | Valerie Wilmer interviews Lee Young |
| Jan 19 | d.b. | p. 12 | B.H. movie in works |
| Feb | Metronome | p. 29 | Stanley Dance interviews Ram Ramirez |
| Apr 13 | d.b. | p. 15 | B.H. died without leaving a will |
| Aug | J.J. | p. 16 | B.H. & Lester Young discography 1937-41 by Michael G. Shera |
| Oct 12 | d.b. | p. 14 | Louis McKay complaint against A.G.V.A. |
| Nov 15 | Jazz News | p. 7 | Peggy Lee by Kitty Grimes |
| Dec 21 | d.b. | p. 19 | B.H. elected to 'Hall of Fame' |
| Dec 21 | d.b. | p. 42 | 'The Essential B.H.' r.r. |

**1962**

| | | | |
|---|---|---|---|
| Feb 1 | d.b. | pp. 1, 18, 20, 24 | 'The Voice of Jazz' L. Feather |
| Mar 29 | d.b. | p. 22 | Abbey Lincoln on B.H. |
| April | J.J. | p. 9 | B.H. with Snooky Young in Detroit |
| May 10 | d.b. | p. 44 | Joe Guy died late 1961 |
| May 16 | Jazz News | p. 11 | 'The Golden Years' r.r. George Ellis |
| June | Jazz Scene | pp. 10, 12, 32 | The Essential B.H. by Max Jones |
| June 21 | d.b. | p. 22 | 'The Golden Years' r.r. Don De Michael |
| July | Jazz Scene | pp. 16-22 | The Essential B.H. (Part 2) by Max Jones |
| July 4 | Jazz News | p. 2 | Reacting to Lady Day by Danny Halperin |
| July 5 | d.b. | p. 11 | Don Friedman sues M.G.M. over Carnegie Album |
| Aug | J.J. | p. 7 | Lucille Armstrong mentions B.H. |
| Aug | J.J. | pp. 17-18 | Survey of B.H.'s Columbia-Clef recordings |
| Sept | Coda | pp. 27-29 | 'The Golden Years' r.r. Ron Anger |
| Oct 24 | Jazz News | p. 5 | Yolande Bevan to star in NBC special on B.H. |
| Dec | Jazz Scene | p. 32 | B.H. on Commodore, r.r. Charles Fox |

**1963**

| | | | |
|---|---|---|---|
| d.b. year book (Music 63) | | pp. 73-75 | Thoughts on Female Jazz Singers by Barbara Gardner |
| Jan 3 | d.b. | p. 30 | 'Lady Love' r.r. John S. Wilson |
| Feb | Jazz | p. 21 | Bob Thiele reminiscing |
| July 4 | d.b. | p. 12 | Chico Hamilton sues Verve over B.H. album |
| July-Aug | Jazz Scene | p. 40 | 'Lady Love' r.r. Burnett James |
| Aug | Jazz Monthly | p. 10 | Babs Gonzales wrote song for B.H. |
| Sept | J.J. | p. 7 | Babs Gonzales on B.H. |
| Oct | Jazz | p. 27 | 'A Lady Well Remembered', by Dan Morgenstern |
| Nov 23 | M.M. | p. 12 | Leonard Feather on B.H. |

**1964**

| | | | |
|---|---|---|---|
| Jan 4 | M.M. | p. 12 | Leonard Feather on B.H. |
| Oct 22 | d.b. | p. 27 | 'Boston Recordings' r.r. John S. Wilson |
| Nov | J.J. | p. 27 | Jimmy Witherspoon on B.H. |
| Dec 5 | M.M. | p. 12 | 'Lady Day' film to be produced |

**1965**

| | | | |
|---|---|---|---|
| Apr 22 | d.b. | p. 27 | Count Basie Band background |
| May 1 | M.M. | p. 6 | Mal Waldron on B.H. |
| July 15 | d.b. | p. 21 | B.H. 1947 concert recalled |
| Sept 11 | M.M. | p. 10 | 'Lady Day' r.r. Max Jones |
| Nov 18 | d.b. | p. 20 | Ella on B.H. and 'Lover Man' recordings |

**1966**

| | | | |
|---|---|---|---|
| d.b. year book (Music '66) | | pp.90,107,109 | Background to Onyx Club |
| Feb | J.J. | pp. 18-19 | 'Quality Jazz by B.H.' G.E. Lambert |
| Feb | Jazz Monthly | p. 26 | George James reminisces about 52nd Street |
| Mar 19 | M.M. | p. 12 | B.H.'s 1944 recordings r.r. Max Jones |
| July | Jazz Monthly | pp. 11-12 | B.H. on Decca r.r. G.E. Lambert |
| July 14 | d.b. | p. 33 | 'The Golden Years VOL II' r.r. |
| Aug | Jazz | p. 15 | Tony Scott's photograph of B.H. |

**1967**

| | | | |
|---|---|---|---|
| d.b. year book (Music '67) | | pp. 75-76 | B.H. at Cafe Society |
| Feb | Bulletin du Hot Club de France | | 'The Golden Years' r.r. Hugues Panassié (see also Bulletin issues 91, 104, 120) |
| Apr | Storyville | pp. 20-24 | Fine and Mellow |
| Nov 2 | d.b. | p. 13 | Repeal of New York Cabaret Card law |
| Nov 16 | d.b. | p. 41 | L.F.B.T. Tony Bennett on B.H. |

**1968**

| | | | |
|---|---|---|---|
| d.b. year book (Music '68) | | pp. 77-81 | 'The Famous Door' by George Hoefer |
| Jan | Jazz Monthly | pp. 28-29 | 'The Golden Years' r.r. George Ellis |
| May 2 | d.b. | p. 25 | John Guarneri on Onyx Club memories |
| Oct | J.J. | pp. 22, 23, 40 | 'B.H. Actress without an act'. Martin Williams |
| Dec | Coda | p. 38 | David Susskind to produce B.H. movie |
| Dec | Crescendo | p. 23 | Red Norvo on B.H. |
| Dec 12 | d.b. | p. 18 | Carmen McRae on B.H. |

**1969**

| | | | |
|---|---|---|---|
| Feb 6 | d.b. | p. 30 | L.F.B.T, Dionne Warwick on B.H. |
| Apr 3 | d.b. | pp. 17, 18 | Dan Morgenstern on Lester Young |
| Oct | J.J. | p. 26 | Basics No. 34. B.H. by Barrie McRae |

**1970**

| | | | |
|---|---|---|---|
| June | J.J. | p. 9 | Carol Sloane on B.H. |

**1971**

| | | | |
|---|---|---|---|
| d.b. year book (Music '71) | | p. 73 | Lester Young discography by Dan Morgenstern |
| Mar 18 | d.b. | p. 12 | Jo Jones interview by L.K. McMilland |
| May | Jazz Hot | pp. 1, 3, 5-8, 17 | B.H. by Mimi Perrin |

| Aug 19 | d.b. | p. 26 | 'The Lady Lives' r.r. John McDonough |
| Oct | Coda | pp. 2-9 | Bobby Henderson by Johnny Simmen |
| | | | (later published in 'Der Jazz freund') |

## 1972

| d.b. year book (Music '72) | | pp. 11, 12, 34 | The Miracle of Lady Day by Henry Pleasants |
|---|---|---|---|
| Mar 25 | M.M. | p. 36 | 'Lady Day Lives' r.r. Max Jones |
| Mar 30 | d.b. | p. 27 | L.F.B.T. Roberta Flack on B.H. |
| Apr | Matrix (96) | pp. 14-15 | B.H.'s Alternative Takes by Jack Millar (see also issues 97 and 98) |
| June-July | Storyville | p. 185 | Mrs. Banga & Mr. Marshall by Johnny Simmen |
| Aug 12 | M.M. | p. 44 | B.H. The Best of All? by Max Jones |
| Sept | J.J. | p. 8 | Big Nick Nicholas on B.H. |
| Nov 4 | M.M. | p. 20 | Film opens at Loew's in New York |
| Nov 11 | M.M. | p. 11 | Michael Watts rev. *Lady Sings The Blues* film |
| Nov 23 | d.b. | p. 11 | Dan Morgenstern rev. *Lady Sings The Blues* film |
| Dec 2 | M.M. | p. 63 | Truth Takes A Holiday – Leonard Feather |
| Dec 21 | d.b. | pp. 22, 26-7 | Re-issue Round-up by Dan Morgenstern |

## 1973

| Jan | Ebony | pp. 110-116 | Lady Didn't Always Sing The Blues: Charles L. Sanders |
|---|---|---|---|
| Mar 17 | M.M. | p. 34 | The Legend of Lady Day |
| Mar 25 | Sunday Times (London) | p. 30 | The Lady As She Lived by Derek Jewell |
| Mar 29 | d.b. | pp. 16, 17 27-9 | A Lady Named Billie and I, by Milt Gabler |
| Spring | Discographical Forum (32) | pp. 3-6 | Discography of B.H. airshots by Jack Millar |
| Apr | Jazz & Blues | pp. 14-15 | Ten Lessons with Tony Scott, by Alun Morgan |
| Apr 8 | Observer (London) | p. 35 | Billie and the Blues, by George Melly |
| May 10 | d.b. | p. 31 | L.F.B.T. Stan Getz on B.H. |
| May 19 | Socialist Worker (London) | p. 11 | A Badly Packaged Holiday, Barry Almeida |
| June | Jazz Hot | pp. 4-7 | B.H.'s Career |
| June | Coda | pp. 12-14 | The B.H. Story – John Norris, Irv Lutsky. |
| June 21 | d.b. | p. 12 | B.H. exhibition at N.Y. Jazz Museum |
| July 7 | M.M. | p. 44 | Louis McKay in shooting incident |
| Aug | Jazz & Blues | pp. 8-10 | Two views of Lester Young, by John Hammond. |
| Sept | Jazz & Blues | pp. 4-6 | B.H. A Continuing Musical Conception by Jack Cooke |

## 1974

| May | Coda | pp. 2-14 | Kenneth L. Hollon by Johnny Simmen (also appeared in 'Le Point du Jazz') |
|---|---|---|---|
| June | Into Jazz | p. 37 | For The Record, by Brian Priestley |
| Nov | Matrix (105) | pp. 7-8 | B.H.'s Alternative Masters by Jack Millar |

# Index

263